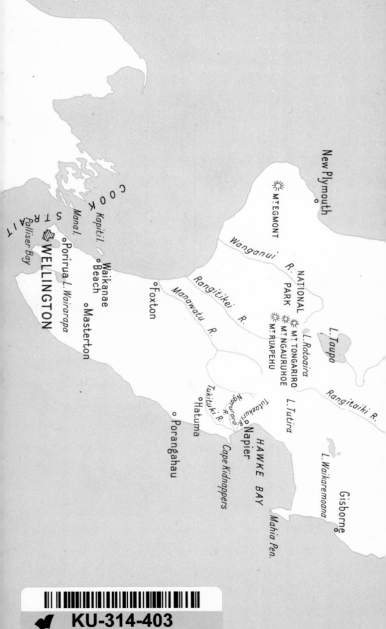

New Plymouth

Mt Egmont

Wanganui R.

NATIONAL PARK

Mt Tongariro
Mt Ngauruhoe
Mt Ruapehu

L. Rotoaira

L. Taupo

Rangitaiki R.

L. Waikaremoana

Gisborne

Rangitikei R.

Manawatu R.

Foxton

Tukituki R.

Ngaruroro R.

Tutaekuri R.

L. Tutira

Napier

HAWKE BAY

Cape Kidnappers

Mahia Pen.

Hatuma

Porangahau

COOK STRAIT

Kapiti I.

Mana I.

Waikanae Beach

WELLINGTON

Porirua L. Wairarapa

Masterton

Palliser Bay

A FIELD GUIDE
TO THE BIRDS OF
NEW ZEALAND

A FIELD GUIDE
TO THE BIRDS OF
NEW ZEALAND
AND OUTLYING ISLANDS

by

R. A. Falla, R. B. Sibson
and E. G. Turbott

with 18 plates and
63 line-drawings
by Chloe Talbot-Kelly

COLLINS
St. James's Place, London

First Edition 1966
Second Edition 1970

ISBN 0 00 212022 4

© *New Zealand Ornithological Society, 1966*
Printed in Great Britain
Collins Clear-Type Press
London and Glasgow

CONTENTS

CONTENTS

CONTENTS

PLATES

New Zealand and its outlying islands

PREFACE

Encouraged by the success of the *Checklist of New Zealand Birds*, published in 1953, the Council of the Ornithological Society of New Zealand in 1959 asked the three authors to collaborate in compiling a practical field-guide for the birds of the New Zealand region. It was a timely decision, for the last few decades have been exciting. An increase of critical ornithology in areas formerly rather inaccessible has shown that several unique endemic species are not as rare as was supposed and has added more transequatorial migrants to the already long New Zealand list. At the same time five self-introduced species from Australia appear to have established themselves in clearly empty ecological niches, and several other comparatively recent trans-Tasman newcomers are steadily increasing. The decline in many native birds, so marked in the nineteenth century, seems to have been arrested. Most in fact are holding their own; some have turned the corner and are utilising new habitats, such as hydro-electric dams, reclaimed salt-marshes, man-made forests of exotic pines, swamp-lands now choked with willow and alder.

Scope and Aim

For the purposes of this field-guide the New Zealand region extends from the Kermadec Islands in Lat. 29° S. to Macquarie Island, Lat. 55° S. (map opposite). Its aim is to enable the serious student, the visitor, the sailor and, perhaps above all the amateur naturalist, who enjoys watching and identifying birds for the fun of the thing and to satisfy his curiosity, to know what bird he is watching and what birds to expect, anywhere on and around the many islands which make up New Zealand. Here perhaps the first *caveat* should be sounded about the difficulty of identifying with certainty many of the petrels and shearwaters that will be seen at sea.

Extinction and Survival

An ornithologist visiting New Zealand one thousand years ago would have been astounded and delighted at the number and variety of flightless birds which have been able to evolve in the virtual absence of carnivorous predators. But the long peace of this South Pacific avian paradise was rudely broken by the arrival of meat-hungry Polynesian seafarers—Sir Peter Buck's " Vikings of the Sunrise." Bone by bone, archæologist and zoologist are piecing together the sadly fascinating story of the extinction of the Moas and some other flightless birds. Altogether of the twenty-seven accepted species or forms of Moa, twenty-two have now been found in association with the middens or hunting-camps of Polynesian man. Some even of the bigger Moas of the genus *Dinornis* survived into the seventeenth century; but when the first European explorers arrived,

11

the giant birds were only a legend, though a few specimens of one of the smallest species may have survived till the nineteenth century. Fortunately all the flightless birds were not equally vulnerable. The Takahe, dramatically rediscovered in 1948, had escaped destruction in its mountain fastnesses—while Wekas and three species of Kiwi (still not uncommon locally) survived the impact of Polynesian man unscathed.

In the nineteenth century the land-hunger of European settlers, mainly of British stock, led to the hasty felling of vast areas of bush and to the draining of swamps. Was it not said that a typical pioneer was born with an axe in one hand and a firestick in the other; and that a cow-cocky would sell his soul for an extra blade of cocksfoot? Inevitably the numbers of forest-haunting birds were reduced; but the number of actual extinctions was small, the only loss of a mainland forest species being that of the Huia, which persisted into the first decade of the twentieth century. Some species now extinct on the main islands survive and thrive on offshore island sanctuaries, e.g. the Stitchbird on Little Barrier; the Saddleback on Hen and Big South Cape Islands; the Shore Plover on South-east Island in the Chathams.

Of course, uncontrolled shooting, based on the philosophy of the inexhaustible, contributed to the general decline. Wekas commonly went into the pot; Kakas were esteemed a delicacy; and the *pièce de résistance* of a bushmens' feast might be a pig stuffed with Native Pigeons and Tuis. The endemic ducks and plovers and the so-called Native Quail provided a tasty meal for hungry colonists. In the Auckland Islands shipwrecked mariners probably ate the Merganser to the point of extinction. Rats, black (*rattus*) and brown (*norvegicus*) which came ashore from ships, mustelids deliberately introduced, dogs and domestic cats, abandoned or gone feral, became an additional menace, especially to flightless or ground-nesting birds, which had no experience of eluding mammalian predators. These " parasites on the Pakeha " still constitute the gravest threat to such colonies of petrels, e.g. the rare Westland Petrel, as survive on the main islands. The effect of introduced deer and opossums on native birds has yet to be assessed. Another danger was disease passed on from domestic poultry or introduced birds. This may partially account for the sudden decline of such different species as Brown Teal, Red-crowned Parakeet and Weka. The range of the Blue Duck seems to have been narrowed by the muddying of formerly clear bush streams.

Much more of the original forest has been permanently reserved— mainly as high country protection forest and National Park—than would have been forecast by an observer in the nineteenth century; and thus the story fortunately is not one of unrelieved gloom. The fast dwindling of some species and the virtual disappearance of others forced the government to act. Protective laws were passed and enforced. The commercial collecting of skins and eggs, trapping of passerines and parrots and their sale or export to aviculturists were strictly prohibited. The season for shooting any ducks was limited to a few weeks in May. The rarer endemic ducks have been absolutely protected for many years and are likely to remain so. In 1894 Little Barrier became the first of many off-shore island sanctuaries. Since 1940 a ban upon the shooting of shore birds has had a most beneficial effect upon the numbers of waders, both endemic and migratory.

Actually very few native species are now in serious danger of extinction, the elusive Kakapo perhaps being an exception. Some species have clearly benefited from European methods of farming and opening up the country. Among these may be named: Grey Warbler, Kingfisher, Harrier, Paradise Duck, the three gulls, Pukeko, Pied Stilt and probably South Island Pied Oystercatcher, Banded Dotterel, Wrybill and Welcome Swallow.

Because New Zealand does not possess, and never did possess, the rich variety of passerines and forest-birds such as may be found in Australia or on one of the great continental land masses, casual visitors who see little but the fertile farmlands of the North and South Islands and may make a brief stay at one of the National Parks, are apt to complain that as far as birds go, the landscape is dominated by aliens. It is indeed true that among the commonest birds in the country must be reckoned most of the dozen or so English passerines which were introduced nearly a hundred years ago mainly from sentiment, with perhaps some thought of utility. But such a visitor has only to visit the coast, preferably at an estuary with the tide coming in, or one of the well-bushed off-shore islands to realise something of the richness of the birdlife, exemplified in one curious way by the 1000-mile overlap of parrots and penguins; for the breeding range of the Little Blue Penguin extends north of Lat. 35° S., and parakeets have successfully colonised many bleak sub-antarctic islands as far as Antipodes and Auckland Islands in Lat. 50° S. Not without reason has it been remarked that the true glory of New Zealand birds is best seen and appreciated in her coastal waters; for there are still many quiet places, far from the madding crowd, where the mind can become, in Darwin's phrase, " a chaos of delight " at the abundance and variety of birds which pass before the eye or perplex the ear.

Nomenclature

The common vernacular name is given first, followed by local or Maori names, if any. For the scientific name the use of binomials instead of trinomials may occasion some surprise among critical readers. The aim has been simplicity. The geography of the New Zealand region, i.e. its length, composition and isolation, has favoured the formation of local races or subspecies. The general rule of the authors has been to use the subspecific name for " strong " races, e.g. Chatham Island Mollymawk, Brown Teal, Hudsonian Godwit, Blackfronted Tern; and the specific name for " weak " subspecies, e.g. White Heron, Little Egret, Bellbird, Fantail; and to mention relationships in the text. The order closely follows that used in the 1953 Checklist, beginning with the Kiwis and ending with the passerines.

Treatment

Those species which breed in New Zealand are treated under four headings (*a*) Description, (*b*) Voice, (*c*) Habitat and Range, (*d*) Breeding. For migrants and stragglers from outside the New Zealand region the section on breeding is omitted.

(*a*) The description begins with a measurement in inches of the length of the flying bird from the tip of the bill to the tip of the tail or, in a few instances, of the legs extending beyond the tail. Salient or diagnostic features are printed in italics. Notes on carriage, posture, behaviour, where judged helpful, are included.

(*b*) Syllabification along traditional lines has been attempted. A well-trained ear is invaluable. Many waders and night-flying migrants can be accurately identified by ear without being seen. In thick bush and swamp Kokako and Fernbird, to name but two elusive species, will not be seen easily, although their presence may be revealed by their distinctive calls. In general, the voices and calls of New Zealand birds are badly in need of study. This is especially true of petrels and seabirds. Some tape-recordings have been made and are most instructive.

(*c*) There are many types of habitat in New Zealand. Perusal of this section will give some idea of their almost infinite variety. In New Zealand many species with a wide distribution in Australia and/or Asia reach the south-east limit of their range. Thus of the ten Ardeidae on the New Zealand list none is endemic, i.e. confined to New Zealand only. Finally, New Zealand is within the regular range of many waders and petrels whose breeding grounds are between 6000 and 8000 miles distant; the waders coming annually from arctic Asia and arctic America; the petrels, as is proved by banding, from as far as the Antarctic coast of the south Atlantic.

(*d*) A summary is here given of what is known of the nesting habits and behaviour of those species which breed in New Zealand. There are many gaps. It is hoped they will prove a challenge.

Although we have not followed in all respects the pattern of the famous Peterson Field Guides, we are extremely grateful to Roger Tory Peterson for allowing us to follow his system as far as the text is concerned. Indeed, the Peterson Field Guides have been an example to us in the whole conception and preparation of this book.

Division of Labour

In preparing the text each of the three authors undertook certain families or natural groups. Dr. Falla was the obvious choice to describe the penguins, albatrosses, petrels, shags and gulls. Graham Turbott contributed the text on the kiwis, ducks, native pigeon, parrots, native owls, Kingfisher and native passerines. I have been responsible for the grebes, tropic-birds, gannets, frigate-birds, herons, ibises, hawks, rails, waders, terns, skuas, cuckoos, introduced pigeons, owls and passerines and stragglers. There has been throughout a free exchange of ideas. As editor, it has been my pleasant task to try to secure a general uniformity of treatment, but minor differences of emphasis and style may remain.

Any gross discrepancies should be laid firmly at the editor's door.   For the illustrations we have been fortunate in having the services of Miss Talbot Kelly, who has lived for some time in New Zealand and has seen in the living flesh many of the birds described.   The illustrations were prepared in consultation with Dr. Falla and myself and with the invaluable help of the Bird Room at the British Museum of Natural History.

PREFACE TO SECOND EDITION

In the five years that have elapsed since the text for the first edition of the Field Guide was completed, enough new material has accrued to justify a revised second edition.

The status of some breeding species, particularly recent successful colonists from Australia, has changed so spectacularly that what was written about their distribution and numbers in 1963–64 is now quite inaccurate.

Expeditions to outlying groups of islands such as the Kermadec, Chatham, Snares and Auckland Islands have brought back new information, some of which is included.

One " lost " species has been rediscovered and several migratory or wandering species have been added to the official New Zealand list.

Additional seasonal observations made not only at such keypoints as Farewell Spit and the Southland lagoons, but also in other well-known harbours and estuaries, tend to confirm that most of the rarer migratory species, which are already listed for New Zealand, should be considered not as casual vagrants but as regular annual visitors.

At the same time the opportunity has been taken to remove some inconsistencies of treatment and to correct some obvious errors.

The authors wish to thank all who have submitted lists of fresh data or suggested emendations, in particular A. Blackburn, A. T. Edgar, B. D. Heather, D. V. Merton, M. F. Soper.

It is hoped that an up-to-date Field Guide will stimulate the study of birds in New Zealand and emphasise the need for general conservation.

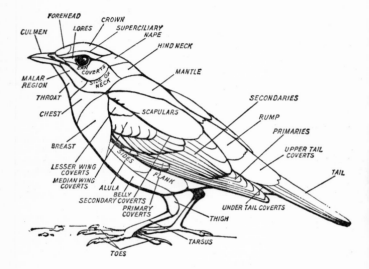

THE PLUMAGE OF A BIRD

KIWIS: Apterygidae

Kiwis are flightless birds of robust build standing at most fourteen inches high. Their position is evidently that of an early offshoot from the evolutionary line of the ratite birds (moa, emu, ostrich, etc.). They probably branched off at an early stage, and their ancestors are believed to have reached New Zealand at about the same time as those of another group of ratites restricted to New Zealand: the extinct moas. The kiwis are unique amongst the ratites in their small size and adaptations to life on the forest floor, the most noteworthy being the long bill used to obtain worms and other food items in the soft ground.

They are entirely nocturnal. With this is associated weak sight and the development of tactile bristles round the mouth. The long, sensitive bill and the facial bristles are probably the main organs enabling them to move about by night on the forest floor, often in dense undergrowth and fallen debris. The sense of smell of the kiwis is considered to be strongly developed but this should be accepted tentatively pending further investigation. Expiration through the nostrils can be heard as the birds explore the ground for food; the nostrils are situated on the sides at the tip of the bill. To obtain insect larvæ, and especially worms, when located underground, kiwis plunge the bill deep into the earth, often right up to the " hilt "; the bill is also used to pick up fallen forest fruits and ground insects, both of which are important items of diet. The tip of the upper mandible overlaps the lower. The wings of the kiwis consist of remnants hidden beneath the plumage which is loose and hangs in a hair-like fashion. There are no tail feathers and in the resting or walking positions the body with its loose plumage has a distinctive rounded appearance; occasionally the bird may adopt a standing position with bill on the ground so that a tripod is formed by bill and legs together.

There are three species; such information as is available suggests that all three are much alike in mode of life and habits. The early settlement of New Zealand, which except in mountain regions brought about a tremendous reduction of forest, caused the extinction of the kiwis in many areas but they have thrived in all large bush areas, and even in comparatively small bush remnants. It is especially notable that kiwis now inhabit semi-cleared scrub country and even rough farmland near the forest. They have thus survived in spite of environmental modification, introduction of carnivores and other factors which adversely affected several flightless New Zealand birds.

Although not generally seen, they indicate their presence by their penetrating calls after dark. They are sometimes killed on roads near the bush by traffic at night; dogs or opossum traps (though required by legislation to be set with special precautions to avoid ground birds) account for a few. Various kiwis injured in this way have been kept in captivity and much has been learned of their habits; they have also been bred in captivity. They become accustomed to taking food by day.

When released in daylight they run with clumsy but powerful strides, and apparently see well enough to enable them to avoid obstacles.

In proportion to the size of the bird, the egg is very big.

BROWN KIWI *Apteryx australis*

Maori name: Kiwi; tokoeka   (Stewart Island).

Description: 18″–22″. General colour dark grey streaked with reddish-brown and black (feathers grey at the base, terminal portion brown with black tips); the amount of reddish-brown less on the head, which is greyish; bill pale (ivory white to pinkish); legs pale to dark brown.

There is a sex difference in size (all three species), the maximum size of the female being greater, with a much longer bill.

North Island Kiwi (*Apteryx australis mantelli*)

Voice: Male a shrill whistle *ki-wi*; female a remarkably hoarse cry, apparently coming from " deep down in the throat." (The calls of males of the three subspecies of Brown Kiwis differ in tape-recordings; the two notes are of the same pitch in both North and South Island subspecies, but are more rapidly delivered in the latter, while in the Stewart Island subspecies the second is a descending note.)

Habitat and range: Originally common in all forest areas, but the South Island subspecies apparently absent on Banks Peninsula (which was originally forested) and on the Canterbury Plains. Settlement has resulted in a reduction of range as mentioned above: now in many forest areas in the North Island but more restricted in the South Island (no recent records from the south-eastern South Island). Common in Fiordland where it reaches subalpine and alpine zones. In the western and northern South Island now absent or rare (perhaps originally out-numbered or replaced by the two species of Spotted Kiwi in these areas).

Particularly in the North Island, recorded recently in modified conditions; nests have been found in rough farmland under logs and in scrub.

Breeding: Nests in holes, e.g. amongst dense vegetation, in a hollow log, between roots of forest trees, sometimes partly excavated by the birds. Observations in captivity of North Island Brown Kiwis have given the incubation period as 75–80 days; incubation by male. Laying July–February. Eggs (clutch one or two in North Island subspecies, one in remaining subspecies) ivory white or greenish, and highly glazed.

Three subspecies are recognised: the North Island Brown Kiwi (*A. a. mantelli*) differs from both South Island Brown Kiwi (*A. a. australis*) and Stewart Island Brown Kiwi (*A. a. lawryi*) in the stiffened tips of the feathers (harsher to the touch). The North Island and Stewart Island subspecies both have distinctly reddish-brown plumage, especially on the back, the South Island Brown Kiwi being a duller brown; the two southern subspecies are larger on the average than the North Island subspecies. Introduced to Kapiti Island (*mantelli* and *australis*) and Little Barrier Island (*mantelli*).

LITTLE SPOTTED KIWI *Apteryx oweni*

Description: 14″–18″. Body is irregularly banded and mottled with brownish-black on a faintly buffy pale grey background; head grey; bill pale as in the Brown Kiwi, and feet pale brown to flesh-white.

Voice: No recent description, but older accounts suggest that the calls of both male and female are like those of the Brown Kiwi.

Habitat and range: Range of the two species of Spotted Kiwi is the western districts of the South Island. In certain areas their range overlaps, or originally overlapped, that of the South Island Brown Kiwi. The present species extends farther both to south (southern Fiordland) and north-east (Marlborough) than the Great Spotted. It has been

displaced by settlement from much of Marlborough. In the North Island one record: a specimen from Tararua Range (Mt. Hector) in 1875, but sub-fossil bones indicate a wide distribution in comparatively recent times. Introduced to Kapiti Island where it is well established. **Breeding:** No difference from the Brown Kiwi according to early accounts; clutch one. No recent records.

GREAT SPOTTED KIWI *Apteryx haasti*

Maori name: Roa.

Description: 18″–22″. Like the Little Spotted, but distinguished by the *strong chestnut tinge* on the back; bill ivory white to pinkish; feet dark to pale brown, claws brown or white.

Voice: In areas where it is the common and, as far as is known, the only species the calls heard do not differ from those of the Brown Kiwi described above.

Habitat and range: According to recent records fairly abundant in forests of western Nelson (especially the Gouland Downs area) and Westland; some doubt as to its occurrence in Westland south of Okarito and in Fiordland. This species has probably suffered comparatively little reduction in range through settlement. It may now be expanding, as there are numerous recent records from the main divide at Arthur's Pass and Lewis Pass; it occurs here at present on both sides of the divide in high altitude beech forest.

Breeding: Only early records, but in the main features evidently similar to the Brown Kiwi. Clutch one, rarely two.

PENGUINS: Spheniscidae

With the addition of the circumpolar species found at Macquarie Island, the New Zealand region has representatives of five of the six genera of penguins, the exception being *Spheniscus*. The breeding range of the smallest (*Eudyptula*) extends from North Cape and Spirits Bay south to Stewart Island.

Within the sub-antarctic belt are several species of *Eudyptes* and the endemic *Megadyptes*. Only the small birds of the genus *Eudyptula* nest in caves and burrows, the others are surface nesters and all of them, except the Fiordland Crested Penguin and *Megadyptes*, tend to form large colonies. The Fiordland Crested Penguin also has a tendency to seek covered nesting shelter.

KING PENGUIN *Aptenodytes patagonicus*   *Pl. 1*

Description: 36″. The head and the neck are dark glossy black merging on the nape to a pale blue-grey which is the prevailing tone of the dorsal plumage. Underparts, as in all penguins, mainly satin white but a pale golden yellow tinge on the breast deepens on the foreneck to orange-yellow and extends in two lozenge-shaped patches to the region of the ears. Bill, black; mandibular plates, orange-rose; feet, black.

Male and female are similar in plumage. Immature birds in first plumage have the same pattern as the adult with much paler yellow colours. Chicks are clothed in smoky brown down, uniform over the whole of the body, and this is retained for some months in the nestling period.

Voice: Resonant squawk; and a somewhat more shrill trumpeting with a whistling quality during intake of breath.

Habitat and range: In the New Zealand region breeds only at Macquarie Island. Stragglers sometime appear at sub-antarctic islands farther north. In the circumpolar range of the King Penguin no well-defined races have been recognised.

Breeding: Strongly colonial. Colonies may cover acres. The single pyriform egg is pale greenish white, chalky outside. Incubation periods, 7½ weeks. The egg is incubated between the feet in a fold of skin.

YELLOW-EYED PENGUIN *Megadyptes antipodes* *Pl. 1*

Maori name: Hoiho.

Description: 30″. The general dorsal colour is slaty grey. The forehead and crown, pale golden with black shaft stripes. A band of yellow feathers commences above the eye and encircles the crown posteriorly. Chin and throat brownish-white which is weakly defined from the satin white of the underparts. Cheeks pale golden, throat and sides of neck brown. Bill flesh coloured, dull reddish-brown on the culmen and towards the tip of the mandibles. Feet pale flesh coloured; iris yellow.

Immature birds in their first year differ from adults in having the yellow band confined to the sides of the head and not encircling the crown. The chin and throat also are only faintly marked but are mainly white. Chicks in down are uniformly dark smoky brown, the texture of the down being fine, rather short and generally more compact than that of the King Penguin.

Voice: Yellow-eyed Penguins have a considerable range of calls, including a full trumpet. A contact call note of two syllables, the first one slurred, is closely similar to the cry of the Weka.

Habitat and range: The breeding range is from Cape Wanbrow, Oamaru, south to Campbell Island, but the species has not been recorded from Snares, Antipodes or Bounty Islands. Formerly *Megadyptes* may have bred farther north, and immature birds have a wandering distribution which includes Banks Peninsula and, rarely, Cook Strait. Otherwise the species is sedentary and there is no indication of true migration.

Breeding: Nesting begins in September and continues until the young are fully fledged about February. Moult takes place later in the same area and the birds are generally present throughout the year. Sites for nests are scattered in the shelter of scrub or low forest at varying distances from the sea and widely scattered within suitable habitat.

The full clutch is two eggs and normally two chicks are reared. Incubation period 40–50 days; fledging 110–115 days.

GENTOO PENGUIN   *Pygoscelis papua*[1]   *Pl. 1*

Description: 30″. General dorsal colour dark slate grey each feather with a bluish-grey tip. Head and neck black with a tendency to ashy grey on the throat. A wide band of white feathers crosses the crown between the eyes and there is usually a scattering of small white plumes as spots about the head and neck. Underparts pure white. Bill black; sides of mandible orange; feet orange; iris brown.

Females are similar in plumage to the males but slightly smaller and the orange coloration of the beak and feet is either paler or tinged with pink.

The immature plumage has the throat mottled with white and the white crescent on the crown is poorly defined, being represented in some examples by irregular white patches only just above the eyes.

The downy young are dark above and white below, the general pattern being similar to that of the adult plumage.

Voice: Trumpeting, braying on two notes by inhaling and exhaling; also hissing.

Habitat and range: With a circumpolar distribution, Gentoo Penguins are found as breeders in the New Zealand region only at Macquarie Island, where they are resident and sedentary. Unlike the King Penguin which occurs in the same region, they have not been recorded as stragglers at points farther north; except one recently at Campbell I.

Breeding: Gentoos nest at varying distances from the sea on inland flats or low hillocks of easy gradient. At Macquarie Island they do not form very large colonies; but loosely-knit groups of 20 to 100 nests are scattered around the coastal belt of the island. Two eggs are laid and usually two chicks reared.

LITTLE BLUE PENGUIN   *Eudyptula minor*   *Pl. 7*

Maori name: Korora.

Description: 16″. Three distinct subspecies appear to be separable. The southern *minor* is described first.

Dorsal surface deep slate blue, each feather with a flattened black shaft, chin, throat, foreneck and underparts pure white. Bill black; feet pale flesh colour, black on the soles; eyes silver grey. Male and female similar, but the bill of the male is stouter. Immature birds in first plumage have smaller bills and the blue of the dorsal plumage is brighter. Young in down are a dark sooty brown dorsally with an ill-defined patch of whitish down on the underparts. Blue Penguins of the

[1] The circumpolar, truly antarctic Adelie Penguin (*Pygoscelis adeliae*) has been reported twice in the New Zealand region. An adult female came ashore on Macquarie Island in November 1950; and a dried corpse was found near Long Point on the Marlborough coast in December 1962.

middle region, i.e. about Cook St. (subsp. not named), are uniformly larger; their bills are stouter and longer; and the blue tone of the plumage is lighter even in the darkest examples. In their pale plumage and white flipper marks some are not very different from *albosignata*.

The northern subspecies *novaehollandiae* has a more slender bill, narrower at the base. It closely resembles the common Fairy Penguins of eastern Australia.

Voice: Blue Penguins have a wide range of calls and are more vocal than any of the larger penguins. Sounds range from mewing notes not unlike those of a cat, to loud screams, trumpetings and deep-toned growls. These are uttered when the bird is ashore at night. The only sounds normally heard at sea are duck-like quacks.

Habitat and range: *Minor* has a breeding range very close to the Sub-Antarctic Convergence from the Chatham Islands westward to the Otago Peninsula; and thence through Stewart Island extending up the greater part of the west coast of the South Island. The unnamed subspecies of the middle region breeds around the coasts of both North and South Islands from the eastern entrance to Cook Strait through to the South Taranaki Bight, Marlborough Sounds and Nelson, south to North Canterbury.

The northern subspecies is found mainly north of 40° S. Lat. as far as Spirits Bay and North Cape, but not Three Kings.

Breeding: Nests are to be found from high-water mark to points inland of several hundred yards distance and sometimes several hundred feet in altitude. Nests are rarely on the surface and usually in ready-made cavities or burrows which the birds either take over from petrels and enlarge or which they may dig themselves if the soil is soft enough. Two eggs are laid and usually two chicks reared. Incubation period *c*. 39 days; fledging 51–58 days.

WHITE-FLIPPERED PENGUIN *Eudyptula albosignata*
Description: 16½″. This is the most robust of the four forms and is also palest on the back, which is pale slaty grey. The flipper has a broad white edge dorsally, and in males a central white patch which often joins the two white bands.

Habitat and range: Breeds around the shores of Banks Peninsula in Canterbury and in considerable numbers at Motunau Island, North Canterbury, where some of the Cook Strait Blue Penguin may occur.

Voice: As in other forms.

Breeding: Incubation period: *c*. 38 days (O'Brien).

ROCKHOPPER PENGUIN *Eudyptes crestatus*   *Pl. 1*
Description: 25″. The general dorsal colour is dark slate with a bright bluish tinge on the back and an intensification of the blackish-grey about the head. Chin, throat and cheeks dark blackish slate. The

crown in which the feathers are elongated appears even darker contrasting with the narrow golden yellow eyebrow strip, commencing behind the nasal feathers and extending along the sides of the crown to form a long crest. Underparts pure white. Bill, dull orange red. Iris geranium. Feet white; soles black. The female is similar in plumage to the male but has a much smaller bill and apparently an eye of slightly less diameter. Immature birds differ in having the chin ashy white and only a faint suggestion of the superciliary crest. Downy young are dark smoky grey above and white below.

Voice: A loud braying yell.

Habitat and range: In the New Zealand sub-antarctic zone is found breeding at Macquarie, Auckland, Campbell and Antipodes Islands, with small numbers at Snares and Bounties associated with other species of crested penguin.

Breeding: This species forms nesting colonies on steep and broken coast-line either utilising caves and cavities for nesting places or using terraces and open areas, sometimes to a considerable height above sea-level. Two eggs are laid of which the first is considerably smaller, and the smaller egg does not receive the same amount of care and attention, being sometimes trodden into the debris of the nest. However, in a certain proportion of nests both eggs may hatch and, rather rarely, two chicks can be reared.

FIORDLAND CRESTED PENGUIN *Eudyptes pachyrhynchus*
Pl. 1

Description: 28″. Forehead and crown bluish black. The rest of the upperparts dark bluish grey. The chin and throat and cheeks are a dark slaty grey but the feathers have white bases and at the bulge of the cheek below the eye these are exposed in four or five parallel whitish streaks. A rather wide pale yellow line of feathers runs back from the nasal angle above each eye and terminates in a lengthened crest. Bill reddish brown. Eye bright reddish brown. Feet whitish with black soles.

The female is similar in plumage but has a less robust bill than the male. There is no visible bare skin about the gape as in all other New Zealand forms of crested penguin. In immature plumage of the first year the superciliary stripe is poorly developed and indicated only by a few pale cream feathers. The chin and throat are whitish. Plumage otherwise as in adult. The downy young have thick sooty brown down above and dirty white below.

Voice: As in Rockhopper but of a lower tone and more hoarse.

Habitat and range: The range of this species is north of the Sub-Tropical Convergence and extends from the coasts of Otago, western coast of Stewart Island, the Solander Islands and from western Southland through all the fiords north to Okarito and south Westland including Jackson Bay. Unsuccessful attempts at nesting have been recorded from as far north as Cook Strait.

Breeding: Throughout the greater part of the nesting range, these penguins build in caves or in deep cavities beneath the roots of trees in coastal forest. They are seldom seen standing about in the open during daylight hours and conspicuous nesting groups may be met with only on Big Solander Island. Two eggs are laid, the first usually slightly smaller than the second but under normal nesting conditions both are hatched and two chicks frequently reared. Eggs may be found in July and chicks in August.

SNARES CRESTED PENGUIN *Eudyptes atratus* Pl. 1

Description: 29″. Superficially similar to the Fiordland Crested Penguin but darker in colour especially about the chin, throat and cheeks which are almost black, the feathers being dark based and not white based as in the last species. The superciliary yellow crest is brighter, if somewhat narrower, and is more extended and bushy at the free end. Bill light reddish brown. Eye bright reddish brown. Feet flesh colour with black soles.

The female is similar with a slightly smaller bill. Immature birds, which have darker bills, are whitish and mottled about the throat and the superciliary crest is represented only by a few yellowish feathers interspersed with black. Nestling down is smoky brown above, white below.

At all ages and especially in the adults, a fleshy exposed line of pale naked skin extends from the gape round the bases of all the bill plates.

Voice: "A staccato bark that sounds in the distance like someone chopping wood; soft musical whistles that may give way to a series of guttural quacks reminiscent of an old drake in a farmyard; harsh screams of anger or alarm, and a number of grunts that sound in the distance like humans talking." (Stead.)

Habitat and range: Known to breed only at the Snares Islands but has been recorded

The undersides of Penguin flippers
a. Eudyptes sclateri
b. Eudyptes schlegeli
c. Eudyptes atratus
d. Eudyptes crestatus moseleyi
e. Eudyptes pachyrhynchus
f. Eudyptes crestatus filholi

as a straggler from Antipodes and points along the New Zealand coast north to Banks Peninsula. It is possible that the now extinct crested penguin of the Chatham Islands was of this form or closely allied to it.
Breeding: This species forms dense and compact nesting colonies in clearings a short distance from the sea on the Snares Islands. The clearings are usually along the line of small creeks or waterways and form open patches in the heavy coastal scrub which clothes the main Snares Island. A mile or so away on the Western Reef, where there is no vegetation, the nests on bare rock are very similar in disposition and concentration to that of the Erect-crested Penguin at Bounty Islands. Two eggs are laid and two chicks frequently reared. The laying dates are in September. The young are fully fledged by the end of January.

ERECT-CRESTED PENGUIN *Eudyptes sclateri*
Description: 28″. The dorsal plumage in this species is very dark bluish black, with feathers of the chin, throat, cheeks, head and crown appearing almost jet black. They are however faintly blue-edged on the crown. The crest is comparatively short. The feathers when erected by muscular contraction tend to rise up into a bristle rising at a steep angle from the region of the gape about the eye to the back of the crown. Bill reddish brown. Eye dark reddish brown. Feet fleshy white with black soles.
The female is slightly smaller but otherwise similar in plumage. In immature plumage of the first year the throat is mottled with white and grey feathers and the incipient crest is hardly developed. The downy young are sooty black above and white below.
Voice: Rather a deep-toned squawk or resonant yell. Generally similar to that of other crested penguins.
Habitat and range: Breeding distribution is at its most dense at the Bounty Islands where practically no other species is nesting: almost as abundant at Antipodes Island where Rockhoppers also occur; and in much smaller numbers associated with Rockhoppers at Campbell and Auckland Islands. As a straggler it has occurred as far south as Macquarie Island and on winter migration has been noted at sea off the coasts of Canterbury and Cook Strait. Immature and moulting birds have been recorded as far north as North Cape. Breeding has also been attempted at Otago Peninsula.
Breeding: Either in dense colonies of their own kind or associated with large numbers of Rockhoppers, Erect-crested Penguins make their nests on the rock surface or ledges a short distance above high-water mark. They seldom ascend to altitudes reached by several of the other related species. They are normally found incubating only one egg (late in October) but it is reliably recorded that two eggs are laid and the first one almost immediately discarded or kicked out of the nest.

ROYAL PENGUIN *Eudyptes schlegeli*   *Pl. 1*
Description: 30″. The dorsal plumage is light bluish grey. The underparts pure white. There is considerable variation in the pattern

of facial and head plumage. In most males the forehead, chin, throat and sides of the head and neck are white like the underparts with a faint stain of yellow near the gape. In others a small triangular patch of dark feathers appears as a spot in the middle of the throat. In others this extends to a completely grey area throughout the cheeks and round the eye and in a few examples this is entirely dark slaty grey attaining a condition indistinguishable from that of the closely related Macaroni Penguin (*Eudyptes chrysolophus*) of the South Atlantic and Indian Oceans. The adult crest consists of golden orange feathers springing from the middle and sides of the crown and bright black extremities. The longest of these are nearly 3″ long and they either lie back along the crown or droop down on both sides behind the eyes. Eyes bright geranium red. Bill light reddish brown. Feet flesh colour with black soles.

Females resemble the males except that few, if any of them, have the extreme white face and all are somewhat smaller in the dimensions of the bill. Immature birds in their first year show exactly the same range of facial pattern but the crest feathers are incipient and short and are not fully developed until after the third year. Chicks in down are smoky brown above and white below.

Voice: A deep-throated bray.

Habitat and range: Endemic at Macquarie Island. Stragglers are rarely recorded as far north as the New Zealand coast but have been met with fairly regularly at Campbell Island and occasionally in Otago.

Breeding: Around the coast of Macquarie Island, Royal Penguins tend to form very large colonies of up to half a million birds in closely packed groups. Some of these are on flattish coastal terraces and others on rocky face sites similar to those of the Rockhoppers. In one or two valleys the birds trek some distance inland and occupy areas of the valley basins associated with the tributary systems of small streams. Only one egg is incubated and one chick reared but again there are records of a first laid egg being regularly discarded at the time the second egg is laid. Incubation period, *c.* 6 weeks.

GREBES: Podicipedidae

Grebes comprise a small cosmopolitan family of lobe-footed waterbirds with the feet set far back. They are expert divers. Superficially they resemble ducks, but are at once distinguished by their pointed bills and " tailless " appearance. Two species breed in New Zealand.

CRESTED GREBE *Podiceps australis*
  Local names: Puteketeke, Topknot Shag.
  Description: 20″. Upperparts darkish brown; underparts satiny white. Unmistakable in summer plumage when blackish " horns " and rufous frill (tippets) are developed. In winter cheeks and throat

are white. Neck straight and slender. Bill (2¼″) sharply-pointed. Reluctant to take wing. Flight which is direct and low with head and neck held stiffly forward, rather below level of body, reveals a surprising amount of white in the wing. Sexes alike.

Voice: When agitated near the nest, a series of hoarse, wailing calls.

Habitat and range: Lowland and subalpine lakes of the South Island, most plentiful in South Westland. Appears to be rather sedentary, but sometimes reported in winter on coastal and estuarine waters. No recent records from the North Island.

Breeding: Nest usually a floating structure of rushes and waterweeds attached to reeds, sunken branches or a drooping bough; sometimes on land under overhanging cover. Eggs 3–5, pale bluish chalky, quickly becoming stained. Both sexes incubate: period *c.* 23 days. Young grebes in striped downy plumage frequently ride on the backs of their parents. The courtship of the New Zealand race of the Crested Grebe

has not been studied. Yet in the words of Julian Huxley, " The grebes have wonderful mutual ceremonies—their courtship is as strange and fantastic as that of any gaudy tropical creature."

H. R. McKenzie watched a pair displaying, while accompanied by well-grown young.

DABCHICK *Podiceps rufopectus*
Local names: Diver, Weweia.

Description: 11″. Top of head and hindneck black glossed with green and faintly streaked; cheeks less dusky with eye showing conspicuously white; upperparts blackish-brown; foreneck and breast rufous; under-parts silvery with flanks dusty brown. Dark silky feathers take the place of a tail; but seen from behind the tail-end looks almost white and fluffed up. Bill (1″) relatively stout. Neck slender when extended.

Voice: A rather shrill sibilant *wee-ee-ee* (hence Maori name). A nest building pair communicated by a series of low-pitched *tuk-tuk-tuk* notes (Edgar).

Habitat and range: Widely distributed in the North Island; locally plentiful, especially on the lakes of the Volcanic Plateau up to nearly 3000 feet and on the sand-dune pools of the north and south peninsulas of Kaipara. Rather a sedentary species; but there is some evidence of autumn wandering, and new dams and reservoirs are being colonised, probably by young birds. On the larger lakes of the Volcanic Plateau loose winter flocks may appear. Dabchicks seem to avoid shallow lowland lakes heavily infested with eels.

Now very scarce in the South Island where it has quite disappeared from many former haunts.

Breeding: Nest " a flimsy, clumsily-built but bulky structure " of waterlogged material anchored to overhanging branches or rushes but sometimes on a solid ledge or platform; even reported in a boat-shed.

Breeding season August–May. Clutch 2–3; eggs white, chalky; quickly yellowish-brown with stain. When a sitting bird slips off the nest, it deftly covers the eggs with weed. Downy nestlings curiously variegated, take to water soon after hatching; often rest by riding on parents' backs.

ALBATROSSES: Diomedeidae

The largest of the petrel family and amongst the largest of living birds, albatrosses are also noted for their perfection of gliding flight. Except in the Pacific Ocean they are restricted to the southern hemisphere. Identification resolves itself into field characters which can be detected when the bird is on the wing as few people have the opportunity or occasion to see albatrosses when they are settled ashore, nesting places with very few exceptions being on uninhabited and often inaccessible islands. There are two very large species, the Wandering Albatross and the Royal Albatross confined to the southern hemisphere and several more of smaller size frequently called Mollymawks to distinguish them from the larger birds. The breeding places of members of this family in New Zealand seas are all south of latitude 44°.

WANDERING ALBATROSS *Diomedea exulans* *Pl. 3*
Maori name: Toroa.
Description: 30″–50″. Beginning their flying life with plumage which is uniformly dark brown except for contrasting white patches on the face and complete underwing, Wandering Albatrosses go through a series of plumage changes which present a bewildering variety of pattern until in old males of the larger of the forms the plumage appears almost entirely white except for the black wing-tips. The series of diagrams accompanying the text gives some indication of the range of pattern that may be expected. Beaks in life are pink with a yellowish tip, eyelids pale powder blue, feet a fleshy white with purple veining and eyes dark brown.
Voice: The only sound heard at sea is a hoarse croak, made when they are fighting for scraps. During display, besides beak-clappering, they gobble, neigh and squeal.
Habitat and range: Wandering Albatrosses have a wide oceanic range throughout the southern ocean between latitudes 22°–66° south. Immature birds and non-breeders are at sea throughout the year and many of them probably circumnavigate the globe in high latitudes. Their breeding distribution in the New Zealand region includes Antipodes Island, Campbell Island, Auckland Islands (*exulans*) and at Macquarie Island a breeding population of the large snowy circumpolar form (*chionoptera*), which is found also breeding in the South Indian and South Atlantic Oceans.
Breeding: This starts in late January and for each pair continues throughout twelve months until the single fledgling flies some time in the following January. Adults then miss a year before breeding again. The nest is a well-built mound of tussock and short lengths of vegetation with a plentiful supply of earth for binding. A single elongated white egg is laid; incubation period 66 days and the young bird remains on the nest for about seven months or longer. While still clothed in nestling down it is a very pale grey which becomes much faded by the time it gives place to the chocolate brown immature plumage.

ROYAL ALBATROSS *Diomedea epomophora* *Pl. 3*
Maori name: Toroa.
Description: 30″–50″. As with the Wandering Albatross, there are two races separated by size, the larger race *epomophora* having a more southerly distribution and attaining a much whiter adult plumage. At no stage is the plumage dark as in the Wandering Albatross and young birds are very similar to adults. The whole body except the

wings is pure white and the amount of black on the wings varies from total coverage to a pattern heavily flecked with white. Bill horn coloured faintly pink in life; cutting edges of both mandibles black: eyelids black, feet whitish, purple veined.

Voice: As in Wandering Albatross.

Habitat and range: The smaller race (*sanfordi*) nests at Chatham Islands and on Otago Peninsula; the larger at Campbell, where it is very plentiful, and Auckland Islands. Distribution at sea is not generally so widespread as that of the Wandering Albatross but examples of both forms have been observed or collected off the coasts of South America.

Breeding: The cycle follows much the same pattern as that of the Wanderer but the season is about two months earlier, eggs being laid in November, hatching early in February with the young departing in September. The southern race is about three weeks later. The young at all stages of down are pure white and the first full-fledged condition differs from the adult only in having some dark barring across the shoulders.

BLACK-BROWED MOLLYMAWK: *Diomedea melanophris Pls. 4, 5*

Description: 20″–25″. Adult plumage is pure white except for black wings and mantle, dark grey tail and a smudge of smoky grey about the eye. In adult birds the bill is yellow with a pink tip, feet are pale bluish white. Immature birds have a darker bill and there is some blackish feathering under the wings giving the pattern shown in accompanying plates (4 and 5). The distinctive race of Black-browed Mollymawk (*impavida*) breeding as far as is known only in the New Zealand area, has a pale honey-coloured eye when adult, whereas the slightly larger circumpolar race (*melanophris*) has a dark eye at all ages.

Voice: As with most mollymawks a loud plaintive cry, like the bah of a sheep, is characteristic of this species when at the nest.

Habitat and range: From their sub-antarctic nesting places these mollymawks range north to New Zealand coastal waters and their range to the southward goes to the northern limits of the pack ice throughout the year. The New Zealand race breeds at Campbell Island and apparently in smaller numbers at Antipodes Island. The circumpolar race breeds at Macquarie Island.

Breeding: This begins in October and lasts till the end of March or early April. Nests are mounds with a cup-shaped depression and most of the nests are in close proximity in breeding colonies. Frequently the Black-browed Mollymawk occupies sections of areas already used by Grey-headed Mollymawks or alternatively there may be a few Grey-heads associated with larger colonies of Black-brows. The egg is elongated, white with pinkish speckles at the larger end.

Incubation period *c.* 56 days and the single chick is fed by both parents. Nestling down is pale grey.

GREY-HEADED MOLLYMAWK: *Diomedea chrysostoma Pls. 4, 5*

Description: 20″–25″. The adult bird has a dark grey head and neck, well defined from the white plumage of the rest of the underparts. There is some white feathering under the wing in a pattern shown in the text figure and in other respects the plumage of the upperparts is similar to that of other mollymawks. The *bill*, however, is distinguished by *dark central stripe edged above and below with rich yellow shading to a bright pink tip*. A dark brown eye set in the midst of the grey plumage of the head is relieved by a half-circle of white feathers at the back of the eyelid. The bill of the immature bird is dusky.

Voice: As in other mollymawks.

Habitat and range: Another circumpolar species of which no races have been clearly defined. The bird appears to have a more restricted wandering distribution at sea than the Black-browed Mollymawk but the breeding range appears to be almost exactly the same and the one species is seldom found nesting without the other also being present.

Breeding: Can be described as almost exactly the same as that of the Black-brow except that it starts about two weeks earlier and the young are distinguished by having down of a slightly darker shade of grey. They fledge and leave the nest two weeks or so before the companion species.

YELLOW-NOSED MOLLYMAWK   *Diomedea chlororhynchus*

Description: 20″–25″. The smallest of the mollymawks resembling the others in plumage pattern except that the *underwing, mainly white, has a dark anterior border slightly wider than the dark posterior one*. The head and neck in adults and young are white like the underparts except that in fresh adult plumage there is a grey smudge on the cheeks. *Adult bill black with the ridge of the culmen yellow deepening to scarlet near the tip*. The immature bill is entirely black. Eyes brown; feet pale fleshy grey.

Voice: The usual bleat.

Habitat and range: Inhabiting the less cold northerly section of the west wind belt, this mollymawk, breeding only at the Tristan da Cunha group in the Atlantic and St. Paul and Amsterdam in the Indian Ocean, ranges normally eastward as far as the Tasman Sea; but has been sighted several times near the Three Kings, in the outer waters of the Hauraki Gulf and at least once near Cuvier Island.

BULLER'S MOLLYMAWK   *Diomedea bulleri*   *Pls. 4, 5*

Description: 25″. This is another small mollymawk of slightly stouter build than the Yellow-nosed. Superficially it resembles the Grey-headed with a central dark band separating the yellow of the upper and lower surfaces of the bill. Cheeks and hind neck are grey but the *forehead is white*. The plumage otherwise is normal as in all mollymawks, the underwing pattern having much the same dark bordering as is found in the Yellow-nosed. Immature birds have a nondescript blackish-grey bill darker towards the tip and somewhat blotchy markings on the neck.

Plate 1

PENGUINS

Voice: Not distinguishable from the sheep-like bleat of the other species.
Habitat and range: Breeding only in New Zealand seas in waters along the convergence, a few examples have been found in the Humboldt current region of South America. Feeding range south to 50°.
Breeding: There are anomalies in the breeding season in that at the Chatham Islands the birds are reported to follow the normal cycle of egg-laying in October-November, with the young fully fledged about April or May. Elsewhere at Solander Island and the Snares the laying period is February, with young fledged and flying in August.

SHY (WHITE-CAPPED) MOLLYMAWK *Diomedea cauta*

Description: 30″–35″. The largest of the mollymawks approaching in size some of the smaller races of Wandering and Royal Albatross. This and the next two mollymawks differ from the others in that the underwing is practically pure white with a narrow dark border all around. They have the usual pure white body, black wings and mantle and grey tail. The bill is indistinctly coloured, being pale greenish-grey changing to yellow at tip. There is a thin flesh orange stripe outlining the base of the lower mandible. Apart from the dark eyebrow line, head and neck are pure white in adult males, with a slight dusting of grey on the cheek of females. Bills in immature birds are generally duller and darker.
Habitat and range: Shy Mollymawks have been recorded all round the southern hemisphere, but as breeding birds only to the south of Australia and New Zealand.
Breeding: Australian breeding islands are in Bass Strait and off the southern tip of Tasmania. The New Zealand breeding station is at the Auckland Islands. The breeding season is from October, when eggs are laid until late February or early March, when the young depart.

GREY-BACKED (BOUNTY ISLAND) MOLLYMAWK *Pls. 4, 5*
Diomedea salvini

Description; 25″–30″. Usually regarded as a subspecies of the Shy Mollymawk, the Grey-backed is distinctive enough in appearance to be treated separately. Its bill is noticeably darker along the central area, paler on the culmen and mandible. There is a well-defined patch of grey spreading past the cheeks and down and around the neck. The mantle feathers are paler grey than in any other mollymawk and contrast noticeably with the dark wings.
Habitat and range: This race has also been recorded as a wanderer in all southern seas.
Breeding: Breeds only in New Zealand where it nests at the Bounty Islands and at the Snares (Western Reef). Nesting season, as for the Shy Mollymawk.

CHATHAM ISLAND MOLLYMAWK *Diomedea eremita Pl. 4*
Description: 25″–30″. No doubt properly regarded as another subspecies of the Shy Mollymawk, this one is even more distinctive in

appearance. It is slightly smaller than either *cauta* or *salvini* and much darker in overall pigmentation. The crown is pale grey and the cheeks and neck even darker grey, making very little contrast with the mantle. The *bill* is perhaps the most distinctive feature, being *rich chrome yellow all over*.

Habitat and range: Restricted as far as is known to the Chatham Islands where it breeds on Pyramid Rock ranging to adjacent seas. There are a few records from the coast of New Zealand but not apparently any farther afield.

LIGHT-MANTLED SOOTY ALBATROSS *Phoebetria* *Pl. 3*
palpebrata

Description: 25″–30″. In this distinctive species the entire plumage is dark except for the small half-circle of white feathers on the eyelid. Main body plumage light pearly brown shading to intense chocolate on the head and cheeks, wings and tail dark brown. *Tail wedge-shaped.* Bill black with pale blue fleshy line on the mandibular sulcus. Eyes dark hazel; feet pale fleshy white. The immature bird is similar in plumage but the bill usually lacks the pale blue line.

Voice: At nesting places a distinctive call, seldom heard at sea, consists of two clear notes which may be transcribed as " Pee-oo." Hence its vernacular name current among sealers and seafarers.

Habitat and range: There are two races of Sooty Albatross in the southern hemisphere and the Light-mantled is the only one known to occur in New Zealand seas. Breeding at Auckland, Campbell, Antipodes and Macquarie Islands, Sooty Albatrosses range widely along a narrow latitudinal belt south to the Antarctic Circle and very rarely north of 40° S. It is thus not a common bird off the coasts of New Zealand and does not frequent inshore waters.

Breeding: Nests are situated on cliff ledges and the small terraces of steep slopes. Usually solitary and very rarely in groups of three or four on suitable ledges. Like those of mollymawks they are steep-sided columns of mud and vegetation; the single egg laid in October, hatches early in January; the young are attended until able to fly in late April or early May.

PETRELS, SHEARWATERS AND FULMARS: Procellariidae

GIANT PETREL *Macronectes giganteus*

Other Names: Nelly, Stinker, Black Molly.

Description: 20″–30″. Males are noticeably larger than females and have heavier bills. Somewhat variable in colour, adult Giant Petrels in average plumage are dull rusty brown, much paler on the face, throat and neck. As the brown feathers have weak pigmentation they

fade rapidly and a mottled variable appearance is not uncommon. Bills vary from horn colour to greenish and feet are from dull brown to almost black. There is also variability in the colour of the eye which may be brown flecked or dull greyish-white. Immature birds in at least their first and second years are a rich glossy brown without the fading variations. The pale beak and dark feet are fairly uniformly so and the eye also is dark. A distinctive feature of the bird's appearance is the heavy bill with the elongated single nasal tube. The white form with scattered black feathers in its plumage is common at Macquarie, but rather rare in the coastal waters of New Zealand proper.

Voice: A hoarse, wheezy croak.

Habitat and range: Mainly scavengers, Giant Petrels are amongst the best documented of ocean wanderers. They have been banded at various breeding places and many recoveries have helped to indicate the extensive wanderings of immature birds in particular. The species is circumpolar in the southern hemisphere and in New Zealand seas is found breeding at Chatham, Stewart, Snares, Auckland, Campbell, Antipodes and Macquarie Islands.

Breeding: The laying season extends over a period from August to October.[1] A single white egg is laid on a roughly constructed nest lacking the elaborate build-up of albatrosses and mollymawks. Chicks, when hatched, show the two colour phases found in the adult population and a proportion of them have pure white down, the rest with pattern of grey and white. On leaving the nesting places the young tend to move in a northerly direction and down-wind from the breeding places. A large non-breeding population is thus to be found at sea as far north as Lat. 30° S. Scavenger flocks congregate about whaling stations, coastal meat works, and other sources of offal. These groups are shown by banded birds to include individuals from almost all the known breeding places in the southern hemisphere.

CAPE PIGEON   *Daption capensis*

Description: 16″. This is one of the few members of the petrel family with a strongly contrasting pattern and is too well known to need detailed description. Head, neck, cheeks, are dark blackish-brown. The back is strongly spotted with black on white, upper tail-coverts white, tip of tail black. There is a broad white bar on the black wings and this often appears as three irregular white lozenge-shaped patches. Underparts white; bill black; feet black; with an occasional splash of bluish-white on the webs.

Voice: Often a harsh cackle from flocks at sea. At the nest, among a variety of softer calls, the most notable is a prolonged whirring coo.

[1] Early and late breeders at Macquarie Island may be different races (Warham).

Habitat and range: The oceanic range is extremely wide from the antarctic ice to Lat. 25° S. As scavenging flocks, large concentrations of Cape Pigeons are common throughout the year off the coast as far north as Cook Strait coming boldly into inshore waters where offal from whaling stations and other sources is available. A few in winter enter the Bay of Plenty and Hauraki Gulf.

Breeding: Cape Pigeons breed from the coasts of Antarctica through many high latitude sub-antarctic islands, with a few more northerly outposts at nearly all the New Zealand sub-antarctic islands. The most northerly known is at the Snares. In their sub-antarctic nesting places the birds are almost all inaccessible on high ledges. A single white egg is laid on a rough nest of chips of rock and the chick is reared in the usual way through guard stages by the parents. Egg dates from the New Zealand region are early October, hatching in December with the young flying in late March–early April—in plumage not readily distinguishable from adults.

SILVER-GREY (ANTARCTIC) FULMAR *Fulmarus glacialoides*
Pl. 7

Description: 17″. This bird is the southern counterpart of the common Fulmar of the northern hemisphere and is similar in appearance being slightly larger and only a little paler in general coloration. Head, neck and underparts are mainly white with a little shading of grey on the hind neck. Back and tail are pearly grey, wings with dark primaries, a pale white patch showing on the upper surface when the bird is in flight. Bill is pinkish horn colour with a bluish tinge on the nasal tube. Feet pale with some darker patches on the outer toes.

Habitat and range: The Silver-grey Fulmar breeds only south of the Antarctic Circle. In New Zealand waters it has been recorded often enough to be regarded as a regular straggler. The most northerly records are: 3 found dead on the Auckland west coast (1949, 1954, 1959); 1 alive off Cape Runaway, Bay of Plenty on 23/8/62.

BLUE PETREL *Halobaena caerulea*   Pl. 7
Description: 12″. This petrel conforms closely in appearance with the prions described later. In flight the upper surface appears bluish-grey with a dark marking extending from the blackish primaries

Blue Petrel

to the carpal flexure at an angle across the lower secondaries and connected by a dark patch on the rump to the similar pattern of the other wing. This forms an inverted " w. " Upper tail-coverts and tail are the same blue-grey as the back, but *the tip of the tail is pure white.* On the crown the feathers darken to a cap which is almost black. There is a mottled forehead, mainly white, underparts including under-wing, pure white; bill black; feet pale blue with pinkish webs.

Habitat and range: Blue Petrels are probably circumpolar in the southern hemisphere and the origin of the birds frequently found throughout winter on New Zealand coasts may be any of the breeding places known from the South Atlantic and South Indian Oceans. They are not known to breed for certain in the New Zealand area although nesting at Macquarie Island is strongly suspected as they are found there throughout the breeding season and remains are plentiful in older deposits on the shore. There is a normal summer breeding season with eggs in October and young flying late February-early March. Beachcombing has shown that Blue Petrels may be present in the Tasman Sea from May to October. In 1954 between these months, eighteen were picked up on the Auckland west coast.

PRIONS The group of petrels which make up this genus is peculiar to the southern hemisphere. It has given much trouble to systematists who are unable to agree on the best classification to express relationships. On superficial view, all prions, or whale-birds as they are sometimes known in sealers' usage, look very much alike, only the extremes of the large Broadbilled Prion and the smaller Fairy Prions being distinguishable on sight at sea. A study of birds from breeding places shows that there is an almost bewildering variety of distinguishable forms, if minute details of bill sizes and plumage characters are taken into account. It is considered that the subdivision given here will enable most observers to place a specimen in the right species.

BROAD-BILLED PRION *Pachyptila vittata*
Other names: Parara, Blue Billy (Chathams).
Description: 11″–12″. Upperparts mainly grey-blue, slightly darker on the crown with blackish patches behind and below the eye, and

dark areas of the wing forming the pattern already described for the Blue Petrel. The upper tail-coverts are the same shade as the back. Tail feathers likewise, but broadly tipped with black terminally. Bill, which is nearly as broad as it is long, is usually steel grey above and bluish along the side of the mandible. A few individuals have bluish bill plates above also as all the smaller prions have. The generally darker bill and large head, are features which permit the Broad-billed Prion to be identified sometimes at close quarters. Eyes brown, feet blue with pale webs.

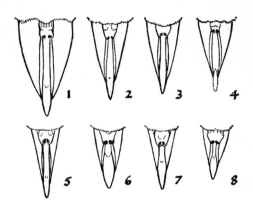

1. Broad-billed Prion, *Pachyptila vittata*
2. Lesser Broad-billed Prion, *P. salvini*
3. Crozet Island Prion, *P. salvini crozeti*
4. Auckland Island Prion, *P. desolata alter*
5. Narrow-billed Prion, *P. belcheri*
6. Fulmar Prion, *P. crassirostris*
7. Fairy Prion, *P. turtur*
8. Lesser (Southern) Fairy Prion, *P. turtur fallai*

Voice: A dove-like coo with some guttural undertones.
Habitat and range: Broad-billed Prions have a restricted breeding range along the convergence region of all the southern oceans. The New Zealand populations are found nesting from the mainland coasts of Foveaux Strait and the south-western fiords through the Stewart Island region, including the Snares, and at Chatham Islands. This species does not wander very far except for ranging in winter into northern New Zealand waters.
Breeding: Egg dates early September, hatching October-November, and young flying in December and January. Incubation period *c.* 56 days; fledging *c.* 7 weeks.

LESSER BROAD-BILLED PRION *Pachyptila salvini*

Description: 11". As for Broad-billed Prion but with narrower bill, the upper plates of which in life are always bluish and not steel grey.

Habitat and range: Recorded in New Zealand only as a winter visitor, the Lesser Broad-billed Prion and several forms very similar to it may be found at sea or blown ashore in very large numbers along the west coasts of New Zealand. There is no evidence that any forms of this prion breed in the New Zealand area and their origin must be the South Indian Ocean. Most New Zealand specimens are immature, many in fresh first-year plumage.

ANTARCTIC PRION *Pachyptila desolata*

Description: 10½". In plumage as for Broad-billed Prion. The specific distinctions are in the form of the bill which is moderately wide, that is, width about half the length; the sides of the bill seen from above are fairly straight without convexity; the *lamellæ* or fringe of thin plates, well developed in Broad-billed and Lesser Broad-billed Prions, are *small* and *not usually visible* at the gape when the bill is closed.

Habitat and range: Although races of the Antarctic Prion are known to nest at Auckland Islands (*P.d. alter*) and Macquarie Island, the flocks found in New Zealand seas throughout the winter are composed for the most part of the distinguishable races breeding much farther west in the subantarctic zone.

NARROW-BILLED PRION *Pachyptila belcheri*

Description: 10". Plumage not distinguishable from the species already described. The *very narrow bill*, with width less than half the length, is the distinguishing character. This prion could not be distinguished on sight at sea.

Habitat and range: The known breeding range is Kerguelen and Falkland Islands but Narrow-billed Prions are regular winter visitors to New Zealand seas. It has been ascertained that large mixed flocks of prions ranging as far north as the Kermadec Islands include many of this species.

FAIRY PRION *Pachyptila turtur*

Maori name: Titiwainui (Stewart Is.)

Description: 9". In general, this species is like the others but is smaller, more stockily built, with a relatively smaller head and generally lacking in any darker tone on the crown. The most useful distinguishing mark, however, is the *greater extent of black at the end of the tail*. When the bird is on the wing this band appears to be fully half the exposed tail and, in fact, it may be ascertained from a specimen in the hand that the tips of the upper tail-coverts are also blackish in this species of prion only. Bill blue, feet bluish with pale webs.

Habitat and range: This is the common resident breeding prion of New Zealand and South Australian seas. Found on islands off the coast from Poor Knights to the Snares, and at the Chatham Islands.

A small sub-antarctic race (*fallai*) occurs at Antipodes Islands and there are several forms distinguishable on some inshore islands, e.g. Motunau. Flocks are at sea throughout the year and there appears to be no extensive migratory movement either north or south of the main breeding range. A vagrant in the South Atlantic.

Breeding: Eggs are laid from late September through October; and young, hatching early in December, are fledged at the end of January when the main exodus flights occur. Incubation period *c.* 55 days; fledging *c.* 7 weeks.

FULMAR PRION *Pachyptila crassirostris*

Description: 9½″. Very similar to Fairy Prion in plumage pattern, but more sturdily built, usually a shade paler overall and distinguished by a *robust swelling of the bill plates*. Actual measurements are not very helpful in distinguishing this form from the others, but the shape of the bill is diagnostic.

Habitat and range: Fulmar Prions range farther south than Fairy Prions. They nest at Chatham Islands on two steep rocky islets and at Auckland Islands in the New Zealand area. Another race occurs on Bounty Island where they nest in fairly exposed crevices.

FLESH-FOOTED SHEARWATER *Puffinus carneipes* Pl. 6

Description: 18″. An all brown shearwater distinguishable on sight by its *pale beak*, darker only at the tip, and the pale *flesh-coloured feet*. In plumage, these birds are not noticeably different from any other dark shearwaters but they are more compactly built than any others in the New Zealand area and are likely to be confused only with the still blacker *Procellaria parkinsoni*.

Voice: As with most petrels, vocal activity is mainly on shore at the nesting place. A variety of calls includes a cat-like mew.

Habitat and range: This is a migrant shearwater breeding only in the southern hemisphere but normally absent in the northern hemisphere during the non-breeding season. Breeding places in the New Zealand area range from the Hen and Chickens Islands to the region of Cook Strait. At sea the range is southward to the latitude of the Chatham Islands and off the New Zealand coast in the same belt.

Breeding: Laying dates are from late November to early December, hatching starting in mid-January and fledglings taking their departure in April. Nestling down is uniformly dark grey and the first plumage of young birds is similar to that of adults.

WEDGE-TAILED SHEARWATER *Puffinus pacificus* Pl. 6

Other name: Black Burrower (Raoul).

Description: 18″. An all brown shearwater with a long wedge-shaped tail, pale feet, and a dull compressed bill more slender in outline than that of the Flesh-footed Shearwater with which it might otherwise be confused. The breeding birds of the Kermadecs all seem to be of the dark phase.

Voice: Strange and weird, resembling the growls and snarls of fighting cats.

Habitat and range: Widely distributed over the tropical Pacific and Indian Oceans. Known to breed in the New Zealand region only at the Kermadecs; and rarely recorded farther south. A specimen of a white-breasted form, picked up at Makara on 26/1/61, is thought to be from a breeding area in the north Pacific.

Breeding: Adults return and start cleaning out burrows in October. Eggs mostly in early December; young hatched generally by the end of January; a few birds may linger at breeding grounds till early June.

BULLER'S SHEARWATER *Puffinus bulleri*   Pl. 6

Description: 18″. A large wedge-tailed shearwater with distinctive plumage pattern. Crown, hind neck, and mantle are dark, shading to grey on the back and on the upper wing-coverts. The pattern of primaries and the outer part of secondaries forms an inverted " w " pattern separated from the dark wedge-shaped tail by grey upper tail-coverts. Underparts, including underwing, pure white, bill bluish-grey dark on the ridge, feet flesh colour, dark on the outer sides.

Voice: Heard only at the nesting places, a mewing call is the main feature with some low cackling notes.

Habitat and range: The main breeding place at the Poor Knights Islands is the centre of a wide dispersal throughout New Zealand seas from early September to mid-May as far south as Banks Peninsula and the western approaches to Cook Strait. Migrates to the north Pacific in the off-season. In summer conspicuously abundant in the Hauraki Gulf and Bay of Plenty.

Breeding: Late November—early December is the laying period; hatching in January and fledglings ready to leave at the beginning of April.

SOOTY SHEARWATER *Puffinus griseus*   Pl. 6

Other names: Muttonbird, Titi.

Description: 17″. Another shearwater all brown except for the greyish tinge of the underparts and the sprinkling of white and mottled feathers in the underwing coverts. As the bill is dark grey and the feet dark lilac with brown markings on the outer side, the general impression is of a dark bird, except for the conspicuous silvery flash of the underwing coverts.

Voice: The predominant sounds are " oo " and " ah " in various combinations in which the tempo increases and the series frequently ends with a yell.

Habitat and range: With a wide breeding range in the south temperate zones and extensive migrations to the northern hemisphere, this is one of the best known of shearwaters. Apart from the little known nesting regions of South America, the largest breeding concentration is in New Zealand seas mainly south of 44° S. and extending to Macquarie Island, 55° S. Smaller breeding colonies are scattered as far north as the Three Kings Islands. In the Stewart Island area, there is extreme density of population and a restricted commercial industry known as mutton-birding.

Breeding: Adults come ashore in October and start cleaning out burrows. Eggs laid mid-November to early December; hatching mostly in late January; young leave late April or early May. Incubation period *c.* 8 weeks; fledging 86–106 days. Both parents incubate.

SHORT-TAILED SHEARWATER (Tasmanian Muttonbird) *Pl. 6*
Puffinus tenuirostris

Description: 15″. Similar to the Sooty Shearwater in colour of plumage but usually lacking the pale areas under the wings. Bill and feet similar in colour, but the bill is proportionately shorter in this species and the general smaller size is also a useful field character.

Habitat and range: Cool temperate waters of the Australian coast with concentration of breeding at islands in Bass Strait where there is a regular industry similar to that conducted in New Zealand with the other species. Egg dates, general life history and departure dates are similar and there is a mass migration to the northern hemisphere. This has been well documented by banding studies in Australia and significant recoveries. In some years many are " wrecked " on the long west coast as they set out on their northward migration. Judged by the frequency of strandings, Tasmanian Muttonbirds regularly occur also in summer in the outer waters of the Hauraki Gulf and Bay of Plenty. Three were watched closely at the Poor Knights on 20/12/58 as they fed among Red-billed Gulls. (R. B. S.)

FLUTTERING SHEARWATER *Puffinus gavia*   *Pl. 6*
Maori name: Pakaha.

Description: 13″. One of the smaller shearwaters, brown above and white below. The brown is seldom of dark tone except in fresh moulted birds and becomes somewhat faded and rusty for most of the year. In the region of the neck there is a faintly mottled darkish collar and breast patch; underwing-coverts are conspicuously white and the undertail-coverts likewise. Legs and feet dark on the outer side and pale fleshy in the inner surfaces; bill darkish olive appearing blackish at a distance. Fluttering Shearwaters spend much time resting on the surface of the sea and in flight they skim the water with a rapid wing-action. In high winds or a rough sea, they assume the rising and falling gliding flight characteristic of most shearwaters. When feeding they also dive frequently and can swim well under water.

Voice: Exceptionally strong for a bird of such small size. A cackling call is sometimes heard even when the birds are feeding or resting at sea. On their approach to nesting grounds after dark, they are very noisy with a rapid staccato repetition of a call which can roughly be rendered by one of the Maori names for the bird " Pakaha " with the emphasis on the last syllable. " The normal full call sounded like *kahów kahów kahów kahów, kehék kehék kehék kehék—errr*; the *Kehek* is sharper, faster and slightly higher pitched than the *kahow*; and the final *errr* tails off as a rather drawn-out note at a lower pitch. There are many variants." (Edgar)

Habitat and range: Cool temperate waters of the New Zealand coast. Known to breed at many islands from Three Kings to Cook Strait. Their normal feeding range is not far off shore and they regularly penetrate the deeper inlets and harbours. Also recorded from the eastern seaboard of Australia, but not as a breeder.

Breeding: The first adults return to the breeding islands in August. Eggs, September–October. Young birds leave December–January.

HUTTON'S SHEARWATER *Puffinus huttoni* Pl. 6

Description: 14″. Very similar to the Fluttering Shearwater in appearance and habits. Its area of distribution is rather more southerly, although formerly it was not distinguished from it. The plumage pattern is the same except for a few scattered dusky underwing-coverts and these, together with the fact that the plumage is of a uniformly darker brown, give Hutton's Shearwater the general appearance of a darker bird altogether. *Brown flecks on lateral undertail-coverts.* The bill is slightly longer and more slender than in the average Fluttering Shearwater, but in other respects *huttoni* is almost indistinguishable.

Voice: Apparently similar to that of the Fluttering Shearwater but has only been recorded from stray birds held in the hand. From these it appears to have a slightly harsher and deeper tone, although the sequence of notes is the same.

Habitat and range: Abundant in Cook Strait and ranges down the east coast of the South Island. There are unconfirmed records from Snares Island but these are based on a series of commercially collected skins, of which the origin seems to be doubtful. The only known breeding place, discovered by G. Harrow in 1965, is at more than 4000 ft. a.s.l. in the Seaward Kaikouras. The breeding season is fully two months later than that of the Fluttering Shearwater. Young birds fresh from the nests on their first flight are regularly taken on board ships in Cook Strait or found along the adjacent shoreline in the latter half of March each year. Only rarely wrecked as far north as the Auckland west coast. Outside New Zealand occurs regularly off the coast of South Australia, with casual records as far as Western Australia.

ALLIED (LITTLE) SHEARWATER *Puffinus assimilis* Pl. 6

There are several well-marked subspecies from different breeding localities from the sub-antarctic to the sub-tropics. Three actually breed in the New Zealand region.

The following description relates to the North Island race *haurakiensis*.

Description: 12″. The smallest of the New Zealand shearwaters; dark bluish-black above and pure white below. The pattern is well defined except for a slight mottling about the cheek and ear patch.

Feet pale bluish with fleshy webs; bill dull lead blue and black along the ridge and tip.

Voice: The normal call is a rapid *kakakakakakak–urrr* repeated; the *urrr* sounding as if uttered while drawing breath. (Edgar.)

Habitat and range: Known as a breeding bird only on islands off the north-east coast of the Auckland Province and in the Bay of Plenty. This subspecies does not seem to range much beyond its breeding area and is replaced both north and south by birds of lighter build and smaller size in the sub-tropics and by a heavier and more stoutly built race in the sub-antarctic. There are small differences of measurement and plumage characters by which they can be distinguished in the hand or as museum specimens; but for field identification, it is not possible to define subspecies.

Breeding: Colonies consist of rather scattered groupings of burrows in terrain that is often fairly heavily wooded. The season extends through the winter, the birds occupying the nesting burrows from about April, with eggs in May and June and most of the young on the wing by the end of October. On Meyer I. young with little down remaining may still be in the burrows in mid-November.

NORTH ATLANTIC SHEARWATER   *Puffinus borealis*
Description: 18″. This large shearwater, dull brown above, white below, has been recorded only once in New Zealand as a straggler, a dead bird being found on Foxton Beach in January 1934. It is described briefly here in case additional strays should turn up, as there is a general trend for Atlantic petrels to drift occasionally south of the Cape of Good Hope and reach Australia or New Zealand. It is somewhat similar to the Grey Petrel but could be distinguished at sea by the decidedly darker brown colour of the head and back, the mottled upper tail-coverts, black tail and pure white under-surface of the wings. The *bill is dull yellow,* darker at the tip and the feet flesh colour stained brown on the outer toe and outer surface of the tarsus.

GREY PETREL   *Procellaria cinerea*   *Pl. 6*
Description: 19″. The general colour of the upper surface is ashy grey, darker on the crown, wings and tail. Underparts are white merging into the darker upper surface without any strongly defined line. Underwing-coverts are grey and this is a good field character when the bird is seen on the wing. The bill is parti-coloured having horn-coloured nail and tip, side plate and bottom of the lower mandible. The blackish areas are the nostril, the ridge just in front of it and the dark sulcus on the lower mandible. Feet dull flesh colour, darker on the outer side, webs distinctly yellowish.

Habitat and range: This is a bird of the southern oceans and a circumpolar breeder. In the New Zealand area breeds plentifully at Antipodes Island and in smaller numbers at Campbell Island. They occur at Macquarie Island and probably breed there but have not yet been recorded at the Auckland Islands. At sea they keep to the regions of cooler water and so are found only occasionally off the main coastline. Only rarely cast ashore as far north as Muriwai.

Breeding: A winter breeder. Eggs in May, the young leaving the nesting grounds early in November.

BLACK PETREL *Procellaria parkinsoni* *Pl. 6*

Description: 17″. Entire plumage is dark blackish brown, feet black and the bill is parti-coloured. It is bluish horn on the nostril, side plates and mandible with a dark line along the ridge of the culmen and dark tip.

Voice: Incoming birds around the summit of Little Barrier seemed to be silent; but a staccato rapidly-reiterated angry-sounding *clack-clack-clack-clack-clack* was traced to birds sitting at burrows. A soft deep-toned hissing call has also been recorded.

Habitat and range: Black Petrels are known to breed on the tops of Little Barrier and Great Barrier and on a few bush-clad mountain-tops some distance inland in Taranaki, Nelson, Westland, Fiordland and Stewart Island. Evidently migratory. Occurs as a non-breeder in the region of the Galapagos Islands.

Breeding: A late breeder. Eggs laid in December and the young flying in May and June.

WESTLAND BLACK PETREL *Procellaria westlandica* *Pl. 6*

Description: 20″. The entirely dark plumage is exactly similar to that of the Black Petrel, as are the bill and feet. There is, if anything, less tendency to bluish horn on the lighter parts of the bill and most specimens are yellowish horn.

Voice: Comparatively silent over land and near its nesting places. Sounds have been noted only when the birds are handled when they utter a wheezy alarm note (R.A.F.). But A.B. heard much noise and repeated clacking.

Distribution and habitat: Known to breed on coastal ranges a mile or two inland along a section of the west coast of the South Island between Barrytown and Punakaiki. At sea they have been observed off the west coast and in Cook Strait; and they range across the Tasman to eastern Australia. The most northerly records are of two found ashore in New South Wales and of two wrecked at Muriwai on the Auckland west coast.

Breeding: A winter breeder. Eggs in May, the young flying in November.

WHITE-CHINNED PETREL (Cape Hen) *Procellaria* *Pl. 6*
aequinoctialis

Description: 20″. Entire plumage dark blackish brown, feet black, bill yellowish horn with black nostril, black along the ridge of the culmen and along the immediate sulcus of the lower mandible. A variable amount of white chin, sometimes reduced to one or two feathers between the mandibles at the base and sometimes more extensive on one side than the other distinguishes the New Zealand race, from those of the South Indian and South Atlantic Oceans, which usually have more white on the chin.

Voice: A clacking sound is made from within the burrow and is said to be uttered also by birds sitting at the mouth of the burrow. Hence the old sealers' name, " Shoemaker."

Habitat and range: A circumpolar, mainly sub-antarctic species, breeding in the New Zealand region at Macquarie, Campbell, Antipodes and Auckland Islands. Favours the cold water zone and not common off the coast of the main islands. Occasionally stranded as far north as Muriwai.

Breeding: Breeds in the southern summer. Burrows are conspicuously large. Many of them are in wet situations with water seeping out of the tunnels; but the nest is usually built up beyond the water-level. Eggs in December; the young leaving April–May.

GREY-FACED PETREL *Pterodroma macroptera*   *Pl. 7*
   Other names: Oi. Great-winged Petrel.
   Description: 16″. Entire plumage blackish brown, pale grey on the forehead, face and throat, feet and bill black. On the wing this bird is a strong and rapid flier wheeling in broad arcs.
   Voice: Heard only at nesting grounds, a whistling call with a guttural undertone rendered roughly by the Maori name.
   Habitat and range: Forages widely over the Tasman and South Pacific eastwards nearly to Pitcairn. Other subspecies with less grey on the face occur in the south Atlantic and Indian Oceans in about the same latitudinal belt. Breeds on most off-shore islands and still on a few mainland cliffs within the triangle formed by Three Kings, Waikato Heads and East Cape.
   Breeding: A winter breeder. Eggs from May onwards, many hatching by the end of August. Young leave, November–January. This is the traditional muttonbird of the North Island Maoris, the taking season being in November.

WHITE-HEADED PETREL *Pterodroma lessoni*   *Pl. 7*
   Description: 17″. Body white, very faintly grey on the crown and hind neck, slightly darker on the back and tail, wings greyish brown and blackish mark through the eye; bill black, feet parti-coloured, being fleshy pink with brown on the outer toe and terminally on the webs.
   Voice: Vocal only at the nesting places, where it has a deep-throated purring call.
   Habitat and range: In the New Zealand region breeds at Auckland, Antipodes and Macquarie Islands; and in the south Indian Ocean at Kerguelen. Fairly common at sea to the south of New Zealand, ranging farther north in winter to about Lat. 34° S. where it sometimes associates with *macroptera*. Regularly recorded as a beach casualty, especially on the west coast of the North Island.

Plate 2

PARAKEETS, PARROTS, KINGFISHER

Breeding: Nesting season extends from November to April, most eggs hatching in late January or early February.

SUNDAY ISLAND PETREL *Pterodroma cervicalis*
Description: 17″ Plumage mainly white with a dark blackish cap and black wings and tail; scapulars and upperwing-coverts frosty grey; bill black; feet parti-coloured. Strikingly different from other petrels of this region by virtue of its black cap and white collar.
Habitat and range: Known only from the vicinity of the Kermadecs where it breeds on Raoul. Probably closely related to *externa* of the south-east Pacific.
Breeding: Returns to Raoul in October; laying begins in December; young fly in late May and June.

BIRD OF PROVIDENCE *Pterodroma solandri*
Description: 16″. A greyish brown petrel, mottled on face and forehead and having a distinctive *whitish patch at the base of primaries* visible when the bird is in flight. This helps to distinguish it from the Grey-faced petrel.
Habitat and range: Formerly bred in great numbers at Norfolk Island, but now reported extinct there. Breeds in winter at Lord Howe Island. It is curious that a petrel which breeds so close, is known in New Zealand only from a single specimen stranded at Muriwai in 1921.

PHOENIX PETREL *Pterodroma alba*
Description: 15″. Dark brown above and white below, the bases of the primaries being only slightly whitish, feet parti-coloured, that is pale fleshy with terminal dark patches on the webs and outer toe. A rather conspicuous field character is the broad *dark band on the chest*.
Habitat and range: Ranges widely in the tropical Pacific mainly south of the equator; westwards to the Kermadecs where four were found on the forest floor of Raoul Island in March 1913. Otherwise not known from New Zealand seas.

KERMADEC PETREL *Pterodroma neglecta*
Description: 15″. There are three phases of body plumage in this species with some intermediates. They have been described as dark, intermediate and light forms. In the dark form the plumage is brownish grey, the only relief in pattern being the white bases to the primaries which occur uniformly in all phases and at sea show as a pale patch in the extended wing. Wings are otherwise dark brown in all three phases. The intermediate form has a palish body and is often mottled about the face. The pale form is almost white on head and neck and over the rest of the body with the exception of the wings and tail; and except for its wing markings looks at sea something like a small version of the White-headed Petrel. Bills are black in all forms; feet usually

parti-coloured, being dark at their extremities, greyish flesh on legs in the intermediate form and pale flesh in the pale form.

Voice: A long-drawn *eeow* often loud, beginning on a high note and descending, commonly followed by three leisurely *yoks*. Brooding birds sometimes make a low, steady purr, lasting more than a minute.

Habitat and range: Has a wide breeding range in the sub-tropical Pacific from Lord Howe east to Juan Fernandez. In the New Zealand regions breeds at Raoul and Herald Islets, very rarely straying as far south as the North Island.

Breeding: Nesting takes place all year round on the Herald Islets Egg laying appears to be at its peak in February. Incubation period 50–52 days.

MOTTLED PETREL *Pterodroma inexpectata*   *Pl. 7*
Other names: Korure, Rainbird.
Description: 13″. The main tone of the plumage is a dark frosty grey. When the wings are spread there is an obscure blacker tone forming an inverted " w " pattern. The upper surface of the tail is grey like the back, the face is white with mottled transition to the dark grey of the crown, a dark mark through the eye, underparts white except for a broad grey patch on the lower breast and belly. Bill black, feet parti-coloured.
Voice: A high-pitched *ti-ti-ti* rapidly and continuously repeated. Another call is a deep resonant bugle-note of two syllables, *Goo-oo*. (Stead.)
Habitat and range: Compared with its former breeding range, which included both North and South Islands, now much restricted; its main centre of distribution being outlying islands in Foveaux Strait, off Stewart Island and at the Snares. Has a very wide oceanic range, southward to the edge of the pack ice; and northward in the southern winter to the Aleutian Islands. Not easily seen off the coasts of the main islands.
Breeding: Burrow-cleaning in November; eggs by mid-December; young flying in April.

KERGUELEN PETREL *Pterodroma brevirostris*   *Pl. 7*
Description: 13″. Almost uniformly dark frosty grey with little variation except for slight mottling on forehead and flanks on some specimens. Compared with the bills of other pterodromas, the black bill of this species is narrow and compressed. Feet purplish flesh colour, darker on the outside.
Habitat and range: Breeds in the sub-antarctic belt of the Atlantic and Indian Oceans, ranging eastwards in autumn. Only known in New Zealand from about two dozen beach casualties; but may be fairly numerous in the Tasman in some winters, e.g. 1954, when 8 were found wrecked on the Auckland west coast in July and August.

PYCROFT'S PETREL *Pterodroma pycrofti* *Pl. 7*

Description: 11". Crown, hind neck, back and central tail medium grey. Forehead and all underparts including underwing-coverts and undertail-coverts are white; the outer webs of the outer tail feathers likewise are white. Feet pale fleshy blue, darker on the outer toe. Generally smaller than Cook's Petrel, with shorter bill and wings, but with a proportionately longer tail. Very hard to distinguish at sea from *cooki* or other members of sub-genus *Cookilaria*.

Voice: Somewhat similar to that of *cooki*, but thinner and higher pitched; a *tzi-tzi-tzi-tzi* with a buzzing undertone when several birds are overhead calling together. Fleming distinguishes two types of cry, one a soft *ti-ti-ti-ti*; the other somewhat lower and louder *té-té-té-té*. On the ground a bass grunt and a pleasant low crooning note appear to be part of courtship.

Habitat and range: Oceanic range unknown. Breeds at Hen and Chickens Islands and Poor Knights; and in 1962 discovered in some numbers on Red Mercury. Probably a migrant leaving home waters in April and returning about October.

Breeding: All the islands on which these petrels are known to breed are well-forested. The burrows may be well inland. The laying season is very short, most eggs appearing in the last week of November.

GOULD'S PETREL *Pterodroma leucoptera* *Pl. 7*

Description: 12". Upperparts dark, almost black on crown and nape, much lighter grey on the shoulders, back and central tail. Forehead, underparts, including underwing-coverts, white; feet bluish with dark terminal patches on the webs and the outer toe, bill black. Distinguishable from several other *Cookilarias* by the darker crown and nape.

Habitat and range: Not known to breed in the New Zealand region; but among 12 specimens, picked up dead on beaches, of which 10 came ashore at Muriwai in April 1942, representatives of two races are distinguishable. The provenance of the ten which were wrecked together is unknown. A later Muriwai specimen, January 1946, is identical with the breeding birds of Cabbage Tree Island, New South Wales. The most southerly record is of one ashore at Otaki in June 1961.

STEJNEGER'S PETREL *Pterodroma longirostris*

Description: 11". Head and nape blackish, back frosty grey, wings black and tail dark grey except for some white mottling on the outer web of the outer feathers. Forehead and underparts including underwing-coverts and undertail-coverts white, feet bluish, darker on the outer webs. The bird is very similar except for its smaller size to Gould's Petrel.

Habitat and range: Known to breed only at Masafuera in the eastern temperate Pacific. Non-breeders in moult occur regularly in the North Pacific and off Japan. In the summer of 1961–2, three were recovered from New Zealand beaches, one at Baring Head, Cook Strait, in December; and two at Ohope, Bay of Plenty, in January.

COOK'S PETREL *Pterodroma cooki* *Pl. 7*

Maori name: Titi.

Description: 12″. Crown, hind neck, back and upper tail pale grey. Forehead white with scalation merging into the grey of the crown. Underparts including underwing-coverts and undertail-coverts, white; feet pale blue, slightly stained with brown on the outer toe; bill black. Wings are darker grey than the back, but, when extended, they show a continuing dark pattern like an inverted " w." The strong wheeling flight of Cook's Petrel presents to the eye in turn the characteristic pattern of the back and the pure white under-surface.

Voice: Over their breeding ground at night, Cook's Petrels make a surprising variety of sounds; the commonest being a rapidly repeated *ti-ti-ti* or *whik-kek-kek*. Others described are: a goatlike bleating; a slow deliberate *kek-kek-kek*; a less frequent *hwit-wit*; a cat-like *purrp*; a *borrr* with well-rolled " r's." From the burrows comes an undertone of purring and crooning.

Ti-ti-ti or *kek-kek-kek* calls heard frequently on summer nights over Northland are believed to come from Cook's Petrels based on Little Barrier, as they fly to or from feeding grounds in the Tasman.

Habitat and range: The two known breeding stations, Little Barrier and Codfish Islands, are 800 miles apart; and different average measurements seem to indicate two distinct populations. The range at sea outside the breeding season is extensive. They are known as migrants during the southern winter along the coast of South America, Mexico and California.

Breeding: On Little Barrier, the burrows are mostly on the high forested slopes above 1000 feet. Burrow-cleaning in October; eggs from early November; young fly in March and April, sometimes crashing in the suburbs of Auckland, perhaps dazed by the city lights. At Codfish Island, where the colony is now very small, the breeding season seems to be some weeks later.

CHATHAM ISLAND PETREL *Pterodroma axillaris*

Maori name: Ranguru.

Description: 12″. Superficially, similar to Cook's Petrel, but differing in being rather darker and having feet of a different colour. Crown, hind neck, back and upper tail are medium grey and the wings blackish. Forehead and underparts pure white, but the *axillaries are black*, a distinctive mark when the bird is on the wing. Bill short, stout, black; feet fleshy colour with terminal dark patches on the webs and outer toe. Now treated, probably correctly, as a strong race of *hypoleuca*.

Habitat and range: Known to breed only at South-east Island, and not definitely recorded away from the Chathams, even as a straggler.

BLACK-WINGED PETREL *Pterodroma nigripennis* *Pl. 7*

Description: 12″. Crown, hind neck, back and the upper-tail, medium grey, wings blackish, forehead and underparts, including underwing-coverts, white. Bill short, stout, black; feet fleshy colour with terminal dark patches on the webs and outer toe. On the wing, can be distinguished from the Chatham Island Petrel by the white axillaries, the *underwing showing white with a firm black edging*.

Now treated as a race of *hypoleuca*.

In the north Tasman in February pairs (? of young adults) have been noted indulging in spirited chases, perhaps courtship flights; often soaring considerably higher than 100 feet.

Voice: A shrill high-pitched *tee-tee-tee*, audible even by day both at sea and over its breeding grounds.

Habitat and range: Its main breeding stations are at the Kermadecs and Norfolk Island—where it flies about the cliffs in broad daylight—and whence it ranges west to Lord Howe and eastwards into the Pacific across the Wellington–Panama shipping route. Discovered breeding at Three Kings Islands in 1945; now known to breed on all major islands in that group. Reported as flying on board ships in mid-ocean probably more frequently than any other petrel of its size. Seldom found storm-wrecked in New Zealand proper; but the great gale of mid-April 1968 cast more than forty ashore in the region of Hawkes Bay and Cook Strait.

Breeding: Returning birds are first heard at Kermadecs in October; burrow-cleaning in November; eggs laid from mid-December to mid-January; young leave towards the end of April.

STORM PETRELS: Hydrobatidae

LEACH'S FORK-TAILED STORM PETREL   *Oceanodroma leucorhoa*

Description: 7½″. Plumage blackish brown, the secondaries paler at the tips and forming a dull rusty band on the upper wing. Upper-tail coverts white, forming a band on the rump. Bill, legs and feet black; iris brown. The feature that distinguishes Leach's petrel on the wing is that a " V " shaped wedge of dark plumage invades the white tail band in front. This is variable in extent, sometimes almost dividing the white patch into two, but the irregularity of marking is always clearly visible.

Habitat and range: Leach's Petrel has a wide breeding range in the northern hemisphere in both Atlantic and Pacific Oceans. The one New Zealand specimen, washed ashore at Muriwai in winter 1922, is not distinguishable from typical specimens of the Atlantic form.

WILSON'S STORM PETREL   *Oceanites oceanicus*

Description: 7½″. Plumage black except for the pale brownish patch on the greater wing coverts and secondaries and a *white rump patch* formed by the upper tail-coverts extending to the lower flanks on either side. Iris brown; bill black; feet black, *with middle portion of the webs yellow*. Tail square; legs very long.

Habitat and range: The circumpolar race of Wilson's Petrel which breeds in Antarctica seems to be the largest of several. In the southern winter it migrates through Atlantic, Pacific and Indian Ocean tropics to the northern hemisphere. Birds taken in New Zealand, where the species is known only as a straggler, have invariably been of the large Antarctic form (*exasperatus*) and not of the smaller races that are

Wilson's Storm Petrel

Grey-backed Storm Petrel

known to breed in Chile, Patagonia and Kerguelen.

GREY-BACKED STORM PETREL

Garrodia nereis

Description: 7″. A diminutive species without white on the rump. Head, neck, throat and upper breast dark greyish black. The back is ashy grey with pale white edges, giving a scalloped appearance, and this colour continues to include the upper tail-coverts and the upper part of the tail which is also grey. The tail terminates in a dark band and the wings, with the exception of the secondary coverts which are pale grey, are dark brownish black. Breast and underparts, including undertail-coverts and the central wing-coverts, white.

Voice: A high-pitched twittering is made by birds on the wing over the nesting-grounds.

Habitat and range: A circumpolar species breeding at many sub-antarctic islands, including Chathams, Antipodes, Auckland Islands and probably Campbell. Ranging north in winter to about Lat. 36° S.; but rarely reported.

Breeding: The season extends from October to February or March. Burrows, like " rat-holes," have been found in a belt of *Anisotome* among sitting mollymawks on Disappointment Island; succulent vegetation of *Cotula* on Pyramid Rock. Elsewhere, the burrow may be in the heart of clumps of tussock.

BLACK-BELLIED STORM PETREL *Fregetta tropica* [1]

Description: 8″. General colour sooty black, brownish grey on the secondary wing-coverts. There is a slight contrast between the ashy tone of the head and the browner tone of the mantle. The upper tail-coverts are white and some of the feathers of the rump are white based and white tipped. *Flanks on both sides are also white*, as are most of the axillaries and a mottled area of the central wing-coverts. There are white bases to the feathers of the throat and in worn plumage this results in a whitish throat patch. Bill black; iris brown; legs and feet black. At sea, this petrel has an erratic flight and tends to zigzag, more so than Wilson's Petrel which it much resembles. In swinging from side to side, it exposes the under-surface of the body so that *the extensive white flank patches* are clearly seen, giving the appearance of a white bellied pattern, unless the thin, dark central line of the belly feathers can be detected.

Voice: A piercingly shrill piping note repeated singly at intervals of four or six seconds. " This call might be imitated on a piccolo fife in tbe key of G or F." (Eaton on this species at Kerguelen Island.)

Habitat and range: A circumpolar species breeding at many sub-antarctic islands, including Auckland, Bounty and Antipodes Islands, off which it is commonly seen at sea. Stragglers reach Lat. 36° S.; but are seldom reported.

Breeding: Seems to be a late nester at the Auckland Islands where Stead found eggs only slightly incubated on 1st February. At Kerguelen Island, the season seems to be some weeks earlier.

WHITE-FACED STORM PETREL *Pelagodroma marina*

Other names: Takahikare-moana, Skipjack, Jesus Christ Bird (shortened to " J. C. Bird "), Dancing Dolly.

Description: 8″. Crown, nape and patch below the eye smoky greyish-brown, mantle and back and upper wing-coverts, brownish. Rump and upper tail-coverts grey; tail and wings blackish brown. The lores and a line above the eye, chin, throat and underparts including underwing-coverts, and the inner webs of primaries, white. Iris brown; bill black; feet black; webs yellowish or dull ochre with pink veins. The only storm-petrel commonly seen in coastal waters; easily distinguished by its wholly white underparts. Occasionally during a flat calm may be seen sitting on the sea, riding high, with wings and tail held at quite a sharp angle. Rump and upper tail-coverts in the well-marked Kermadec race (*albiclunis*) are white.

Voice: At a nesting colony after dark an animated twittering.

[1] The specific name is a bad misnomer, as this species is the cold water representative of the sub-tropical White-bellied Storm Petrel (*Fregetta grallaria*), known in New Zealand only from a single straggler, although it breeds at Lord Howe Island and in the Kermadecs (Macauley Island).

Habitat and range: The common subspecies (*maoriana*) of the New Zealand region breeds on many islands and islets from the Three Kings to the Chatham and Auckland Islands. Apparently absent from late-April to early August; destination unknown, but has occurred near Galapagos Is.

Breeding: On some islands the colonies are dense; and after dark the returning birds drop in like a snowstorm, bouncing daintily on a mat of ice-plant or low-growing taupata as if they were at sea. The egg is white with faint pinkish-brown specks at the larger end. Eggs, in the north mostly in second half of October; young leave mostly in February; but one still in a burrow at the Noises on 9th March (R. B. S.). On Whero, the peak of egg-laying was about 6th November (Richdale). Incubation period 55–56 days; fledging 52–67 days. Near nesting colonies Harriers, Black-backed Gulls and Southern Skuas take their toll.

DIVING PETRELS: Pelecanoididae

This specialised group of the petrels, or tube-nosed swimmers, is confined to the southern hemisphere. They are small stocky birds, all much alike, with short powerful wings which they use under water for swimming and in the air for rapid whirring flight near the surface of the sea, into which they frequently dive. They are apparently flightless during a short period of moult. Dark above and white below, they resemble superficially the Little Auks of the northern hemisphere, but are true petrels both in structure and habits.

DIVING PETREL *Pelecanoides urinatrix*

Local names: Dipchick, Kuaka (Stewart Island only).
Description: $7\frac{1}{2}''$–8″. Crown, neck, back, tail and upper surface of wings black, except for white edges on new secondaries. Cheeks grey. Underparts pure white, smoky under the wings. Bill black; legs blue.

The northern subspecies *urinatrix* is slightly larger than the southern *chathamensis*. In the subantarctic subspecies, *exsul*, the bill is proportionately wider at the base so that the sides looked at from above are less parallel. Usually, but not always, the grey speckling on the breast and foreneck is more pronounced.

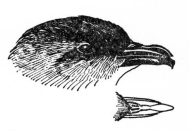

Voice: Silent at sea; but wailing, chattering, cooing and mewing in the air over nesting places at night, with a considerable range of powerful calls.

57

Habitat and range: Typical *urinatrix* is found in coastal waters from Three Kings to Cook Strait, breeding in burrows on many offshore islets; *chathamensis* ranges from Cook Strait to about Lat. 47° S., breeding on offshore islets at Chatham, Stewart, Solander and Snares Islands; *exsul* occurs in subantarctic seas south of Lat. 48° S., breeding at Antipodes and Auckland Islands, probably at Campbell Island and straggling to Macquarie Island.

Breeding: In the north the season is from August to December. Incubation period, five weeks. The first down of the chicks is pale; the second darker grey. In full first plumage, the young resemble the adults. With *chathamensis* the season comes about a month later; and in the subantarctic islands it lasts from October to February.

SOUTH GEORGIAN DIVING PETREL *Pelecanoides*
georgicus

Description: 6½″–7″. Crown, neck, back, tail and upper surface of wings black, except for patches of white scapulars, white edges to secondaries and white inner webs to the outer wing feathers seen when the wings are spread. Bill black above, bluish along the edges of the mandibles; feet pale blue.

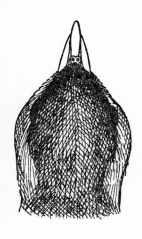

Voice: Not recorded for the New Zealand race.

Habitat and range: This is an antarctic diving-petrel of circumpolar range, occurring in New Zealand seas, as far as is known, only at the Auckland Islands, where it is now exceedingly rare. Nothing is known of its distribution at sea nor the extent of its feeding range, except that it has not been detected amongst large flocks of diving petrels in coastal waters and possibly is more pelagic.

Breeding: The season is from October to February and the sequence appears to be similar to that of other diving petrels, except that at the Auckland Islands burrows have been found to be shallower and in more sandy soil than those of *exsul*. They were first collected in 1840 on Enderby Island, where the sandy coastal areas have since been much consolidated by trampling of cattle and reburrowed by rabbits. The only colony now known to exist is on a small islet, and the burrows are round a fringe of consolidated sand.

TROPIC BIRDS: Phaethontidae

A small family (3 species) of beautiful white seabirds, superficially pigeon-like, well-named because they are confined almost exclusively to the tropics. In adult birds the two central tail feathers are very much elongated. Hence they are also known as Bo'sun Birds after the "marlin-spike" in the tail. Tropic Birds range far from their nesting grounds and may appear suddenly, approaching with a steady flapping flight, and briefly escorting a ship when it is far from land.

Of the two species which occur in the south-west Pacific, one, the Red-tailed, breeds at the Kermadecs and may range to S. Lat. 38°; the White-tailed (*P. lepturus*) has not been satisfactorily recorded in New Zealand waters.

RED-TAILED TROPIC BIRD   *Phaethon rubricauda*

Other names: Amokura, Strawtail.

Description: 18", plus up to 16" according to the elongation of the *two scarlet central tail-feathers*. Plumage mainly white with a pinkish hue; but there is a conspicuous black crescent before and over eye; the tail-feathers and longer wing-feathers have black shafts; and some feathers on flanks and under tail have black centres. Bill yellow or coral red with black streak through nostrils; feet black. Young have upperparts broadly barred with black; bill black; legs yellowish or bluish-white; central tail-feathers undeveloped.

Voice: A harsh grating sound, repeated two or three times, is frequently heard in fine weather at the breeding grounds. A shrill, rasping call has been heard from birds circling a ship.

Habitat and range: The breeding range of the sub-species of the western Pacific (*roseotincta*) extends from northern Queensland to Lord Howe, Norfolk and the Kermadec Islands. Recent sightings suggest that in summer some regularly reach the outer waters of

the Hauraki Gulf and Bay of Plenty and may penetrate the Tasman as far as Lat. 38° S.

Breeding: At the Kermadecs most eggs are laid between mid-December and mid-January. Clutch one; egg commonly pinkish, closely blotched reddish-brown; nest a mere hollow on a ledge of a cliff. Incubation period *c.* 35 days. Most birds leave the breeding grounds in April and May; a few linger over the winter months; most return in October.

GANNETS AND BOOBIES: Sulidae

The members of this family are large strong-flying seabirds (wing-span over 5½ ft.) related to the shags and pelicans; but somewhat gooselike when resting on the sea or standing near their nests. Physically they are especially characterised by their stout, pointed conical bills, an area of bare skin on face and throat and their wedge-shaped tails. The family is mainly tropical and its tropical species are commonly known as Boobies, while those which frequent cooler waters are the true Gannets.

They nest in colonies, most of which are on small islands. Their food, mainly fish, is obtained by diving and their almost vertical plunges from a considerable height can be truly spectacular.

The Australian Gannet is the commonest of the really big seabirds around the coast of the North Island, but south of Cook Strait it becomes rather scarce. Two tropical boobies at the southern limit of their range reach the northern waters of New Zealand.

Included in the same order (*Pelecaniformes*) are the true pelicans. An Australian Pelican (*Pelecanus conspicillatus*) was shot on the Wanganui River in 1890. Sub-fossil bones, found at Waikaremoana, Poukawa and Grassmere, may indicate that formerly pelicans occurred more frequently.

AUSTRALIAN GANNET *Sula serrator*

Local name: Takapu.

Description: 36″. " The finest and most majestic of the birds of coastal waters." (Buddle.) Mainly white; crown and nape pastel yellow; primaries, secondaries and at least four, occasionally as many as ten, central tail feathers black. Bill and bare skin of face, bluish grey; feet dark brown, with vivid light green lines running down to the toes.

The nestling at first black and naked becomes fluffy white in just over a month. By three months it is mainly brown on the upper surface of neck, body, wings and tail, but a white dot at the end of each feather gives a generally speckled appearance. Under surfaces are mainly white.

Flight strong and direct; also glides, soars and planes. Catches its prey both by steep plunges from up to 100 feet and also by shallow low-angled torpedo-like dives.

Voice: Even in the hatching egg the chick yaps like a small puppy. Later the voice deepens but it is still like a short, sharp bark and is used

mainly to greet a parent returning with food. Adults at sea are generally silent, but a gruff *aak-aak* and a softer throaty *kook-kook-kook* have been heard. On nearing their nesting sites adults may utter a pleasantly rhythmic throaty call, produced by a very rapid movement back and forward of the tongue as in *ooh-lah-ooh-lah-ooh-lah*. A not unmusical quavering *kee-er-up*, *kee-eree* or *skee-ree* is also described.

Habitat and range: According to a census taken in 1946–7, *c.* 21,000 pairs were then breeding in New Zealand, but in ten of the colonies which have since been checked the count is now higher, so that the estimated breeding population in 1961 was 27,000 pairs which together with roosting non-breeders would make the total number of adults about 60,000.

The colonies with one notable exception at Cape Kidnappers, are on small islands, mostly north of Lat. 38° S.; but two very small colonies, Nuggets and Little Solander, are in much colder water at Lat. 46½° S.

Adults are common in coastal waters, sometimes penetrating muddy creeks, around the North Island throughout the year. In the vicinity of the colonies Gannets may often be seen flying in lines, especially when returning to roost at night. The formations, which are often roughly V-shaped, with one arm longer than the other, vary in size from a few birds to over eighty.

Few mottled immatures are seen after May; for on leaving the nest most of them set off across the Tasman to spend two or three years around the Australian coast south from Queensland and west to the Indian Ocean, before returning to New Zealand to breed.

The Australian breeding colonies are confined to the region of Bass Strait and Tasmania. Closely allied forms are found in the North Atlantic (*S. bassana*) and around South Africa (*S. capensis*).

Breeding: Banding has shown that a few Gannets return to their home colony at the end of their third year, and some have been found breeding at the end of their fourth. Most breed in their fifth year or later; a few are eight years old when found breeding for the first time. The nest is a mound of seaweed, soft plants, earth and guano. In the north eggs are laid from late August to early December; in the south over a month later. Only one egg is laid, but if it is lost in the early stages of incubation, a second may be laid about five weeks later. Parents take turns in incubating for 43 days. Fledging, 15½ weeks. Within six months of departing the young loose some of their mottled plumage, and within a year they resemble adults but are not as white on the body or as yellow on the head, and the dark feathers of the wings and tail do not present the same contrast as in the adults.

BROWN BOOBY   *Sula leucogaster*
Description: 28″–30″. Adults with dark chocolate brown plumage and white belly are unmistakable, *the sharp line of demarcation being on the lower breast.* In flight the

white axillaries and median under wing-coverts become visible. Naked face of skin and throat greenish yellow or bluish; bill yellowish or bluish; feet pale yellow. In immatures the bill can be shining bluish horn-colour and the feet bright orange-yellow; the underparts are smudged brown, but a sharp line usually separates the darker breast from the lighter belly and the contrasting pattern of the underwing is helpful in distinguishing them from the mottled immatures of *S. serrator*.

Habitat and range: Though the subspecies *plotus* is the commonest of the tropical boobies in the south-west Pacific, it has seldom been recorded from New Zealand; but increased sightings since the 1950s may indicate that Brown Boobies, probably immature non-breeders, visit our northern waters every summer. One is known to have frequented the Hauraki Gulf for three consecutive seasons and to have roosted with the Gannets on Horuhoru. Brown Boobies have been recorded as far south as Napier and Otaki.

BLUE-FACED BOOBY   *Sula dactylatra*
Other name: Masked Gannet.
Description: 34″. Largely white and at first glance rather like *S. serrator*; but the tail and flight feathers are dark brown, appearing in flight as a *broad black band on the rear edge of the wing.* Head white; beak stout and yellow; naked skin on face and throat blue-black; feet

greenish blue. Immatures are mainly white, but head, throat, mantle, upper wing surface and tail are brown.

Habitat and range: The subspecies *personata* is widespread in the western and central Pacific; only recorded in New Zealand from the Kermadecs where it breeds.

Breeding: Nest a slight hollow in the ground. Eggs August–November. Clutch commonly two, but only one young is reared.

SHAGS OR CORMORANTS:
Phalacrocoracidae

Birds of this group are well represented in New Zealand. The number of species recognised depends on the form of classification adopted, and on an extreme view, sixteen forms can be recognised. A useful sub-division can be made of those having black feet. There are four of these, and they are all associated, to some extent, with freshwater habitat, although they also occur coastally. On the other hand, there are six or seven races of sub-antarctic shags with pink feet and one with yellow feet which are exclusively marine, some of them inhabiting outlying oceanic islands. In the latter group, a field identification key must concern itself mainly with the facial markings and colours. Like the Penguins, the pink-footed shags seem to have their main recognition characters in the head, the body plumage otherwise being remarkably uniform and similar throughout. The eggs of all shags are whitish or very pale bluish or greenish with a chalky encrustation.

Closely related to the Shags are the Darters (*Anhingidae*), distinguished by their sharp-pointed bills and long snaky necks. In 1874 the skin of a freshly dead Australian Darter (*Anhinga novaehollandiae*) was found nailed up inside an old shed at Hokitika. This waterbird is rare in New South Wales and unrecorded in Tasmania.

BLACK SHAG *Phalacrocorax carbo*   *Pl. 8*

Maori name: Kawau.

Description: 35″. The adult in breeding plumage has generally black plumage glossed with oil green. There is a well-developed crest of black feathers extending on to the nape. The upper back plumage is dull bronze brown, each feather widely bordered with dark green. The naked gular pouch is narrowly bordered with white feathers and there are narrow white filo-plumes on the head and neck in breeding plumage, also a large patch of white feathers on each flank. The skin about the eye and the gular sac yellowish. Bill greyish brown. Iris green. Legs and feet blackish. The white filo-plumes on the neck and the thigh patches are transitory and seasonal, being found usually in May and October.

The plumage of the female, which is smaller, is similar. In immature

Plate 3

ALBATROSSES IN FLIGHT

Plate 4
MOLLYMAWKS IN FLIGHT

birds in their first year, the underparts are dirty white and the facial colours not strongly developed. The young, hatched naked, are later covered with a blackish down.

Voice: A hoarse croak and a wheezy whistling note, as recorded for this species elsewhere.

Habitat and range: The Australian race (*novaehollandiae*) of this cosmopolitan cormorant ranges throughout the main islands, inland to mountain lakes and streams, and eastwards to the Chathams; stragglers penetrating south to Campbell and Macquarie Islands. Most feeding appears to be inland; but in autumn and early winter flocks, numbering hundreds of birds, may fish sheltered tidal waters such as the Firth of Thames.

Breeding: Nesting colonies are commonly in clumps of tall trees or on the ledges of inland cliffs and river-gorges; some colonies are on coastal cliffs or off-shore rockstacks. Nests with eggs or young may be found at almost any season. Clutch 3–4. Precise information on incubation and fledging periods is lacking. The young, hatched naked, are later covered with a blackish down. A high proportion of the fish brought to the young consists of freshwater eels.

PIED SHAG *Phalacrocorax varius*   *Pl. 8*
Maori name: Karuhiruhi
Description: 32″. Upperparts, including top of the head and hind neck are black glossed with dark green. Dorsal wing feathers are bronze grey with a greenish gloss, each feather bordered with black. Sides of the head, chin, throat and underparts pure white. Iris sea-green, a bright yellow spot of bare skin in front of the eye, naked blue skin around the eye, and gular sac yellow. Bill, dark horn colour, with some variable marking. Legs and feet black.

In the first year, immature plumage upperparts are somewhat browner and the pale underparts are mottled with occasional brown feathers.

Voice: Varies from a deep croak to a light and monotonous wheezy call.

Habitat and range: Restricted to the warmer parts of New Zealand, being most plentiful in the north; but the range is discontinuous, viz: Northland, Hauraki Gulf and Bay of Plenty where many off-shore islands possess breeding colonies; virtually absent from Hawke's Bay and the Wellington coast; occurring again in the Marlborough Sounds and around Nelson with a small group nesting on the coast of North Canterbury; not found again until Stewart Island. Pied Shags rarely venture inland and their food consists mostly of estuarine fishes.

Breeding: The typical colony is in trees, especially pohutukawas in the north, on an exposed sea-cliff; but a few colonies are in trees beside freshwater lakes which are near the coast, e.g. Pupuke, Takapuna; Lake Paritu, one of the crater lakes on Mayor Island, and Lake Rotorua, nearly two miles inland from the Kaikoura coast. At Lake Pupuke, nesting goes on throughout the year, with two peak seasons of egg laying, August–September and March–April; and apparently as many pairs breed in autumn as in spring. Clutch 2–4. After the naked stage, chicks have white down on the underparts.

LITTLE BLACK SHAG *Phalacrocorax sulcirostris*   *Pl. 8*
Description: 24″. Generally smaller but otherwise similar to the Big Black Shag. The entire plumage is black with a dull oil green gloss and the usual dark bordered ashy feathers on the shoulders and wing-coverts. There are seasonal white plumules on the side of the head and about the eye in the breeding season, but they are not clearly visible at a distance, and no white thigh patches are developed. The rather long bill (1¾″) is dull lead colour, appearing black at a distance. The iris is deep emerald green. Occasionally, there is a bluish-purple tinge about the skin of the face; otherwise this is the most sombrely plumaged of all the New Zealand shags. Females are similar to males, and immature birds differ only in being slightly duller.
Habitat and range: An Australian species, which has tended to escape notice in New Zealand; but actually not uncommon and probably increasing in the northern part of the North Island; occasionally reported from Wellington and Hawke's Bay and more rarely from the South Island. In early winter, there appears to be a northward movement into coastal waters of the Bay of Plenty, Hauraki Gulf, Manukau and Northland. One characteristic of this species is to hunt in packs, presumably rounding up fish. A flock, containing anything from a dozen to 150 birds, will swim round a lake or about an estuary diving. As birds surface and find that they are at the rear of the flock they fly over the main body and dive again to be in the forefront of the chase.
Breeding: So far has been found breeding at only two lakes, Waikare, a large colony; and Pupuke, a few pairs, the nests being in trees; but almost certainly breeds regularly in the Bay of Plenty and Rangaunu Bay and probably elsewhere, even on rocky islets offshore. Competition with other shags may force it to breed rather late, i.e. about midsummer or in early autumn. Clutch 2–5, commonly 3. Chicks clothed in a dark blackish-brown down are not easily distinguished from the young of *carbo* and *brevirostris*. At Lake Waikare, they were fed largely on carp and eels.

LITTLE SHAG *Phalacrocorax melanoleucos brevirostris*   *Pl. 8*
Maori name: Kawaupaka. The name White-throated Shag is also in general use for the most abundant phase of a rather variable species which, at its other extreme, is identical with the Little Pied Shag of Australia. However, as intermediates occur, and the Little Pied form is relatively uncommon, it seems more convenient to treat the New Zealand population as a variable one under a distinctive name.
Description: 22″. In the dark phase the entire plumage is glossy black with the face, cheeks and chin white, a patch which commonly extends to the throat and foreneck. The feathers of the crown are elongated and form a ruff-like crest. The naked skin of the face and the gular pouch are yellow. Bill (1¼″) black above yellowish below. Feet black.

In the other extreme of plumage the entire underparts are pure white.

Most immature birds are dull brownish black over the entire plumage, including the throat, with conspicuously yellow bill and face, although it should be be noted that immature birds of the extreme pied phase are often dull smoky white below. Chicks are covered with blackish-brown down dotted with tufts of white in birds that are ultimately of the pied phase. As a field character, all these Little Shags can be readily distinguished from the Little Black Shag by the fact that the *bill is short and stout and the tail relatively long.*

Voice: Wheezy and guttural. During courtship, low urgent cooings; a muffled sound something between a low bark and a coo.

Habitat and range: The most widespread of the freshwater shags, being found far inland up into the mountains and along the whole coastline south to Stewart Island; recorded as a visitor to most northern off-shore islands but only rarely straggling to sub-antarctic islands. The Little Pied form is most plentiful in Northland where the proportion of Little Pied to White-throated is about 1 to 3 or 4. The food in inland waters includes eels, koura, native freshwater fish, and an assortment of larvæ of aquatic insects.

Breeding: Nests are in trees or shrubs commonly with other species of black-footed shags in swamps, on lakes, in river gorges or on sea-cliffs. These shags have an extended breeding season; but near Auckland, they appear to have a fairly rigid annual breeding cycle with egg laying at a peak in September or early October. Clutch 3 or 4.

NEW ZEALAND KING SHAG *Phalacrocorax carunculatus* Pl. 9
carunculatus

Description: 30″. Head, cheeks, neck, sides, back and outer thigh feathers dull metallic bluish green. Inner scapular regions, scapulars and wing coverts glossed with oil green. Quills and tail blackish brown. A wide white alar bar is formed by the inner median wing coverts. Another white patch appears among the outer scapulars in most specimens, and there is usually a central dorsal patch of white variable in size. No crest. The bill is horny brown. Facial skin and gular pouch, dark reddish brown. Ring round the eye bright blue. Patches of chrome yellow caruncles above the bill at the base. Iris dark hazel. Feet pink. The caruncles are generally larger in males than females. Immature birds in their first plumage have the upperparts mainly dull brown with very little of the greenish gloss in the first plumage. The alar bar and scapular patch, when present, are indicated by paler buffy feathers but the dorsal patch is rarely indicated except by a slight weakness of pigmentation in the middle of the back. Facial colours about the bill have not developed and they remain purplish brown. Nestlings after hatching naked are clothed in dark smoky down.

Voice: The usual croak of which the pitch and tone has not been precisely distinguished from that of other cormorants.

Habitat and range: The habitat is entirely oceanic. The only known nesting places are on rocky islets adjacent to oceanic water which in

Cook Strait contains many elements of the Sub-Tropical Convergence. The food consists of bottom haunting and weed-inhabiting fishes or seasonal crustacean supplies. A radius of about thirty miles encompasses all the known breeding stations from the White Rocks in the east to Trios in the west.

Breeding: Large built-up nests of marine growth and coastal plants are placed on rock platforms and ledges in close proximity. The full clutch of eggs is three and the laying season appears to vary. In a normal year most of the colonies are winter breeders having eggs in June and a considerable batch of fledglings in late August. In some seasons the various separate colonies are out of step by several months and the situation suggests breeding by some groups of birds all the year round although this has not been precisely demonstrated. The numerical strength of the King Shag is only a few hundred birds but its present status is quite healthy and protection is more effective than in the past.

STEWART ISLAND SHAG *Phalacrocorax chalconotus*   *Pl. 9*
Description: 26″–28″. The description given above for the King Shag applies in most details to this species, at least in its pied phase. The southern bird is, however, *dimorphic* and approximately half the populations are entirely and uniformly bronze oily green with the colours of soft parts the same in both phases. The soft part colours are also similar to those of *carunculatus* except that a few yellow to orange papillæ take the place of the robust caruncles of the northern bird. Also the white scapular patch found in the latter, is lacking in *chalconotus*.

Habitat and range: The birds are restricted to coastal waters from Otago Peninsula to Foveaux Strait and Stewart Island. There is a marked cline in the size of birds in this range, those of Otago Peninsula being much larger and heavier and having more pronounced development of papillæ above the beak.

Breeding: Rock-stacks and flat-topped rocks are favoured for the close grouping of nests which are built up into raised cups on a fairly solid base of organic debris and guano. Mated pairs may be of either phase or mixed and although this appears to be indiscriminate, the young develop into the two distinct phases without many intermediate plumages being produced. The only variant that has been noted in a small percentage of examples is an occasional " bronze " bird with irregular scatterings of white feathers, usually on the belly.

CHATHAM ISLAND SHAG *Phalacrocorax onslowi*
Description: 25″. The description given for the King Shag applies also to this species except that the plumage is in all respects more sleek and glossy, with heightened colour and strong metallic reflections. It has well developed orange caruncles and an alar bar of white as well as some white in the scapulars and the dorsal patch. Facial colours are

much brighter than *carunculatus*, being reddish on the cheeks and gular pouch; bright blue ring round the eye; iris brown. The same brown stages of immaturity and nestling down apply equally to this form.

Habitat and range: Found only at the Chatham Islands, this shag has not been known to occur elsewhere and has probably a restricted home range. Nesting sites chosen are similar in all respects to the larger colonies of the other races already described and are to be found around the coasts of the main Chatham Islands and their outliers. They have not been recorded as nesting on the more exposed outlying stacks.

BOUNTY ISLAND SHAG *Phalacrocorax ranfurlyi*

Description: 28". In general plumage and in size similar to the largest examples of the Stewart Island Shag, the bird exclusively inhabiting Bounty Islands differs mainly in having almost entirely bright red facial skin although lacking either caruncles or papillæ. It has both alar bar and dorsal patch although the latter is poorly developed and often broken in the specimens available for study. Its general group relationship, however, seems to be clearly with the *carunculatus, onslowi, chalconotus* group and not with *campbelli* as suggested by a preliminary examination and quoted in the *Checklist of New Zealand Birds* (1953), page 30.

Habitat and range: Restricted to the rocky Bounty Islands and appears to be restricted there to roosting and nesting on a few narrow ledges not already occupied by penguins and mollymawks. As there must be abundant feed in the area, the controlling factor responsible for the comparatively small numbers must be lack of nesting space.

Breeding: Nests are similar to those of the other forms and the full clutch of eggs appears to be three.

Immature plumages are probably indistinguishable from those of the other forms, and nestlings have not been described.

AUCKLAND ISLAND SHAG *Phalacrocorax colensoi*

Description: 25". This bird and the Campbell Island Shag form a group seperable from the other Blue-eyed Shags. In the main, they are smaller and more delicately built. There is no trace of papillæ or carunculation. The general plumage pattern and colour is hardly distinguishable from that of *carunculatus* group. However, the dark feathering on the back and sides of the neck almost meets on the foreneck and in a few examples is joined by a complete dark band. This is variable in the Auckland Island Shag but fixed and regular in the Campbell Island Shag. The gular pouch is red. Facial skin reddish-brown. Ring round the eye mauve or pinkish-violet. The feet are pink as in all the other sub-antarctic cormorants. Iris brown.

Immature birds have the plumage pattern much the same, but instead of the metallic colours have dull lustreless brown and the foreneck is almost always mottled or brown plumaged in immature birds.

In comparison with *carunculatus* the alar bar is much reduced and the white dorsal patch normally missing, although it does occur in a few examples.

Habitat and range: Around the many harbours and inlets of the Auckland Islands and along their eastern coastlines, this shag is plentiful, and occupies a large number of nesting sites which may be changed from year to year. Either coastal rock terraces or a series of narrow ledges may be occupied and the nests are the usual built-up piles of debris and guano. Clutch 3.

There is an abundant food supply of post-larval fishes and kelp-haunting fish as well as a considerable range of surface crustaceans.

CAMPBELL ISLAND SHAG *Phalacrocorax campbelli*

Description: 25". Just separable from the Auckland Island Shag, being of exactly the same size but having less variable plumage pattern and generally darker pigmentation, especially in the colours of soft parts. The remarkable uniformity of plumage is indeed in contrast to the variability of the Auckland Island Shag: although chin and throat are white, there is a black throat band about 3" in depth. The white alar bar is not present nor has the white dorsal patch been recorded. Facial skin and gular pouch are deep red and the eye is dark purple mauve, as distinct from the more pinkish tinge of the Auckland Island Shag.

Habitat and range: Restricted to Campbell Island and its outliers and much less abundant than the Auckland Island form. After the breeding season " rafts " gather in sheltered inlets such as Perseverance Harbour. On 11/8/60 it was estimated that more than 2000 were fishing Tucker Cove.

Breeding: The nesting season for both Auckland and Campbell Island Shags is the same, the earliest eggs appearing in November.

MACQUARIE ISLAND SHAG *Phalacrocorax albiventer purpurascens*

Description: 28". This sub-antarctic cormorant resembles the others in having pink feet; but it clearly belongs to a circumpolar chain of races grouped about *P. albiventer* of the Falkland Islands. The metallic colours are much closer to royal blue than to bluish green. The abundant caruncles are yellow and the ring about the eye bright electric blue set in an area of facial skin and gular pouch of dark brown. There is an alar bar but no record of dorsal white or white scapulars in this form. It differs also from the others in having the dark feathers of the cheek commencing about the gape and not at the base of the lower mandible. This means that the facial pattern is much whiter and the ear opening is to be found along the line of demarcation of the dark and white feathers and not in the dark area as in all the others. Immature birds are brown above and white below, with dull facial colours; nestlings in down are smoky: irises at all ages, brown.

Habitat and range: In the New Zealand region found at Macquarie Island only and does not wander.

Breeding: Forms fairly compact nesting colonies, sometimes on low-lying rocks and occasionally on coastal ledges. There are numerous colonies scattered along the shores of Macquarie Island and other birds are breeding on the more distant outliers north and south. There appears to be a stable population of Macquarie Island Shags and the limiting factor on increase of numbers is probably food supply. None of the sub-antarctic cormorants is migratory and their sedentary range is quite small.

SPOTTED SHAG *Stictocarbo punctatus*   *Pl. 9*

Description: 39″. A very handsome bird in full plumage, but for the greater part of the year it appears in non-breeding dress and there are several stages of plumage in the progress to maturity. In a fully adult bird at the beginning of the breeding season the crown of the head and the longish double crest rising at the forehead and again at the nape are greyish black with a faint metallic gloss. The back of the neck is glossy greenish blue and this dark metallic colour occurs again on the lower back and rump. The scapulars and wing coverts are pale grey, each feather with a round black spot at the extremity. The underparts are silvery grey from the chin to the under-tail-coverts which like the thighs are glossy greenish-black. Two white lateral strips of plumage start at the base of the bill, pass above the eye and are continued down the sides of the neck to the shoulder. There may also be scattered white feathers sprouting from the darker portions of the plumage. Bill long and slender (2¾″), light horn colour. Iris hazel. Naked skin around the eye opalescent blue and green. The gular pouch bright blue and the feet bright orange-yellow. In non-breeding plumage, the clear white areas are invaded by mottled feathers and the conspicuous pattern is effectively broken down.

Immature birds which are dark grey above and very pale grey almost white below, have no conspicuous pattern until they begin to assume the first adult plumage. Their feet also are seldom bright yellow and may be dull brownish-pink.

Voice: Adults croak; nestlings make a thin, reedy whistle and almost musical warble.

Habitat and range: Entirely marine and rather sedentary, occupying throughout the year cliff stations adjacent to fairly deep water from which large quantities of post-larval and small fish may be obtained. Not common in the North Island, where there are two groups of breeding colonies (*a*) in Hauraki Gulf, Noises to Waiheke, Tarakihi and Ponui Islands, and east to the islets off Coromandel Peninsula, (*b*) on the Auckland west coast, Oaia, Ihumoana and Girdwood Point. An irregular winter visitor, presumably from the South Island, to Wellington Harbour (Ward Island), Waikanae and Palliser Bay.

Abundant in the South Island from Marlborough Sounds down the east coast, especially Goose Bay, Banks Peninsula and Otago Peninsula, where long lines of these shags flying between cliffs and feeding grounds make an impressive sight. Smaller scattered colonies on the west coast, as far south as Open Bay Islands, which may in fact be inhabited not by Spotted Shags but by the closely allied Blue Shag. (q.v.)

Breeding: Nests in colonies on ledges, in fissures on steep cliffs or in sea-caves. A fairly substantial nest is made of old sticks, cliff-plants and seaweed. Clutch commonly 3, rarely 4. Incubation period *c.* $4\frac{1}{2}$ weeks. An extended breeding season seems to vary according to locality. The elegant nuptial plumes and colours are lost during incubation.

BLUE SHAG *Stictocarbo steadi*

Probably best treated as a subspecies of the Spotted Shag, the Blue Shag is nevertheless distinguishable by being slightly dark in tone of plumage, having a narrower white line on the sides of the neck in breeding dress and occupying a restricted zone of coastline around Stewart Island and at one or two islands in Foveaux Strait. Some of the plumage characters are clearly trends in the direction of the pattern found in the more distinct Pitt Island Shag of the Chatham group. Little has been recorded about the habits which appear to be similar to those of the Spotted Shag.

PITT ISLAND SHAG *Stictocarbo featherstoni*

Local name: Double-crested Shag.

Description: 25″. This is clearly the Chatham Island representative of the Spotted Shag/Blue Shag group. Very similar to the two already described, but entirely lacking the white neck stripes and much darker altogether. Head, both crests, chin, throat, foreneck and the entire back rump and upper tail-coverts as well as the undertail-coverts and thighs, black glossed with dark greenish-blue. The grey plumage of the wing-coverts and scapulars is of a deep tone with an oil green gloss, each feather having the triangular black spot on the extremity. The rest of the underparts is dark silvery grey and the only white plumes are the scattered filo-plumes on head and neck in breeding condition. The naked skin about the eye is purple. Iris dark hazel. Legs and feet orange.

In the immature plumage there is a strong suffusion of brown tone and no clearly marked pattern except on the scapulars and wing-coverts, which resemble the adult condition.

Habitat and range: Restricted to the Chatham Islands, with its greatest numbers south of Pitt Strait.

Breeding: Favourite nesting sites are in eroded pockets or ledges in vertical cliff faces. Eggs are said to be laid in August. Most nests are deserted by the end of December.

FRIGATE BIRDS: Fregatidae

With their long forked tails and narrow angular wings Frigate Birds are very easily recognised. They are the most aerial of oceanic birds and they are said never to settle on the water. In the tropics they hang poised in the sky, dark sinister shapes, ready to swoop upon other seabirds and to harry them till they force them to disgorge whatever they have caught. Because of their marauding habits they are also called Man-o'-War Birds. Their long slender bills are sharply hooked at the tip.

Five species are recognised all breeding in colonies on tropical islands. Two species, rather different in size, occur in the south-west Pacific; but as they seldom travel far from land, it is not surprising that they reach New Zealand waters only when driven south by tropical cyclones.

In identifying the two species which may occur in New Zealand it is important to note carefully the position and extent of the whitish areas of the underparts.

GREATER FRIGATE BIRD *Fregata minor* [1]

Description: 40″; wing span *c.* 7 ft. Adult male entirely dark, with no white, and with a red distensible gular pouch; female has a grey-ish-white throat and fore-neck and the lower neck, breast and sides of the body are white. In immature birds the head and neck are white and the underparts tinged reddish.

Habitat and range: A very rare straggler from distant tropical breeding grounds south to Cook Strait; *c.* 12. records.

Lesser Frigate Bird (adult male)

[1] The curious may wonder why somewhat anomalously the specific name of the Greater Frigate-bird is *minor*. The adjective survives from the eighteenth century when this bird was called the Lesser Pelican (*Pelecanus minor*).

LESSER FRIGATE BIRD *Fregata ariel*
Other name: Least Man-o'-War.
Description: 31″; wingspan *c.* 6 ft. Plumage generally black with a grey-brown wing bar. *Male has a white patch on either flank under the wing* and a bright red distensible gular pouch; female has throat black and breast buffy white; immature birds have head, neck and breast white mottled with rusty brown.
Habitat and range: Commoner in the south-west Pacific than *F. minor*; breeding from Queensland to Fiji, but rarely wandering to New Zealand; *c.* 10 records mostly from the north during or after tropical blows, but has reached Cook Strait and the Chatham Islands. One in Kaipara Harbour was seen to harry gannets, gulls and terns.

HERONS, EGRETS AND BITTERNS:
Ardeidae

As a general rule herons and egrets are birds of the open; bitterns and night-herons are shy skulkers in reed-beds or thick cover. Nine of the ten species which occur in New Zealand are widely distributed in Australia and/or south-east Asia. In New Zealand they reach the south-east limit of their range. None is peculiar to New Zealand.

Three species, Reef Heron, White-faced Heron and Bittern breed widely in the main islands, the most numerous now being the White-faced Heron, a highly successful recent immigrant. There is a single small breeding colony of White Herons. In the last decade there have been so many records of Little Egret that it is not implausible to suggest that a small breeding colony may be now be established. The status of the Little Bittern is quite unknown. Although the Nankeen Night-heron is very rare, there is reason to believe that a pair may have bred recently near Blenheim. The first Cattle Egret has now been found in New Zealand. This species is spreading so fast in Australia that its arrival here was not altogether surprising.

With their broad wings and slow, heavy flight, herons are especially susceptible to wind drift. A remarkable example, if the record is true, of drifting by an over-carried migrant is that of the Grey Heron (*Ardea cinerea*) said to have come aboard a schooner off the east coast about 1898.

WHITE-FACED HERON *Ardea novaehollandiae*   *Pl. 10*
Other name: Blue Crane.
Description: 26″. Bluish grey with *white on forehead, chin and around eye*; long pale grey plumes on back; under surface light grey with chestnut or bronze feathers on breast; wing quills blackish, *the contrasting tones in the wing showing clearly in flight.* Bill black; legs greenish yellow, *sometimes reddish.*
  Flight leisurely and strong. Can gain height quickly. When not

foraging, often to be seen perched on a post in a vulturine attitude with neck tucked in between hunched shoulders.

Voice: Flight call a guttural *graaw*; "a similar call is used when alighting at the nest but on these occasions it ends with a repeated *gow-gow-gow* which becomes quieter as each syllable is repeated." (Moon.) A higher pitched *wrank* used near the nest seems to be an alarm call.

Habitat and range: This common Australian species, only rarely reported in New Zealand before 1940 when breeding was suspected at Okarito, has become in quarter of a century, the most plentiful heron in the country. Widespread in coastal districts of North and South Islands, but scarce inland above 1000 ft., though it has reached the Volcanic Plateau. Its rapid spread has been aided by the construction of farm-dams which are quickly colonised by the introduced Australian Green Frog (*Hyla aurea*). When nesting is over, flocks of 20 or more are now quite usual at roosts or in sodden paddocks; and as numbers increase, even larger gatherings are being reported in areas where the incoming tide drives them off their feeding grounds; e.g. 75 resting together in mangroves in a Kaipara creek and 82 in marsh pasture along the south shore of Manukau. There may be some northward movement in autumn, viz., in May 1962 more than 400 were counted on Farewell Spit, where few breed.

Now established on some off-shore islands, e.g. Waiheke, Kawau, Ponui, Great Mercury. Has straggled to Mokohinau and Campbell Island.

Breeding First proved in the South Island at Shag River, 1941 and in the North Island at Porirua, 1951. In Northland some pairs are nesting by midwinter. Pairs commonly nest singly; but with increasing numbers a few pairs may form a loose colony. The untidy nest frequently flimsy and surprisingly small, is usually high up in a tree. Exotic pines, especially *Pinus radiata*, are preferred; but gums, cypress (*macrocarpa*), kahikatea, tanekaha, totara, kauri and the tall crowns of manuka are used. In 1962 a pair nested successfully in an old passenger ferry beached on Ponui Island. Eggs, June to December, 3–5, pale blue-green, unglossed. Incubation 25 days; fledging *c*. 6 weeks. Both sexes incubate.

WHITE-NECKED (PACIFIC) HERON *Ardea pacifica*

Description: 36″. Larger and more conspicuous than the White-faced Heron, with which it is likely to associate. *Head, neck and breast white*, lightly shaded with grey; body mainly dark blue-grey with some reddish feathers on back and upper breast; *a white patch on the leading edge of the wing at the bend*, conspicuous in flight. Bill and legs black or dark grey-green.

Wing beat slow and strong.

Habitat and range: A typical heron of inland swamps and waters in Australia; but of irregular occurrence in the south-east coastal region and Tasmania, where periodical irruptions may occur. So far only once recorded in New Zealand, autumn and winter 1952, at Methven.

WHITE HERON *Egretta alba*

Maori name: Kotuku.

Description: 33″. Uniformly white, with elegant dorsal plumes (ospreys or aigrettes) in nuptial dress. Bill yellow, except for a brief period during the nesting season when it is purple-black; skin between eye and bill yellowish green; upper leg (tibia) yellowish; tarsus black, with yellow tinge on the inner side; and with a distinct purplish bloom in nesting season. The double kink in the long thin neck is characteristic.

Voice: In flight a frog-like croak is sometimes uttered.

Habitat and range: An almost cosmopolitan species, common in Australia (subspecies *modesta*) the outlying breeding colony of 12–20 pairs in South Westland being of this race. After the nesting season, these herons disperse all over the country, especially northwards so that there are few lowland lakes, estuaries, coastal lagoons or mangrove creeks which they do not visit at one time or another. Numbers in New Zealand seem to vary between *c.* 50 and *c.* 200. Strong winds at the time of dispersal may reduce the population. Stragglers which reach the sub-antarctic islands may be considered lost beyond reprieve. Local numbers may be substantially augmented by wind-drifted strays from Australia. Thus during and after the winter of 1957 numbers were exceptional. Immature non-breeders commonly summer away from Okarito. In the far north they are particularly partial to Rangaunu Bay, where more than forty have been reported in winter; and 15 have been present even in January (R. B. S.).

Breeding: New Zealand-bred White Herons are evidently strongly conservative. The one known breeding place is near Okarito in a kahikatea swamp through which the sluggish Waitangiroto crawls. Some of the herons' nests are in the crowns of tree-ferns; others in kowhai or kamahi which they share with Little Shags, while Royal Spoonbills prefer the taller kahikateas. It is curious that no colony has been established in any of the big northern harbours, where many White Herons pass the winter and there are areas of swamp-bush which appear quite suitable for nesting.

Eggs, September–October, 3–5, pale bluish-green. Incubation *c.* 25 days; fledging *c.* 6 weeks.

LITTLE EGRET *Egretta garzetta*   *Pl. 10*

Description: 22″. Pure white. In nuptial plumage two long narrow-pointed plumes fall from the nape and there are ornamental filamentous plumes on back and breast. Bill, black with base of lower mandible yellow; bare skin of face yellow; legs black; soles of feet greenish yellow.

In flight gains height quickly with comparatively fast wing-beats; and in the distance, flying away looks not unlike a very white Caspian Tern.

Voice: Nothing recorded in New Zealand.

Habitat and range: A cosmopolitan species with a number of weakly defined subspecies. First recorded in New Zealand in 1951; since when, reported from about twenty coastal lagoons and estuaries between Parengarenga and Bluff; rarely inland. Often solitary; greatest number seen together in New Zealand five. Associates freely along the shore with other herons and the larger waders; but likely to be harassed by gulls.

The reappearance of Little Egrets, winter after winter in certain localities, favoured also by Great White Heron, almost suggests a regular dispersal or migration from a breeding place within New Zealand. But one banded as a nestling in New South Wales in December 1962 was found at the Kakanui River near Oamaru in May 1963.

BLUE REEF HERON *Egretta sacra*

Other names: Blue Crane, Matuku moana.

Description: 26″. Generally slaty grey, darker above, paler below with a tinge of brown on the abdomen; a narrow streak of white on chin and throat. During courtship and nesting long plumes are visible on back and lower neck. Bill brown; skin between bill and eye greenish-yellow; legs yellowish-green.

A bird of coastal rocks and the tideline. Its crouching gait, rather heavy bill and shorter legs give it quite a different silhouette from that of the more graceful White-faced Heron, which is now invading its habitat. In flight which is nearly always low over the water, the uniformity of its colouring is plain to see.

Usually solitary or in pairs; but in the northern harbours flocks of about a dozen may gather at high tide or night-roosts.

Voice: During the breeding season a guttural croaking is made, often accompanied by bill snapping. Alarm note a guttural *crraw* (Moon).

Habitat and range: Sparingly distributed around the rocky coasts of the main islands, but absent from long sandy stretches; commonest north of the Bay of Plenty and Raglan and present on many coastal islands. Very seldom inland, two at L. Taupo in 1961 being quite exceptional. A rare straggler to some sub-antarctic islands, e.g. Chatham.

The wide range of this species includes the coasts of south-east Asia, Australia and Polynesia. The Reef Heron is dimorphic but New Zealand is outside the range of the white phase.

Breeding: Preferably the nest is in a cave on a rocky islet—sometimes several pairs together; it may also be in a crevice or among vegetation on a cliff, on a rotting hulk or a tumbledown jetty.

Eggs, September–February, 2–3, typically 3; pale greenish-blue. Incubation period 25–28 days; fledging *c*. 5½ weeks. Both sexes incubate.

CATTLE EGRET *Bubulcus ibis*   *Pl. 10*

Other name: Buff-backed Heron.

Description: 20″. A small stocky heron with a rather short bill (2¼″)

and neck. At first glance appears wholly white; especially in flight, when easily confused with Little Egret (q.v.). Unmistakable in breeding dress when plumes on crown, nape, back and breast become orange-buff; and legs and bill redden. Juveniles and adults in eclipse are mainly white with *yellow bill* and yellowish or grey-green legs.

Habitually consorts with grazing animals, eating the insects which they disturb and often perching on their backs.

Habitat and range: A vigorous coloniser now widespread in warmer regions of both Old and New Worlds; and still extending its range. The eastern race (*coromanda*) appears to be spreading fast in Australia.

Only recently recorded in New Zealand. A single bird spent the cold winter of 1963, May–September near Christchurch, alternating between two herds of Friesian-Holsteins " on town supply." It may have left the Australian coast in company with Little Egrets. In the spring it developed nuptial plumes. At the same time a second specimen was discovered at L. Ellesmere.

In 1964 reported more widely (once 5 together) in both North and South Islands. One in Stewart Island 1967.

AUSTRALIAN BROWN BITTERN *Botaurus poiciloptilus*

Other names: Brown Bittern, Black-backed Bittern, Matuku, Matuku-hurepo.

Description: 28″. A large brown heron-like bird, normally not easily seen because of its skulking habits; but one surprised in the open may " freeze " in surroundings where it is absurdly obvious. Upperparts dark-brown mottled with golden buff; underparts light buff with dark brown streaks and flecks. Superciliary stripe and throat pale cream. The neck is thickly feathered with a smoky brown expandable ruff. Bill, dark brown above, lighter beneath; skin between eye and bill pale green; legs and feet pale green.

Wings broad and rounded. Rises with long dangling legs. Flies with neck tucked in. Sometimes climbs reeds to survey surroundings. Several bitterns may soar and spiral over their nesting swamp. One has been seen to assume a loon-like attitude and to swim across a deep channel.

Voice: Flight call a hoarse *cr-a-ak*. The resonant boom of the male *woomph*, following an audible intake of breath, may be heard especially in the evening from July to February. A bubbling call, accompanied by a distinct soft flutelike note, is sometimes made by the female as she approaches the nest (Moon).

Habitat and range: Less plentiful than formerly, but still widely distributed in the main islands in marshy places and reedbeds up to more than 1000 ft. a.s.l. at e.g. Taupo and Wakatipu. Young wander in autumn and are quite often flushed on salt-marshes. An occasional visitor to off-shore islands, e.g. Kapiti, Great Mercury. Believed to breed at crater-lake on Mayor Island.

B. poiciloptilus, whose range includes Australia and New Caledonia, is closely related to *B. stellaris* of the Old World.

Plate 5

HEADS AND TOP VIEW OF BILLS OF MOLLYMAWKS

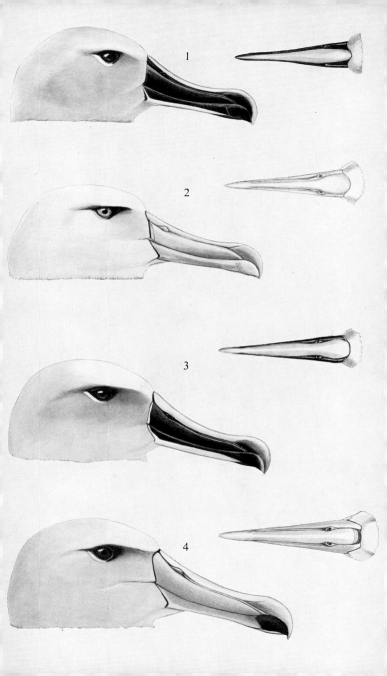

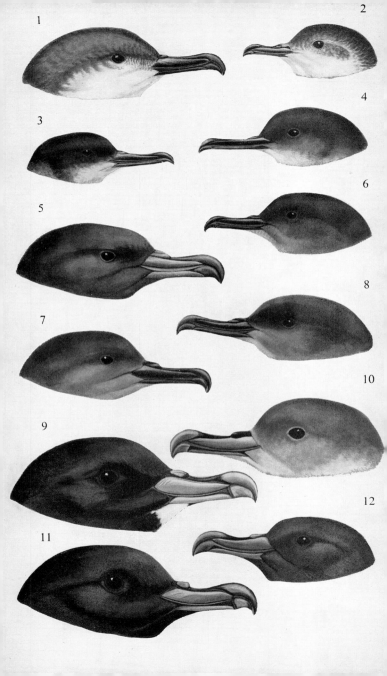

Plate 6

HEADS OF PETRELS AND SHEARWATERS

Breeding: The female builds the nest which is a firm platform of sedge or rush, usually surrounded by water, in a thick reed bed, preferably raupo. Eggs, September to January, 3–5 (typically five in the north) smooth, greenish cream. Incubation period *c.* 25 days. Only the female incubates. Chicks are thinly clad in a long greyish down with silky tips.

NANKEEN (RUFOUS) NIGHT HERON *Nycticorax caledonicus*
Description: 22″. A short-necked heron with beautiful rich chestnut plumage; unmistakable if well seen, but not easily located. Crown and nape, blue-black; back and wings chestnut red; underparts whitish; superciliary streak white; throat and neck rich buff. Bill sharp, stout, black; skin between eyes and bill greenish yellow; legs yellowish to reddish orange. In breeding plumage one, two or three white plumes with brown shafts drop over the nape. Young are dark brown, heavily spotted and streaked with buffy white.
Voice: Said to call harshly at night.
Habitat and range: Widely distributed in Australia and the south-west Pacific; straggling to New Zealand. Some were liberated unsuccessfully near Wellington in 1852. There are very few records for the present century. Young may have been reared near Blenheim, 1957–9. One was present near Kaitaia in 1961, regularly roosting in a pine.

Mainly nocturnal. Spends the day in leafy cover, emerging to feed towards dusk. Night Herons watched at Blenheim were perching well up in the leafy canopy of elm and walnut.

LITTLE BITTERN *Ixobrychus novaezelandiae*
Maori name: Kaoriki.
Description: 12″. Small, secretive and hard to flush. Crown and nape greenish black; hind neck deep chestnut red; back and mantle dark brown; tail black above, slaty below; neck and chest buff with an irregular streak of reddish brown running from the chin and down the foreneck; underparts buff with darker streaks; wings chestnut buff and dark brown, the contrasting pattern very evident in flight. Bill yellowish green with black tip; legs long, green.
Voice: Alarm notes " a peculiar snapping cry " and also " a cry not unlike that of the Kingfisher, though not so loud " (Buller).
Habitat and range: Has commonly been treated as a subspecies of *minutus*, which is widespread in the Old World and Australia; but the few skins in museums are so markedly distinct that it is not easy to dismiss New Zealand Little Bitterns simply as wind-blown strays of *minutus* from Australia.

Twenty recorded in the South Island mostly from Westland, where it probably bred in the extensive swamps and may do so still, though none has been recorded there in the twentieth century. Neither of the two North Island records, Tauranga 1836 and Meremere 1963 is wholly satisfactory.

IBISES AND SPOONBILLS:
Threskiornithidae

The members of this cosmopolitan family of large water-birds bear a superficial resemblance to herons, but are readily distinguishable by the shape of their bills and their manner of flight. The family is strongly represented in Australia whence vagrant Royal Spoonbills have recently established a small breeding colony in South Westland. Two species of ibis occur as irregular stragglers, most often, so it would seem, during periods of prolonged drought in inland Australia, where some mixed breeding colonies contain many thousands of pairs. It is curious that the commonest of the three Australian ibises, the Straw-necked (*Threskiornis spinicollis*) has not yet been reported from New Zealand, though one was seen on Norfolk Island in 1962.

GLOSSY IBIS *Plegadis falcinellus*
Description: 19″–24″. At a distance appears black; actually deep purplish-bronze, darker on wings and tail, with greenish gloss. Bill (5″) strong and arched. In winter head and neck show whitish streaking. Not to be confused with Australian Curlew which is about same size but is mottled brown and has a markedly longer bill. Flies with neck and legs extended and with faster wing-beat than herons and egrets. Can gain height quickly. A flock when descending swiftly make a noise like Shoveler Ducks. Often glides. Seen in a flock, these ibises may show considerable variation in size.
Voice: A harsh grating *gra-a-k* described as a " decidedly corvine prolonged guttural croak." Flocks make subdued grunting sounds.
Habitat and range: The Glossy Ibis is a notorious wanderer, especially when the colonies disperse after the breeding season. To New Zealand, it is a casual visitor widely reported, sometimes appearing in flocks, from the big river swamps of Australia where the race *peregrinus* breeds. They are most likely to visit New Zealand when forced by prolonged drought to seek new feeding grounds. There was a notable irruption in 1953–4, when the biggest flock seen contained 24 birds. Not primarily a bird of the coast but of freshwater swamps and lakesides, likely to remain for some weeks where food is plentiful, e.g. tadpoles. Described as feeding busily like Starlings on marshy ground.

AUSTRALIAN WHITE IBIS *Threskiornis molucca*
Description: 30″. Uniformly dull-white with wings tipped black; head and upper neck of adults bare and black, with nape banded rose-pink; neck of immature birds feathered; bill long (7″) down-curved; legs, black. On the ground the black tips of the folded wings make it appear that this Ibis has a black tail; actually the tail is white. Distinguished at once from all white egrets by shape of bill and manner of flight.

Voice: A short goose-like cry.

Habitat and range: The Australian White Ibis which occasionally reaches New Zealand — scattered irruptions in 1925 and 1957–8—is sometimes considered a race of the Sacred Ibis (*T. aethiopicus*) of ancient Egypt, the range of the species including Africa, India and Australasia. In New Zealand, these ibises have freely associated in swampy places with domestic geese, ducks and fowls, feeding by stabbing their strong bills full length into the soft ground. They fly strongly and roost at night in trees.

ROYAL SPOONBILL *Platalea regia*

Maori name: Kotuku ngutu-papa.

Description: 30″–32″. A large white heron-like bird, distinguishable at once by its *curious black spatulate bill* (7″) slightly decurved. Breeding birds have a drooping crest on the nape and show sandy-buff on the foreneck. Forehead and ocular region bare and black. Legs black. Young birds show some brown in the primaries. Flight strong and direct, with *neck held forward*, not as in herons. Also glides and soars on extended wings. Usually near water in marshes or tidal creeks; but will perch in a tree or on a post. Feeds by sweeping bill from side to side in shallow water as it moves forward. Roosts without friction among waders especially Pied Stilts, at high tide.

Habitat and range: Widespread in Australia whence vagrants have become established in New Zealand. Apparently in the 1940s one or two pairs began to breed in the White Heron sanctuary near Okarito and by 1960 10–12 pairs were known to be nesting. Birds disperse in autumn and have been met with from Parengarenga to Paterson Inlet but rarely inland. A flock of some size (20+) winters in the Manawatu estuary; smaller flocks (up to 6) have started to frequent Rangaunu Bay, Kaipara and Manukau Harbours where non-breeding immature birds have also remained throughout the summer. New blood for the established breeding stock may be coming with further stragglers from Australia.

Breeding: Nests observed in New Zealand have been high, 50–70 ft. in the forks of big swamp trees, e.g. Kahikatea. Eggs 3–4, dull white lightly smeared with brown, November–December.

Note: Another Australian species, the Yellow-billed Spoonbill (*P. flavipes*), slightly larger, 35″, with dull yellow bill and legs has not been recorded in New Zealand, but could well straggle here as it far out-numbers the Royal Spoonbill in some parts of New South Wales.

GEESE, SWANS AND DUCKS:
Anatidae

CANADA GOOSE   *Branta canadensis*
Description: 35″–40″. Body brown above and pale brown to white below; lower back black; band above base of tail and whole of tail-coverts white; tail black; *black* head and neck with a conspicuous *white mark on the cheek*. In flight black tail contrasts with white under tail and rump. When seen on the water with Black Swans the two species may be confused but Canada Goose has shorter and less curved neck; in favourable light the white under tail is visible for some distance. Downy young yellow, shaded brown above. Immature plumage tinged brown.
Voice: Musical double honk delivered on the water and in flight. High-pitched call when disturbed on breeding grounds.
Habitat and range: Introduced from North America as game (the stock probably includes more than one race). Abundant in Canterbury and North Otago, breeding mainly in grassy mountain valleys and high country lakes. In Otago remains mostly in vicinity of the breeding grounds for the winter; Canterbury breeders migrate to lowland estuaries and lakes (mostly to Lake Ellesmere) in May, returning to the high country in early September; some breed on Lake Ellesmere. (Non-breeding Canterbury birds leave the high country in December to moult at Lake Ellesmere; most of these return to the high country in late January, and fly back with the main flocks in May.) Breeds more sparingly in other parts of the South Island. Does not breed in the North Island but stragglers appear in all districts.
Breeding: A mound nest is built where the incubating bird can obtain a wide view; eggs 4–6, October–January, creamy white, incubated by female. When nest is approached, the female lowers her neck to ground level, remaining quite motionless, and nest is detected with the greatest difficulty.

WHITE (MUTE) SWAN   *Cygnus olor*
Description: 60″. Pure white plumage and size, also generally loosely folded wings on the water ensure identification at any distance. Orange bill, with black base and black knob on forehead (knob of male is enlarged in spring). Downy young, pale grey. First plumage brownish-white above, almost white below.
Voice: Has a penetrating trumpeting note, rarely heard; also snort and hiss of annoyance.

Habitat and range: Introduced from Great Britain as an ornamental bird and still exists in a semi-domestic state except on Lake Ellesmere, Canterbury, where there is a considerable breeding population (total of this species on Lake Ellesmere is approximately 200). Small populations (12–20) breed L. Poukawa, Wanstead Lagoon and other lakes in central and southern Hawke's Bay.

Breeding: Nest massive, in raupo, etc., at water's edge, or on stream or lake shore in secluded location; eggs 5–7, September–January. Incubation mainly by female. In Europe, large colonies may be formed but more often singly and highly territorial (only the latter in New Zealand).

BLACK SWAN *Cygnus atratus*

Description: 40″. Black; primaries and secondaries white, producing flashing white wing-tips prominent in flight. Bill crimson, with white band crossing the upper mandible near tip, and extreme tip also white. On the water white flight feathers occasionally show as a patch on the folded wings. Downy cygnet a little darker (brownish-white) than Mute Swan; immature plumage ashy brown, becoming darker after later moults.

Voice: Musical and far-reaching crooning note; also a whistle especially when disturbed on breeding grounds.

Habitat and range: Introduced as an ornamental waterfowl from Australia, and has increased phenomenally in some districts; now the predominating waterfowl on Lake Whangape in lower Waikato; Lake Ellesmere and Chatham Islands (the central lagoon on the main island). In varying numbers in most other districts.

Breeding: A substantial mound nest on river or lake shore, forming colonies on the latter; may be surrounded by tall lakeside vegetation, or in open. The numbers of Black Swans are controlled on Lake Ellesmere by disturbance of undesired colonies and commercial egg-collecting. Clutch up to 15, commonly 4–7, June–December, in some districts also autumn; greenish-white; incubation by both sexes.

PLUMED WHISTLING DUCK (TREE-DUCK)

Dendrocygna eytoni

Description: 17″. Long neck and upright carriage is characteristic. Brown, with buff face, and pink bill and legs. Stiff, yellow flank plumes are held outside the wings. Tail black with a broad buff band at base; abdomen white. Sexes are almost indistinguishable. Head feathers can be erected to a crest when disturbed.

Voice: A loud piping.

Habitat and range: Inland waters; feeds on grass and other vegetation. The alternative name is derived from the habit of commonly perching in trees. A straggler in New Zealand, the three records being: Thames (1871), Kaitangata (1871), Ashburton (1894–6).

PARADISE DUCK   *Tadorna variegata*   *Pl. 15*
   Other names: Putangitangi, Rangitata Goose, Painted Duck.
   Description: 25″. Of intermediate size between the ducks and the larger species (Canada Goose and swans). The female's *conspicuous white head* is generally the first field characteristic recognised (commonly observed in pairs or family groups); body of female mainly bright chestnut. Male predominantly dark; black barred with fine white lines, reddish-brown abdomen, head black with a metallic sheen. Bill and feet black. At a distance on the water recognised by stout build and relatively short neck. In flight, the conspicuous *white coverts form a prominent wing patch* on both upper and under wing. Speculum green. (As in other ducks these wing markings may or may not be visible when the wings are folded.) Runs strongly, legs relatively long.
   First plumage of immatures of both sexes is similar to that of adult male. Downy chick has striking pattern of white and brown.
   Voice: Loud alarm note different in male and female: male a deep *zonk—zonk* . . . and female a shrill, penetrating *zeek—zeek* . . . . In the breeding season the pairs rise and call on sighting an intruder, and the calls are given as a duet in the air or from some high point on the ground. Call carries for some distance—especially the high-pitched call of the female—in mountain valleys, and is thus well known as a cause of disturbance to deer-stalkers.
   Habitat and range: Very widely distributed in the mountains and foothills of the South Island; formerly on lowland streams, lakes and estuaries and still scattered throughout. The largest breeding populations are found on tussock river flats in the South Island's mountain areas. At moulting time in late summer large flocks form on certain lakes and estuaries, and a partial migration may occur from the breeding grounds. In the North Island it originally occurred only in the southern section, but there have been a number of liberations in the centre; now well established and breeding abundantly south of a line approximately from Taihape to East Cape, and is extending its range farther north. Winter visitor to Bay of Plenty, Firth of Thames and more rarely Manukau. There are signs that it will adapt itself to pastoral land if not unduly disturbed. A game bird, but protected in some districts. Liberated and now breeding in Northland.
   Breeding: Nest built of grass and down, well hidden on the ground or up to a height of 20 feet in hollow trees. Eggs 5–11, August–January, cream; female incubates. Often double-brooded.
CAPE BARREN GOOSE   *Cereopsis novaehollandiae*
   Description: 34″. An upstanding, goose-like species (related to Paradise Duck, not to geese); colour *grey*, faintly spotted dark on wing-coverts; tail and end of quills *black*; yellowish-green soft skin (cere) covers base of black bill; feet pink. Sexes alike.
   Voice: Grunt-like (thus local name in Australia " Pig Goose ").
   Habitat and range: Introduced from Australia in 1915; now rare in Australia, being found only on islands off the south and south-western coast. Liberated on Lake Hawea, and subsequently reported (in 1936)

from Lake Hawea and Lake Thomson. Has also been recorded in
Fiordland (1947) although this may be the result of immigration from
Australia. Inhabits grasslands and swampy areas in Australia, feeding
on vegetation.

Breeding: In Australia a grass nest, lined with down, on the ground
in the open; eggs 4–6, June–September, white.

GREY TEAL *Anas gibberifrons*   *Pl. 15*
Maori name: Tete.
Description: 17″. Like the Grey Duck has pale throat, but noticeably
smaller and differs in having no conspicuous eyebrow-and eye-stripes
on the face; from the female Mallard is distinguished by greyer
plumage; from the female Shoveler by more rounded outline, neat
head and small bill. The Grey Teal is distinguished in flight from all
three of the above species by the *prominent white triangle* on the upper
wing in front of speculum, and by having less white on the under wing.
Speculum green, with narrow white bar behind. Bill blue-grey upper
and yellow lower mandible; feet greyish-brown. Sexes alike. Wing
beats are faster than in other New Zealand ducks, and flocks often
wheel rapidly in flight.
Voice: A rapid *cuck-cuck-cuck*, and a muted *eep* given by
adult to young.
Habitat and range: A common species in Australia, but in New Zealand
established in several districts and apparently spreading to new localities
every year. It is probably self-introduced fairly regularly from Australia (an influx is believed to have occurred in the autumn of 1957,
when a banded bird from Victoria was shot in the Waikato district);
there have been established breeding populations for at least 50 years
in the Rotorua and Wairarapa districts, and more recently it has been
observed regularly on lakes and ponds from Manukau to Oreti gravel
pits, breeding (1961) as high as L. Tekapo at 2300 ft. a.s.l. (R. B. S.).
Sometimes visits salt water.
Breeding: On ground under vegetation near water; nest of grasses,
normally lined with down but down sometimes absent; sites recorded
in New Zealand include top of " niggerheads " (*Carex*) (Wairarapa
district) and tree forks (Waikato). Eggs 5–9, September–January, dark
cream.

BROWN DUCK (BROWN TEAL) *Anas chlorotis*   *Pl. 15*
Maori name: Pateke.
Description: 19″. General colour is warm brown. *Male* dark brown
head with green reflections on nape and along a line to eye; *white collar*
(on front portion of neck only) between this and the vivid reddish-brown
breast; some indistinct fine barring on back; a black line passes back
from each shoulder; on flanks is an area of fine wavy lines of alternate
pale and dark, and behind this a *white flank patch*; under tail-coverts
black; speculum green broadly edged behind with black, and behind
this a *white posterior bar*; another narrow bar of buff in front of

speculum. *Female* uniformly brown, head closely freckled with dark brown; wing markings as in male; no white flank. In both sexes, the under wing-coverts partly white; bill bluish-black; feet slate grey.

Some males breed in a dull plumage almost identical with that of the adult female (Peter Scott); it is not known whether these birds ultimately assume the brighter plumage. The immature male is similar to adult female.

Voice: Low *quark* and a high-pitched piping (G. R. Williams).

Habitat and range: Once very widely distributed, especially on swampy streams and ponds and tidal creeks shaded by trees, coming out at night to feed on open ground. Widely taken for food in the early period of European settlement. Various factors probably caused its sharp decline in numbers, especially swamp draining. It is now rare, but there are considerable numbers on Great Barrier Island, and localities where it has persisted in small groups are in North Auckland (Waipu, Kara, Helena Bay, Kerikeri, Takou Bay, Kaeo); Fiordland and Stewart Island. In Fiordland and about Stewart Island its habitat includes sheltered portions of the coast and it may rest and feed in beds of bull-kelp. Dives well, and has strong flight, although it takes to the wing infrequently.

Breeding: Grass, lined with down, in a well-concealed situation near the water; eggs 5–7, July–December, cream.

AUCKLAND ISLAND FLIGHTLESS DUCK *Anas aucklandica*

Description: 17″. Resembles Brown Duck in both sexes, but there is no white collar or dark line on the back in the male; male has only a faint patch (brownish-white) on the flanks; speculum and wing-bars almost absent, reduced to greenish gloss and faintly indicated brownish-white bar at rear edge; abdomen of female whitish. Under wing white mottled with brown in both sexes.

Voice: A piping or whistling note resembling that of the Brown Duck; no other call recorded.

Habitat and range: This form is essentially flightless, with much reduced wings which are of use only to aid the bird when scrambling up to coastal rocks. It feeds regularly amongst kelp on the coast, which is much indented and provides many sheltered locations. Also on the streams and lakes, which are never far from the coast in this group. Like the Brown Duck, habits are nocturnal: feeds on land at night.

A slightly smaller and browner form (*nesiotis*) on Campbell Island, where it was originally only in small numbers, now greatly reduced.

Breeding: Nests on the smaller members of the group, but cats probably now prevent it from breeding on the main island. Nest lined with grass, *Dracophyllum* leaves and down, concealed under vegetation; eggs 3–5, October–December, cream.

GREY DUCK *Anas superciliosa* *Pl. 15*

Maori name: Parera.

Description: 22″. " Grey " plumage (dull brown with a pale greyish or buff crescentic tip on each feather), paler over-all on the lower surface; the distinctive markings are the *pale chin and throat* and *conspicuous striped pattern of the face* (latter consists of dark brown stripe through the eye, and above it a pale buff eyebrow-stripe which divides the eye-stripe from the dark crown); a second dark stripe from the gape across the cheek, but less distinct. *Speculum green,* black borders and *narrow white posterior band*; in front of the speculum a narrow pale buff band, but often indistinct. No difference between the sexes (cf. Mallard). Under wing white; bill dark bluish-grey; feet olive or yellowish-brown.

May be confused with the female Mallard, but in addition to the above plumage characters, the Grey Duck is of somewhat slighter build, the head being larger in proportion.

Voice: The female's loud quacking is familiar, the male having a higher-pitched call like that of the Mallard.

Habitat and range: Universally distributed, and on Kermadec, Chatham, Snares, Auckland, Campbell and Macquarie Islands. Although the modification of swamps and inland waters as the result of settlement, together with other factors, have caused a general decrease in numbers, it remains a common duck in many parts of New Zealand; it is also adaptable, although appearing to need more cover than the introduced Mallard and thus avoiding the more developed farmlands. Habitat includes mountainous areas, estuaries and sheltered inlets, as well as all inland waters. Food is both plant and animal, obtained by typical " up-ending," or dabbling in shallower water, or on land; marine organisms commonly taken on mud in estuaries.

Banding records of movements to date include regular recoveries between the Waikato district and Southland—the longest (700 miles) recorded within New Zealand; and several from Chatham Islands and from Australia.

Breeding: Generally away from water (cf. Mallard) concealed in herbage; frequently in a tree fork or hollow tree; a favourite site is in masses of perching *Astelia*; dry grass and other vegetation is used, with much down as a lining. Eggs 5–11, September–December, greenish-white, or pale cream tinged with green. In this and related ducks incubation is performed by the female.

MALLARD *Anas platyrhynchos* *Pl. 15*

Description: 23″. Although the female may be confused with the Grey Duck, there is a striking difference between the sexes, the *male* being unmistakable, viz. glossy dark green head, white collar, purplish-brown breast, grey body varied with brown, and iridescent black rump; the middle tail feathers are black and the side feathers white, the four centre black feathers curled; *white vertical stripe on flank*; bill greenish-yellow. *Female* mottled brown, *without the pale chin or striking facial* *pattern* present in the Grey Duck (there is a comparatively faint dark line through the eye and indistinct pale eyebrow stripe); the pale tip of each feather much more extensive than in grey duck, and tips strongly buff in colour; bill olive-brown, yellow on sides. In both sexes under wing white; *speculum blue* with black border in front and behind, and a *double wing bar. Feet orange in both sexes.*

Swifter and more irregular flight in comparison with the Grey Duck, and take-off is generally more sudden.

The bright plumage of the male is replaced in summer or autumn, for a period of about a month, by an " eclipse " plumage: this resembles plumage of female, but not evenly mottled, and distinguished further by darker brown (almost black) crown, brownish-black rump and greyish upper surface; curled tail feathers absent. Moult back to the breeding plumage during February–May.

Mallard and Grey Duck readily hybridise, but mainly in districts where there is a high proportion of semi-tame birds (has been recorded especially in Manawatu district and in coastal districts of Canterbury, including Lake Ellesmere). Flocks in parks, etc., consist largely of hybrids; the River Avon, in Christchurch city, has the best-known population. Hybrid plumage varies: a common type has general plumage, especially strong facial pattern, derived from Grey Duck, in combination with the Mallard's conspicuous double wing bar and either orange or orange-tinged feet. Common in the *male* is the above plumage with an additional Mallard feature, viz. black rump and curled middle tail feathers; less commonly the male has a " patchwork " of plumage features (partial green head, etc.) and this *may be mistaken for the eclipse plumage of the pure Mallard drake* (note eclipse plumage is summer–autumn). *Female* may have more mottled general plumage of Mallard female with facial markings derived from the Grey Duck.

Voice: Female has a loud, deep *quark* and softer "conversational" notes; male softer, higher-pitched *quek.*

Habitat and range: Introduced as early as 1867, the stock originating from the British Isles, but did not become established until intensive breeding and liberation was carried out *c.* 1930; since then further introductions have been made from the United States. The stock is thus of mixed origin, and it is not known whether both migratory and sedentary races were included. Research on migration of this species and the Grey Duck in New Zealand shows that while the Grey Duck performs widespread movements (possibly migratory), the Mallard is distinctly sedentary. In general habits the Mallard bears a strong resemblance to the Grey Duck; the two species probably compete for food.

The Mallard is common (predominating over the Grey Duck) in the eastern South Island and southern portion of the North Island (especially Hawke's Bay and Manawatu). It outnumbers the Grey Duck in most closely settled districts. Present on the Chatham Islands but in small numbers.

Breeding: Nests under cover, rarely far from the water, and like the

Grey Duck often chooses a hollow tree or fork; nests may be simply
in tall grass. Constructed of grass (sometimes nest material is practically absent), down being added as incubation progresses. Eggs 10–15,
August–October, greenish- to bluish-white, or creamy. Incubation
28 days, sometimes less.

NEW ZEALAND SHOVELER *Anas rhynchotis*   *Pl. 15*
Other names: Kuruwhengi, Spoonbill, Spoonie
Description: 19″. *Male* is the most colourful New Zealand duck,
striking features being: bluish-grey head combined with black round
base of bill and *vertical white line in front of eye*; *bright chestnut under
surface*, and breast freckled dark-brown and white; *prominent white
patch on flanks*; *pale cobalt blue upper wing-coverts* (and outer webs
scapulars), *green speculum*, the coverts and speculum divided by a
white bar; bright orange-yellow feet; rump and tail-coverts (upper and
under) are black with a green gloss. Adult males show much variation
in extent of white on breast. The plumage of the *female* is mottled
brown, but *wing markings similar to those of male*; feet yellowish-brown.
In both sexes under wing white.
  On the water where the full pattern may not be seen, this species has
a distinctive squat outline—in proportion a *shorter neck and bigger bill*
than the Grey Duck or Mallard. The bright chestnut sides are conspicuous in good light (chestnut distinctly brighter than the purplish-
brown breast coloration in the Mallard drake and more conspicuous at a
distance); white more extensive on flanks than in the Mallard drake.
Female distinguished from Grey Duck by absence of facial pattern, and
from both Grey Duck and Mallard by smaller size and different outline.
  Males in dowdy eclipse plumage somewhat resembles females. Flight
is swift and impulsive, with a tendency to turn suddenly.
Voice: Female *cuck-cuck-cuck* very similar to that of Grey Teal, with
which easily confused; male a muted *clonk* given only in evenings or
when disturbed.
Habitat and range: Spread throughout, and considered to be increasing
in numbers; at the Chatham Islands until *c.* 1925; straggler to the
Auckland Islands. Visits most lakes up to about 2000 ft. a.s.l. (e.g.
Rotoaira); readily colonises new ponds and dams; seldom in small
streams in forested regions such as those favoured by the Grey Duck.
Both animal and plant food are recorded, but there has been little
investigation of its habits.
  A slightly different (duller breast) subspecies in Australia (*rhynchotis*).
Breeding: Recent records mainly in very open grassy sites a short
distance (*c.* 100 yards) from water, often in the ranker patches found
on pasture land; an early record under tussock at some distance from
water (Potts); under a small lupin on a shingle-ridge in a riverbed
(R. B. S.). Occasionally in trees in Australia, but no records of this in
New Zealand. Nest of grass and other vegetation, lined plentifully
with down; eggs 9–13, October–January, pale bluish-white.

BLUE DUCK *Hymenolaimus malacorhynchos*   *Pl. 15*
Maori name: Whio.
Description: 21″. Dove-grey with strong bluish sheen; brownish-grey
on crown; heavily *spotted red-brown* on the breast; on the inner
secondaries each feather has a black margin, and inner secondaries
have narrow white tips; under wing pale grey; *pinkish-white bill* is
a prominent feature, and has a *black tip* (including flexible lobe on each
side); feet dark brown. Female has reduced red-brown spotting on
breast; spots are completely absent in the first immature plumage.
    If it remains motionless seen with difficulty against stones in stream
bed.
Voice: Male has a shrill, somewhat hoarse whistle (denoted by Maori
name); female has a characteristic cry *cra-ack* that has been
appropriately described as a " rattle "; also recorded is a *ra-ra-ruk*.
Habitat and range: North (south of Coromandel Peninsula) and South
Islands: originally to sea-level in areas with turbulent streams, i.e.
fiords and hilly areas; restricted at present mainly to more mountainous
regions where modification of the habitat is at a minimum. Adapted
to feeding upon aquatic insects and obtains much of its food from stones
and boulders amongst rapids, where insect life is abundant. Caddis-fly
larvæ probably form the most important food item. It can dive freely,
even in swifter currents, clinging to boulders while feeding under water.
Emerging adult insects, etc., are also taken on the surface of streams
and lakes. Flight is strong and direct; but when disturbed, will escape
more often by diving and swimming out of sight. In pairs or family
groups throughout the year.
    Remarkably tame, and has thus sometimes been severely depleted
in unfrequented areas, but now that total protection is more generally
observed is believed to be increasing.
Breeding: Under thick vegetation near a stream, often on a steep bank
above water; eggs 4–9, August–November, creamy-white. Downy
young in olive-brown and pale creamy-white down, with narrow stripe
through the eye, are strong divers and swimmers, and accompany
their parents along the stream-beds.

AUSTRALIAN WHITE-EYED DUCK *Aythya australis*
Maori name: Karakahia.
Description: 19″. Like the following species (New Zealand Scaup)
this is a " diving duck," a group in which the legs are set well back on
the body and the body outline is distinctly rounded; diving ducks tend
to swim in the deeper portions of lakes and lagoons, and there dive
for their food. The White-eyed Duck and Scaup are alike in the mainly
dark plumage of the male, but in the present species *white rump and
under tail* are distinctive. In both sexes *wide white wing-stripe across
whole wing*; under wing white. Female brown. The male has a *white*
iris (female *brown*).
Habitat and range: While a number of Australian species have reached
New Zealand during the last 50 years, some settling permanently, this

duck has apparently disappeared after an early period (1867–95) of some abundance in certain districts. It was present in numbers in the lower Waikato, and recorded from Lakes Rotomahana and Tarawera, Manawatu district, Hawke's Bay, Lake Wairarapa, Lake Ellesmere and finally an isolated sight record in 1934 at Hamurana, on Lake Rotorua.

Common in Australia, where it is recorded as taking a wide variety of plant and animal foods.

Breeding: In Australia the nest, a deep cup of water plants, is frequently placed in a bushy shrub above the ground; it is lined with down; eggs 9–14, creamy-white.

NEW ZEALAND SCAUP (BLACK TEAL) *Aythya*
novaeseelandiae Pl. 15

Maori name: Papango.

Description: 16″. *Male* black above with purple sheen (greenish on head), and blackish-brown below; the abdomen with white mottling. *Female* blackish-brown, darker above; in breeding plumage has a white band (sometimes incomplete) on forehead; abdomen mottled with more white than in male. In both sexes, a *broad white wing-bar on secondaries*; under-wing greyish-white with brown mottling; bill bluish-black; feet dark brown. Iris *yellow* in male, *brown* in female.

Readily distinguished by dark plumage and rounded outline; sits high in the water as compared with other ducks, and patters along the surface to take off. Dives for food.

Voice: Male a soft whistle, female a muted quack.

Habitat and range: Lagoons and lakes, including mountain lakes up to *c.* 3000 ft. a.s.l. and numerous small coastal ponds and sand-dune lakes in both islands. It is still found throughout, but numbers greatly reduced following settlement probably both through modification of the habitat and extensive shooting: it is now completely protected. It has increased greatly on North Island hydro lakes, colonising some within a few months after flooding. Established on artificial ponds in some areas.

Flocks of non-breeders persisting throughout the nesting season may indicate that this species does not breed till two or more years old.

Breeding: Nests close to water in dense cover, occasionally under an overhanging bank; material mainly grasses, lined plentifully with down; eggs 5–8, October–March, creamy-white; large for the size of the bird. Commonly nests in close groups. The chicks can dive shortly after hatching, and go down to a considerable depth.

MANED GOOSE (AUSTRALIAN WOOD DUCK)
Chenonetta jubata

Description: 19″. Recognised by goose-like head in association with small size. *Male* has *chocolate head*; mane-like black feathers on the back of the neck; mottled brown and white breast; back, under tail-coverts and tail black; and *blue-grey wing-coverts and flanks*. *Female* mainly mottled and barred brown and white; pale buff face and dark line through the eye; under tail-coverts white. Speculum *green*, with *white bar above and below*, in both sexes; under wing white; dark brown bill and black feet.

Habitat and range: Four records, apparently of stragglers, from Wanaka (1910), and Orawia, Linwood and Wairaki (Southland) (all 1944). In Australia a widespread species, obtaining much of its food on land, including grassland and sometimes crops. Frequently perches on logs or trees.

AUCKLAND ISLAND MERGANSER   *Mergus australis*

Description: 23″. Belongs to the Sea Ducks (Mergini), which include the eider ducks and their relations as well as the mergansers—the latter are distinguished by their slender bills, serrated along the cutting edge on both mandibles. Apart from a species on the eastern coast of South America, the Auckland Island Merganser is the only Sea Duck found in the southern hemisphere. Except that both sexes resemble the female of northern mergansers it is not markedly distinct, and thus probably arose as an offshoot of the northern hemisphere stock comparatively recently. Has been found sub-fossil in the South Island. Plumage *mainly dark greyish-brown*, with *dark red-brown head*; the feathers on the back of the head hair-like forming a crest; *white wing-patch*; under wing white mottled grey; *abdomen with plentiful white mottling*; bill orange-yellow, brown above; feet orange. Note slim shape and narrow bill. Female similar to male, but plumage slightly duller (*note*—both sexes are very like the female of northern species, especially the Red-breasted Merganser, *Mergus serrator*; in all northern mergansers the male has a green head).

Habitat and range: Almost certainly extinct as it has not been recorded since 1905; further, a thorough search in 1942–5 by the coast-watching parties stationed on the Auckland Islands in nearly all localities on Auckland, Adams, Disappointment and other members of the group had no result. Lived mainly on the fiord-like inlets of the east and south coasts, and on the extensive coast of Carnley Harbour, but also on the lower reaches of streams. Only food recorded is fish (a species of *Galaxias*).

Breeding: Nest and eggs not known; downy chick olive-brown above, yellowish-white below with reddish throat and foreneck.

HARRIER-HAWKS AND EAGLES:
Accipitridae

This large cosmopolitan family which in Australia alone numbers nearly twenty species, has only one representative in New Zealand. The common Australian Sea Eagle (*Haliaeetus leucogaster*) might be expected to wander to these islands, but the evidence that it has done so on a number of occasions is inconclusive.

Plate 7

HEADS OF PETRELS

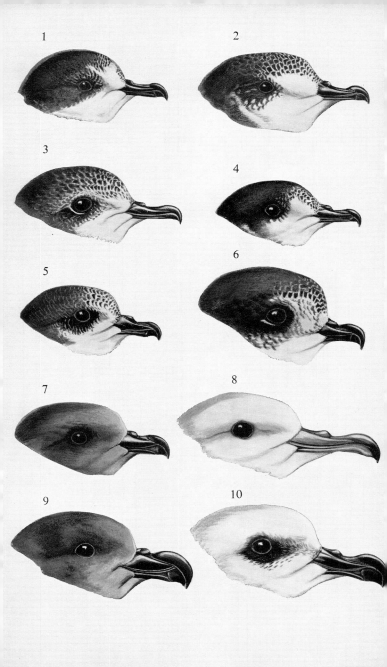

Plate 8

CORMORANTS

HARRIER *Circus approximans*
   Other names: Hawk, Swamp Harrier, Gould's Harrier, Kahu.
   Description: 22″–24″, females being slightly larger than males. Plumage
rather variable. Head and upperparts commonly dark brown, upper
tail-coverts white; usually some white feathers on nape; tail lighter
brown with dark bars; underparts reddish-brown with dark streaks;
legs and feet yellow. Young birds are dark and lack the pale rump;
plumage becomes lighter with age and some old birds, especially males,
are almost grey.
   A bird of open country, quartering the ground with slow, leisurely
flight, sometimes soars in wide effortless circles; often a roadside

scavenger, feeding upon car-killed rabbits, hares, opossums, etc. Will
wade into shallow water after frogs and tadpoles. Persistently badgered
by Australian Magpies where they are present; and often mobbed by
flocks of Starlings.
   Voice: Mewing accompanies playful courtship flights. A high-pitched
squeal *Kee kee kee* is used during display; also by the male to call
the female from the nest.
   Habitat and range: Fairly common throughout, except in heavily
forested districts (up to 5000 ft.); straggling south to Auckland and
Campbell Islands. By opening up great tracts of country and increasing
its food supply, pakeha farming has benefited this hawk which despite
persecution survives in settled districts. Young birds wander in
autumn and there is some evidence that they tend to drift northwards.

Communal ground-roosts in winter may contain scores of birds. The species is found throughout Australia and the south-west Pacific.

Breeding: Courtship flights observable in September. Nest, preferably in a swamp among raupo or niggerheads, often in scrub and fern, sometimes on saltings. Eggs 2–7, commonly 4, white, chalky, October–December; incubation period 31–34 days; fledging about six weeks. The passing of food in mid-air when the female rises from the nest and turns on her back to receive it from the male is sometimes observed.

FALCONS: Falconidae

Falcons with powerful strokes of their long pointed wings are among the fastest of fliers and are noted for the boldness with which they attack and strike down their prey. Of the two species on the New Zealand list, one is endemic, the other is a rare straggler from Australia. It is remarkable that the almost ubiquitous Peregrine Falcon (*F. peregrinus*) has never been known to occur in New Zealand.

NEW ZEALAND FALCON *Falco novaeseelandiae*

Other names: Bush Hawk, Sparrow Hawk, Quail Hawk, Karearea.

Description: 16″–19″. Like many falcons, a variable bird; females generally bigger and more richly coloured than males, but the largest males are bigger than the smallest females. Upperparts brownish-black, darkest on the crown, barred with brown in older birds, chin and throat whitish with dark brown streaks; dark line through eye beneath pale superciliary stripe; dark streak at sides of chin like

drooping moustache. Underparts pale buff to white, striped with dark brown on chess and belly, barred on flanks (adult); dark rufous brown with obscure round spots and splashes of pale buff (imm). Thighs and under tail-coverts rufous brown (" red trousers ") with darker streaks. Legs and feet yellow, claws black. A fierce and fearless predator, preying mostly upon birds, especially now apparently on the common introduced species, and occasionally on small mammals. Intolerant of intruders, particularly of the Harrier on its breeding territory.

Voice: A loud piercing whistle or shrill scream on the wing. Also during play or exercise a series of single *heks* with pauses between.

Habitat and range: Nowhere common

and now very rare north of Rotorua. Found mainly in the back country but scarce above 4000 ft. Young birds wandering in autumn, visit settled country and even urban gardens. Reported as far south as Auckland Islands.

Breeding: Nest usually on the ground on the ledge of a cliff or on a bare slip in steep bush, sometimes in a tree. Eggs 2–4, rich reddish brown with chocolate blotches, typically falconine, October–December; incubation period 30 days.

NANKEEN KESTREL *Falco cenchroides*
Other names: Australian Windhover, Hoverer.
Description: 12″–14″. Above a beautiful cinnamon brown, feathers with black centres; wing quills dark brown; underparts white or light yellowish buff, the breast feathers having narrow brown shaft lines. Rump and tail grey in male, rufous in female with black sub-terminal band and white tip. Legs orange-yellow.

A typical Kestrel distinguished at once by its size, colouring and *habit of hovering*, poised in mid-air with head facing into wind and tail more or less depressed according to the strength of the breeze. Drops by stages. Hunts over open country especially short grass, in search of lizards, large insects, small birds and mammals.

Habitat and range: Widespread in Australia but scarce in Tasmania. Rare straggler to New Zealand, reported only eight times (five in North Island, three in South Island). Worth watching for after strong autumn westerlies on the West Coast.

GAME BIRDS: Galliformes

The only indigenous member of this order, *Coturnix novaezealandiae*, Koreke of the Maoris, became extinct about 1870. It was a close relative of the Stubble Quail (*C. pectoralis*) which is still quite common in Australia.

The following species of game birds have become established in New Zealand with more or less success:

Name	First introduced	Status
Australian Brown Quail (*Synoicus australis*) 7″	1866	North Island. Two races were introduced; but it is possible that these small brown quail had already reached New Zealand unaided, as they occur on many off-shore islands from Mayor and the Aldermen to the Three Kings.
Californian Quail (*Lophortyx californica*) 10″	1865	Locally plentiful in both North and South Islands.

Californian Quail (*Lophortyx californica*)

Name	First introduced	Status
Bobwhite Quail (*Colinus virginianus*) 9″	1894	Now apparently confined to the Wairoa district of Hawke's Bay.
Pheasant (*Phasianus colchicus*)	1842	Fresh liberations are made annually.
Chukor (*Alectoris chukar*) 13″	1926	Two Asiatic races were introduced. Now widespread in hilly country east of the Southern Alps from Nelson to Otago.
Grey Partridge (*Perdix perdix*) 12″	1962	Locally liberated in North and South Islands. Success of experiment not yet proved.
Peacock (*Pavo cristatus*)	1843	Several feral populations in the North Island from Kaipara to Wanganui and Hawke's Bay.
Guinea Fowl (*Numida meleagris*)	1864	Established only locally. Little known.
Turkey (*Meleagris gallopavo*)	Before 1890	Feral in several districts.

NEW ZEALAND QUAIL   *Coturnix novaezealandiae*

Other name: Koreke.

Description: 6″. Above and on flanks warm dark brown, mottled dark brown, each feather centrally streaked with buffy white; paler, mottled dark brown below. *Male* has face (from a line above the eye) and throat *reddish-chestnut* (in female face and throat whitish with dark brown spots).

Note that male is readily distinguishable from that of Australian Brown Quail, as the latter has no chestnut on face and throat; the pale stripes are bolder in the present species; underparts in Australian Brown Quail are barred rather than mottled. The *axillary feathers* (under wings) are *white* in the New Zealand Quail cf. grey in Australian Brown Quail (this can only be seen when specimens are examined).

Voice: Low purring and call *twit, twit, twit, twee-twit* (Potts) (cf. the characteristic double call *ker-wee*, accented on the second syllable, of the Australian Brown Quail).

Habitat and range: Presumed extinct, the last acceptable recorded date being 1875 (Buller). Formerly North, South and Great Barrier Islands, being " excessively abundant in all the open country, and especially on the grass-covered downs of the South Island " (Buller). In the early days of settlement it was widely taken for food (and for sport); other factors contributing to its reduction were widespread burning of native grasslands, and mammalian predators; however, the ultimate cause of its extinction remains difficult to trace.

Food seeds and grass (Buller).

The New Zealand form is subspecifically related to the Australian Stubble Quail, *Coturnix novaezealandiae pectoralis*, and, in view of the persistence—even under modern agricultural conditions—of the latter, the possibility should not be overlooked that an invasion may still occur from Australia (in *pectoralis* general colour is paler, but chestnut throat in male more extensive).

Breeding: Nest a depression lined with grass. Eggs 10–12, yellowish-brown to buff, with heavy spots and blotches of dark brown (cf. Australian Brown Quail, eggs of which are evenly freckled with small dark brown spots).

BROWN QUAIL   *Synoicus ypsilophorus*

Local name: Rat Quail.

Description: 7½″. Two forms of this Australian quail, *ypsilophorus* and *australis*, were introduced in the mid-nineteenth century; but the possibility of there having been natural colonisations should not be ruled out. Sexes alike. Upper parts generally brown, mottled black and chestnut; feathers of back centrally streaked with white; throat buffy white; underparts greyish buff with black zig-zag bars. Females are slightly bigger than males. Crouches, runs and flies briefly on short rounded wings.

Voice: A plaintive long drawn rising whistle—*Ker-wee, ffweep*, or *mooreete* (this being its Australian Aboriginal name).

Habitat and range: Widespread in lowlands of North Island; scarce in the southern half. Locally faithful to swamps or the edges of salt-marshes (? descendants of Tasmanian Swamp Quail). Often seen in Northland along the dusty edges of scrub-fringed roads. Also, rather enigmatically on several offshore islands from Mayor and Aldermen to Three Kings.

Breeding: Nest a slight depression lined with grass and leaves. Eggs October–January, dull white evenly freckled with brown. Fledging *c.* 10 days.

CALIFORNIAN QUAIL *Lophortyx californica*

Description: 9½″–11″. A plump stocky gamebird with a jaunty crest. Male, forehead pale grey; crown dark brown; top-knot plume black and curving forward; back mostly brown; tail grey; throat black encircled by a narrow white band; breast bluish-grey; upper belly buff, feathers edged with black; rich chestnut patch in middle of belly; lower belly buff; flanks brownish-grey streaked conspicuously with white. Female smaller; chiefly brown; belly scaled and flanks streaked as in male; top-knot shorter.

Runs fast, rises with a whirr and glides on short wings stiffly held. Will perch in a tree or watch alertly from an eminence, e.g. fencepost, wall, rock.

Voice: A sharp clucking *tek-tek*; an anxious *whit-whit* when a flock is scattered. Most characteristic is a clear, triple call, variously interpreted as *tobácco*, *chicágo*, *where áre you*; frequently mimicked by Starlings.

Habitat and range: Widely spread in both North and South Islands; and on some settled offshore islands, frequenting both farmlands and scrub.

Breeding: Flocks split up in late winter. Nest commonly in long grass near thick cover of brambles, gorse or fern. Eggs October–December. Clutch 9–16, pyriform creamy white, spotted dark and yellowish-brown. Incubation 22–23 days.

CHUKOR *Alectoris chukar*

Description: 13″. Two of the numerous races of this Asiatic rock partridge were introduced into the South Island and have prospered. For a time *chukar* was considered a race of *A. graeca*, but recent authorities treat them as distinct species.

Upperparts ashy tinged on crown and shoulders with vinous red; a black band across forehead, continuing through eyes and down sides of neck to join above breast; cheeks, chin and throat buffy white; breast ashy tinged with brown; abdomen buff; flanks barred with chestnut and black. Bill and legs bright red.

Voice: Cackles or clucks rather like a barnyard fowl.

Habitat and range: High country mainly east of the Southern Alps from Nelson to Otago, up to 6000 ft., preferring dry rocky faces.

Breeding: Nest usually in a rocky place under shelter, e.g. snowgrass or tussock. Eggs September–February. Clutch 10–18, greyish-freckled with brown spots. Average size of coveys 8–10. In autumn larger flocks are formed.

PHEASANT *Phasianus colchicus*
Description: Males 30–35″; females 21–25″. At least two forms of this popular and colourful game-bird have been introduced, the so-called English Pheasant *colchicus* and the Chinese Ring-necked Pheasant *torquatus*.

Plumage of males is rather variable; but the glossy dark green head and neck, red wattles around eyes and short ear tufts are unmistakable; and most have complete or partial white neck rings. Females are soberly mottled in light brown, chestnut and black; tail shorter than in male, distinctively pointed.

Voice: Male has a loud, abrupt crowing *kok-kok*.
Habitat and range: Widely and frequently released. Appears to thrive best in the coastal scrubland of the north.
Breeding: Polygamous. Nest a hollow scratched by female, scantily lined and usually in thick cover. Eggs 7–15, uniform olive brown, September–January. Incubation *c.* 23 days. Young accompany mother and can fly at *c.* 14 days, though far from full grown.

RAILS, CRATES, WEKAS, GALLINULES AND COOTS: Rallidae

With few exceptions, among which are the Weka, the Pukeko and the Takahe, the rails are a diversified family of secretive, sombre birds of swamp and reed-fringed waterway. The bill varies in dimensions, being long in typical rails (*Rallus*), shorter and thicker in crakes (*Crex* and *Porzana*), reaching its greatest size in the gallinules (*Porphyrio, Notornis*), where it is sub-conical. In some species a bony shield covers the forehead. Rails are characterised by short wings, heavy bodies and long legs. Most species fly only under duress, and some have lost the power of flight. Yet rather surprisingly, despite their short wings, rails have successfully spread to many remote islands, and from ancestral types some very distinct forma have been evolved. All over the world the rails tend to disappear before settlement and the advance of urbanisation.

In New Zealand only one species, the Pukeko, is conspicuously common. The Weka is locally numerous. Three species, Banded Rail, Spotless Crake and Marsh Crake, are widely distributed, but like the Scarlet Pimpernel " demmed elusive." The Australian Coot, though still rare, is expanding its range yearly. The remarkable Takahe, a highly specialised gallinule, survives only in a few remote valleys of Fiordland.

Two distinctive rails of the Chatham Islands, *Rallus dieffenbachi* and *Cabalus modestus*, became extinct in the nineteenth century. The Auckland Island Rail, which was rediscovered in 1966, is doubtfully distinct from a small Australian rail, which is common in Tasmania, *Rallus pectoralis*, the Lewin or Slate-breasted Rail.

An extreme example of ralline wandering is provided by the Corncrake (*Crex crex*) said to have been killed near Nelson about 1865.[1] Among the lost crails of New Zealand known only from sub-fossil bones are: a small weka, a small gallinule, a flightless coot and the giant rails, *Diaphorapteryx* and *Aptornis*.

Included in the same order (Gruiformes) are the Cranes: one unsubstantiated record of the Australian Brolga or Native Companion (*Grus rubicunda*) is the only evidence of a true Crane in New Zealand.

WEKA *Gallirallus australis*

Other names: Woodhen, Woodrail.

Description: 21″. Wekas are large flightless rails with strong bills and feet and reduced wings. The plumage is mainly brown and black, but the tone of the brown and the amount of black vary. On these colour differences, and also on slight differences in size, several forms have been defined.

North Island Weka

The Weka of the North Island (*greyi*) has more grey on the underparts and brown rather than reddish legs, the colour becoming brighter in the breeding season.

The Buff Weka (*hectori*) was found in low rainfall districts east of the main range in the South Island. It became extinct in its old haunts, but throve at Chatham Island, whence 16 were re-introduced in February 1962 to Arthur's Pass National Park.

The Weka of the western region of the South Island from Nelson to Fiordland (*australis*) has a streaked red-brown and black breast. In South Westland and Fiordland it is dimorphic, the dark form showing

[1] The Corncrake, a western palaearctic breeding species, normally migrates to South Africa. The New Zealand occurrence, though suspect, is not impossible. The bird has twice been recorded in Australia; the first from a few miles south of Sydney in June 1893; the second from Jurien Bay, Western Australia, in December 1944.

much more black in the plumage. " Black " Wekas are not uncommon along the Milford Track and range to the top of the Mackinnon Pass (3400 ft. a.s.l.).

The Stewart Island Weka (*scotti*) is slightly smaller. It also is dimorphic, but the dark phase is less black.

The Weka walks deliberately with tail flicking, but can run very fast and swims without hesitation. Inquisitive, omnivorous, a ready snapper-up of unconsidered—or unguarded—trifles, especially if they are bright and shiny. In association with man can become a shameless raider of rubbish-bins and fowl runs. Near the sea frequently feeds on beaches among kelp and tidewrack. A capable rat-killer. Becomes more active at dusk.

Voice: A shrill, far-carrying whistle, *coo-eet*, many times repeated. When one Weka starts calling, others in the vicinity are likely to join in. Also described as a " thin, fairly high-pitched *wee-eek*, *wee-ee-eek*, *wee-ee-ee-eek*, which seemed to sound all round the hills " (Gee).

Habitat and range: Not primarily a swamp bird, preferring drier scrub country or the edge of the forests.

In the North Island the Weka is now confined to the Gisborne district, where it has recently increased and continues to thrive in a variety of habitats, both urban and rural. Its sudden disappearance from districts where it was plentiful is probably to be attributed to disease. In Taranaki its disappearance is dated to 1918. In parts of Northland Wekas were plentiful in 1936 and very hard to find by 1940. In an attempt to re-establish Wekas in some of their old haunts, hundreds have been caught near Gisborne and released in the North Island, where conditions for their survival appear favourable.

In the South Island Wekas are to be found mainly west of the main range. Plentiful in north-west Nelson, especially on Farewell Spit, they are said to be increasing in Westland and becoming plentiful again in parts of Fiordland. The decline of the Buff Weka in Canterbury became apparent about 1917; and the last record known to Stead was in 1924. However, in 1905 this form was introduced to Chatham Island, where it prospered exceedingly. The Weka of the Stewart and adjacent islands is in no danger. This form was introduced to Macquarie Island, where it is now numerous. The Wekas on Kapiti are said to be hybrids of *greyi* and *scotti*. The nearest allies of this endemic species are the flight-less woodrails (*Tricholimnas*) of Lord Howe Island and New Caledonia.

Breeding: Matures early. A pair of North Island Wekas, aged about nine months, nested and reared a chick. Nesting season very extended; eggs commonly September to April, 3–6, typically ralline, creamy-white or pinkish with scattered brown and light purplish blotches. Incubation 20–27 days. Chicks are clad in brownish-black down. Broods commonly reduced to one or two, but a pair may nest repeatedly in a season.

BANDED RAIL   *Rallus philippensis*
Other names: Landrail, Striped Rail, Mohopereru, Mioweka. (The old sealers' name for the Macquarie Island race was Wigeon!)

Description: 12″. A secretive bird, more often heard than seen and most often glimpsed as a disappearing shape, *ventre à terre*. The rich colouring and the subtle pattern of its markings are not easily seen. Upperparts olive brown spotted with black and white; superciliary streak whitish; broad chestnut band through eye to hindneck; another chestnut band across the breast; chin whitish; throat and foreneck grey; underparts black with narrow irregular white bars. Bill reddish-brown; feet brown.

Voice: A creaky *swit-swit* or high-pitched *quee-quee* often heard at dusk. Near the nest a low *kik-kik-kik*. An intruder near the nest is greeted by a growl or throaty croak.

Habitat and range: This species is represented by many races in southeast Asia, Australia and the islands of the south-west Pacific. Apparently once widespread in New Zealand, but now seldom reported except coastally north of Raglan and the Bay of Plenty and in north-west Nelson. Not uncommon along mangrove creeks and the adjacent saltings and sedgy swamps, surviving even in urban surroundings despite rats, cats and tin cans. Still occurs inland in the lower Waikato (Meremere 1962). A scarce resident on some off-shore islands, from Three Kings to Weka-free islets off Stewart Island.

Sometimes in secluded creeks may be observed foraging in the open, especially in rainy weather or when there are downy chicks to feed. May fly a short distance with dangling legs, if suddenly flushed.

Breeding: The nest is well hidden in thick grass or rushes near water. It has also been found supported on the trailing stems of ribbonwood in a tangle of saltmarsh herbage. Eggs September to February, 4–7, buff or pale pinkish marked with dark reddish-brown and purplish-grey spots and blotches. Incubation *c.* 18 days. The chicks are covered with black down. Both sexes incubate. Probably double-brooded.

Note: Dieffenbach's Rail (*Rallus dieffenbachi*), once abundant in the Chatham Islands, was similar to the Banded Rail in so many respects that it may be regarded as a strong subspecies of *philippensis*. The last specimen was obtained in 1840.

AUCKLAND ISLANDS RAIL *Rallus pectoralis*

Description: 8½″. Crown chestnut streaked with black; upperparts chestnut obscurely streaked with blackish-brown; superciliary stripe, cheeks, side of neck and nape rich rufous; chin whitish; throat and breast slate-grey, lower tinged with olive; wings, belly and flanks black barred with white. Bill reddish-brown; legs pinky-grey or light grey-brown.

Voice: A metallic *clink* or *cree-eek* repeated loudly; also a typical ralline grunt. A double note, *kek-kek*, may indicate mild alarm.

Habitat and range: Possibly exterminated by feral cats on the main Auckland Island; surviving on Ewing Island and Adams Island. Clearly a colonist from south-eastern Australia, the local form, the so-called *muelleri*, being doubtfully distinct from typical *pectoralis*.

Breeding: Nest not known in New Zealand. In Australia the nest is a saucer of rushes and grasses, but in a swamp. Eggs 4–6, pale stone, spotted with red and lavender.

SPOTLESS CRAKE *Porzana tabuensis*

Other names: Sooty Rail, Putoto, Puweto.

Description: 8″. Upper surface dark slate merging with chocolate brown; chin greyish; underparts leaden grey; under tail-coverts black

barred with white. Bill black; legs reddish. " Eye " red.

An elegant little rail which " seldom takes wing, and then only for a very short distance; but it runs with rapidity, swims very gracefully and often dives to escape its enemies " (Buller).

Voice: Three distinct calls were noted by Buddle at the Poor Knights:

    (*a*) a high-pitched squeak repeated steadily at short intervals by both birds of a pair;

    (*b*) a very low crooning—the purring note of other authors—audible only at close range, used by the female when in nesting cover, evidently a call to the young;

    (*c*) a harsh scolding *crack-crack-crack* repeated rapidly which seemed to be the male driving the female back to the nest.

Habitat and range: This small dusky rail is generally a skulking denizen of swamps, fresh and saline. Much of our knowledge of its distribution in New Zealand depends on specimens brought in by cats. On Aorangi in the Poor Knights, where there is no true swamp, and also on the Southwest King, it forages on the open forest floor.

The range of the species includes Australia and much of the south-west Pacific, *plumbea* being the name of the southern race which is found 'in Tasmania, southern Australia and New Zealand south to Stewart and Chatham Islands.

Breeding: The nest is seldom found in New Zealand, and our knowledge of nesting habits lean heavily on the findings of Buddle at the Poor Knights.

Nest a bulky, clumsy structure loosely woven of grass or sedge. Apparently several spare nests may be built. Eggs October to December, 2–3, typically three; pinkish-cream, occasionally pale bluish, flecked all over with light brown spots varying considerably in size. Chicks are clothed in a woolly black down, the hair-like tips on back and head having a greenish sheen.

MARSH CRAKE *Porzana pusilla*
Other name: Koitareke.
Description: 7″. The smallest of our rails. Very secretive. Distinguished from Spotless Crake by white markings and brownish colouring. Upper-parts brown spotted with white and streaked with black; breast pale

blue-grey; flanks and abdomen barred with black and white. Bill, legs and feet brownish-green. Sexes similar. One flushed by a dog at Lake Wainono flew with rapid wingbeats for about 100 yards, not rising more than 3 feet.
Voice: Call notes a harsh *krek-krek* or *creak-creak*. A quick jarring trill has also been described.
Habitat and range: A bird of swamps and the thick reedy margins of lakes up to over 1000 ft. a.s.l. (Taupo), it has been widely reported from the main islands and recorded at Stewart and Chatham Islands, but is nowhere common. It falls an easy victim to introduced vermin.

The Marsh Crake ranges very widely over the Eastern Hemisphere. It has been divided into five subspecies, *affinis* being the name given to New Zealand birds.

Breeding: This small elusive rail obviously breeds in many swamps throughout the country; but the nest appears to have been found only once. An egg from Awanui in the Buddle collection, now deposited in the Auckland War Memorial Museum, is dark olive brown. According to Sharland, the clutch in Tasmania is 4–8 and the eggs are brown, spotted olive.

AUSTRALIAN COOT *Fulica atra*

Description: 15″. Plumage appears wholly black; actually upperparts are sooty black and underparts dark grey; *no white under tail*. *Bill* and *frontal shield* pale bluish-grey, *appearing creamy-white* at a distance; legs and feet steel grey with fleshy lobes.

Juveniles lack the frontal shield and have a dusky bill.

Flight laboured at take-off, as feet patter along the surface. Bobs its head while swimming. Dives frequently to bring up weed.

Voice: A variety of calls includes a harsh *crark-crark* and a noise very similar to the sound of someone's chopping with an axe, *kratack*, *krat*, *krat*.

Habitat and range: A cosmopolitan species, represented in Australia and Tasmania by the race *australis*. Rare but increasing in New

Zealand, especially in the last decade. The most aquatic of the rails, frequenting reed-fringed lakes both subalpine and lowland.

In the South Island Coots now occur sparingly from Southland to Marlborough. Breeding has been proved at Lake Hayes (1958), St. Anne's Lagoon, Cheviot (1961), Lakes Alexandrina and Macgregor (1962).

In the North Island Coots were found in 1954 at Tutira, where they have since bred successfully. They have now been reported from other lakes in Hawke's Bay; from Lake Wairarapa (1957); Lake Pupuke (1957–9), Lake Okareka (1962), Virginia Water, Wanganui (1962). On the last two there are now substantial populations.

Gregarious in winter when *c.* 70 have been reported at Lakes Hayes and flocks of 10–12 at Cheviot, Tutira and Horseshoe Lake, Hawke's Bay.

Breeding: Nests at Lake Hayes were placed on a solid foundation in a tangle of willow, made of willow rootlets and lined with raupo. Eggs October to November, 5–7, creamy-white evenly and sparsely marked with small and medium-sized black spots. Incubation *c*. 22 days. The dusky down of nestlings is strikingly tipped orange to orange-rufous; bill crimson with a white line. May be double or treble-brooded like the typical race.

PUKEKO *Porphyrio melanotus*

Other names: Swamp-hen, Pukaki, Pook.

Description: 20″. The most conspicuous of our rails. Head black; upperparts black with green gloss; throat, neck, breast and flanks purplish-blue; abdomen and thighs black; *undertail coverts white. Massive bill and frontal plate scarlet*; legs and feet pale red or orange. Females are slightly smaller than males. Juveniles lack the iridescence and the bright colours.

Walks jauntily and delicately, flirting its tail. Can run fast and, if pressed, swims freely. Flight at first laboured with legs dangling, then strong. Habitually climbs about swamp vegetation. Has a parrot-like habit of sometimes holding its food firmly in one foot.

The species is prone to albinism, complete or partial. A colony containing several buff-coloured birds has been described from the Wairarapa.

Voice: An ear-piercing screech *kwee-ow* seems to be both an alarm note and also a contact note used, e.g. when Pukekos are flying high at night. A variety of sounds emerges from a raupo-swamp which holds a colony of Pukekos: a drawn-out, almost booming *poo-koo-koo-koo*, a sighing *kwee-uk*; a bleating *kwairk*; an anxious *pee-ewk* and agitated *a-yik* or *k-yik* quickly repeated.

Habitat and range: Closely related to the Purple Gallinule which has a very wide range in the Old World. Apparently only locally common in New Zealand before 1850; but increased greatly in second half of nineteenth century and now plentiful in the main islands in swampy places up to 1200 feet, from which it may emerge to raid crops or feed in open grassland. Now on Rotoaira, 1850 ft. a.s.l.

Plate 9
CORMORANTS

Often flies by night. Has recently colonised swamps on some inshore islands, e.g. Waiheke, Great Mercury; and has straggled to Three Kings, Fanal, Little Barrier, Mayor, Campbell Island. Resident on Raoul and Norfolk Islands.

Breeding: The nest, a bulky structure, is normally in marshy surroundings but is sometimes ill-concealed. Eggs 4–7, buff or reddish-stone with dark brown, grey and reddish blotches all over; commonly August to March; but midwinter nesting has been recorded. Incubation period *c.* 24 days; apparently mostly done by male at least during the day-time. Chicks are clad in a silver-tipped black down.

TAKAHE *Notornis mantelli*

Other name: *Moho*.

Description: 25″. A ponderous, flightless, brilliantly coloured gallinule with massive bill and legs. Head, neck, breast and flanks iridescent indigo blue; shoulders peacock blue; mantle, back and rump suffused with shades of green; wings blue (greater coverts) and green (lesser coverts); thighs and abdomen bluish-black; under tail-coverts white.

Plate 10

HERONS, EGRETS, BITTERN

Frontal shield and base of bill scarlet; rest of bill pink; feet red. The plumage of the immature bird contains more brown and is without the brilliant gloss. Sexes similar.

Voice: Alarm call *oomf* repeated slowly. Possibly a contact call is a weka-like duet, *coo-eet* many times repeated by a pair as a two-part canon (Fleming). The cry of the chick is a slow *wee-a* or a repeated wheedle, the parent meanwhile keeping contact by the *cowp-cowp* call.

Habitat and range: Known from the North Island only by sub-fossil bones, though it may have persisted till the nineteenth century. Formerly ranged over much of the South Island, but only four specimens were obtained (1849, 1851, 1879, 1898), all in the south-west. Dramatically rediscovered in 1948 by Dr. Orbell, the Takahe has since been the subject of much expert study. It is now known to survive only west of Lake Te Anau in the Murchison and Kepler Ranges, where its main habitat is the tussock grassland of the valleys at 2000–3000 ft. a.s.l. More especially in winter it enters the adjacent beech forests.

Breeding: The nest is a kind of bower between tussocks of *Danthonia*. Eggs October to March, 1–2, dull cream with brown and mauve blotches. Chicks are covered with a black down and have a white patch on the fore-edge of the wing.

BLACK-TAILED WATERHEN (NATIVE HEN) *Tribonyx ventralis*

Upperparts dark bronze brown; throat and breast bluish-grey; **Description:** 14″. An obvious gallinule, generally dusky, considerably smaller than a Pukeko and not unlike a handsome little bantam.
abdomen black; *conspicuous white spotting on the flanks*; frontal shield and upper mandible dark pea-green; lower mandible orange-red, green towards tip; *legs brick red.*

Runs but seldom flies. Tail carried erect and continuously flicked.

Habitat and range: An Australian species ranging widely in swampy districts, but apparently rather scarce near the south-east coast and replaced in Tasmania by a much larger water-hen, the non-flying *Tribonyx mortieri*.

The Australian Water-hen is known as a nomad, prone to mass movements. Numbers will suddenly arrive in a district after rains and may disappear just as suddenly. The overflow of such irruptions may occasionally reach New Zealand, but the only satisfactory records are of a bird shot at Colac Bay, Southland, in June 1923; and of one which frequented the Tukituki river-bed, near Patangata, Hawke's Bay, in 1957 and 1958. Other specimens lack authenticating data.

WADERS

After the Petrels, the Waders are the largest order of birds on the New Zealand list. They are primarily birds of the coast, though some, e.g. Pied Stilt, Black Stilt, Banded Dotterel, Wrybill, South Island Pied Oystercatcher, move inland to breed, even high into the mountains, and two, the Spur-winged Plover and the Black-fronted Dotterel, are hardly shore-birds at all.

There can be few estuaries on the long New Zealand coastline which are not frequented or visited by a variety of waders in the course of the year; and the study of wader-migration is perhaps one of the most fascinating aspects of ornithology. For the benefit of the beginner, some of the more important areas where waders may be successfully studied are now briefly mentioned.

In the far north, Parengarenga, Rangauna and Kaipara have begun to reveal their secrets and would richly repay regular watching. Manukau and the Firth of Thames are the largest areas which have been worked systematically. Much has been published both on the commoner and the rarer waders for which they provide ideal feeding grounds. Where Bar-tailed Godwits occur in large flocks, other waders will be found. Ohiwa and Tauranga are known as good " godwit harbours " in the Bay of Plenty, and so are Raglan and Aotea west of the Waikato. The sandy beaches and river mouths of the south-west and south-east coasts of the North Island are visited by many passing migrants, and have their quota of breeding Stilts, Dotterels and Oystercatchers. In the South Island, the vast flats inside Farewell Spit are obviously an area of major importance. Nelson is a well-known " godwit harbour." Westland has received little attention, but a harbour such as Okarito must have great possibilities. On the east coast of the South Island, the many river mouths are admirable, but little-studied wader habitats. The Heathcote-Avon estuary is dominated by impressive numbers of Godwits and Oystercatchers. Lake Ellesmere was a wonderfully rich area in the first half of this century, when Edgar Stead was collecting information on the birds of Canterbury, and probably still is. Otago Harbour and nearby inlets attract many waders both resident and migrant. In the far south the lagoons and estuaries along Foveaux Strait support a large and varied population.

For the correct identification of waders it is essential to note not only size, shape, general colour and behaviour; but also the length and shape of the bill; the length and colour of the legs; the flight-pattern, with special regard to markings on back, tail or wings; and, if possible, voice. An added complication is that the plumage of many species varies according to age and season. An obvious example is the Banded Dotterel. Adults in breeding dress may be quite unmistakable; but adults in the post-nuptial moult, when the bands have disappeared, and juveniles look very different. Much the same is true of other species of dotterels which sometimes stray to New Zealand from Australia or Asia and may attach themselves in summer or autumn to flocks of Banded Dotterels which contain moulting adults and bandless juveniles. Only after a very close and critical scrutiny will these rare visitors be acceptably identified. Even the most experienced observers have to check and re-check such occurrences.

Several species also of the migratory arctic waders show striking differences between the comparatively drab colouring of adults in eclipse or first-year birds and the vivid reds, deep blacks and rich variegated spangling of breeding dress. Between January and April the plumages of adult male Godwits, Knots, Curlew Sandpipers, Red-necked Stints, Golden and Grey Plovers, undergo a spectacular change. The plumage of the females too becomes more colourful. Other more subtle changes are less easily detected, e.g. the development of crescentic spots on the flanks of Sharp-tailed Sandpipers or an increase of barring on the underparts of Tattlers. Traces of nuptial colouring are still visible in the plumage of some adults when they return to New Zealand in September or October.

Geographically, the waders of New Zealand fall into three groups:
(a) Those which breed in New Zealand.
(b) Those which breed in Australia and have strayed across the Tasman Sea, perhaps to become established in New Zealand, e.g. Spur-winged Plover, Black-fronted Dotterel.
(c) The trans-equatorial migrants which breed in northern Asia, Siberia and north-west America and, by flying south, avoid winter in the northern hemisphere and enjoy the temperate summer of New Zealand.

(a) Of those which breed in New Zealand, the commonest are Banded Dotterel, Pied Stilt and South Island Pied Oystercatcher. All are migratory within New Zealand so that, if the birdwatcher lives on the coast or is able to visit an estuary, he should soon be able to recognise these three distinctive birds even if they do not breed in his district. It should perhaps be mentioned that even in the North Island, the commonest oystercatcher is the one which breeds on the riverbeds of the South Island and flocks of uniformly marked black and white oystercatchers, occurring in northern New Zealand even in summer, are likely to be migrants from the south.

Some of the waders which breed only in New Zealand must be considered among the rarer birds of the world. The population of Wrybills, estimated from counts of wintering flocks in the northern harbours may be 5000. Much scarcer are the Red-breasted Dotterel with 500–1000 individuals, the Northern (Variable) Oystercatcher, the Black Stilt, the Shore Plover now confined to Southeast Island in the Chathams and the Southern Snipe with its four or five subspecies on remote sub-antarctic islands.

Regular watching of an estuary where migratory waders pause to rest and feed is the kind of field-work which can prove most rewarding. Outside Canterbury there are curiously few records of the Wrybill in the

South Island. On its migrations, it occurs on both west and east coasts of the North Island. The Red-breasted Dotterel is a puzzling bird with a curious distribution. The two areas where it is known to breed are 700 miles apart and there are very few recent reports of this fine dotterel between Foveaux Strait in the south and the Waikato estuary in the north.

The oystercatchers of New Zealand are a notoriously difficult family. Something has already been said of the South Island Pied Oystercatcher, a successful bird with distinctive habits and the representative in New Zealand of the common oystercatcher of the northern hemisphere. Larger and rather scarce is the Northern Oystercatcher, a variable bird of unstable plumage characters, some being black, some fully pied, while there are all sorts of intermediate phases with smudgy markings. The ranges of this and the Black Oystercatcher overlap. It is taxonomically convenient and probably biologically correct to unite the Northern and Black Oystercatchers and regard them as a polymorphic species, with the black form dominant in the south and the mixed form most numerous in the north, though nowhere abundant enough to form big flocks. Quite distinct also is the oystercatcher which inhabits the Chatham Islands.

The Black Stilt which some ornithological workers consider to have been the original stilt of New Zealand before the invasion of the Pied Stilt from Australia, is known to breed in only a few loose colonies which may total 30–40 pairs.

The Spur-winged Plover is an example of a vigorous coloniser, now firmly established in Southland and steadily extending its range.

(b) The field-naturalist should find it worthwhile to familiarise himself with the appearance of the commoner plovers which breed in south-east Australia just in case he is lucky enough to encounter one or more of them as stragglers. In recent years the Red-capped Dotterel has been found sitting on eggs in Canterbury and the Black-fronted Dotterel, which has been reported from widely scattered localities, has started to breed in Hawke's Bay. Climate and terrain being suitable, both these small plovers could become established as breeding species. Indeed they may already have taken the first steps towards becoming naturalised New Zealanders, as the Spur-winged Plover has done. The beautiful Australian Avocet evidently bred in the South Island in the middle of the nineteenth century. Probably collectors, rather than a lack of suitable habitats, are to be blamed for frustrating its efforts to become established.

(c) The third group of waders comprises nearly thirty species. Birds from this group form a very important part of the bird life of our tidal flats which, without them, would be comparatively barren for long periods of the year. These far-travelling visitors come from northern Asia, Siberia and north-west America, arriving from about mid-September and departing in March and April, though flocks of immature non-breeding birds remain throughout our mild winter, growing up and conserving their strength for the time when they, too, will have to face a flight of 6000–8000 miles to reach their breeding grounds.

At least nine species of waders may be considered regular annual migrants from arctic or sub-arctic regions. Of these, the most numerous is the Eastern Bar-tailed Godwit. Absolute protection came in time to save it; for the experience of other lands has shown that the larger shore-birds which form dense flocks are very vulnerable to shooting.[1]

Godwits are sometimes referred to as " snipe " or " curlew." Both these names are quite incorrect. A constant companion of the Godwit is the Knot. Mixed flocks in favoured localities often contain many thousands of these two " fellow-travellers." Third in order of abundance are Turnstones and after them Asiatic Golden Plovers. In a few chosen coastal districts, these two very different birds regularly form sizeable flocks and feed together.

An examination of the classified summarised notes which are published yearly in " Notornis " shows that Sharp-tailed Sandpipers, Red-necked Stints, Curlew Sandpipers, Long-billed Curlews and Whimbrels are regular migrants in small numbers; and few years now pass without reports of Pectoral Sandpiper, Terek Sandpiper and Hudsonian Godwit. Especially in the north, the patient watcher has a fair chance of finding some of the more unusual visitors which, drifted by the wind or caught up with a flock of strong-flying regular migrants, have missed Australia or overshot the normal southern limits of their kind.

The name of Edgar Stead, the great Canterbury naturalist and collector, is closely linked with the discovery that the migration of several species of arctic waders could take them to New Zealand and indeed did so regularly. His impressive list of " firsts " includes Little Whimbrel (1900), Hudsonian Godwit (1902), Curlew Sandpiper (1902), Red-necked Stint (1902), Pectoral Sandpiper (1903), Sanderling (1917), Red-necked Phalarope (1929). It is unfortunate that, since the golden age of Edgar Stead, Lake Ellesmere where most of these birds were collected has not been the scene of much critical ornithology. Fortunately the study of the migratory shore-birds has been maintained with increasing keenness in the north; and, while much has been learnt about the numbers and movements of the commoner species, several arctic waders new to New Zealand have been found and the evidence is that some of them reach New Zealand much more frequently than was formerly supposed. As the result of painstaking field work, Auckland ornithologists now have several " firsts " based on sight records to their credit, viz. Large Sand Dotterel (1943), Grey Plover (1946), Siberian Tattler (1950), Terek Sandpiper (1951), Asiatic Black-tailed Godwit (1952), Oriental Dotterel (1954), Marsh Sandpiper (1959), Broad-Billed Sandpiper (1960). The first Least Sandpiper to be reported in New Zealand was found by R. H. D. Stidolph in Hawke's Bay in 1952. Farewell Spit produced a Mongolian Dotterel in 1961 ; Porirua a Greater Yellowlegs in 1962. Nor is the list of possibilities exhausted. Sooner or later Great Knot, Wood Sandpiper and Common Sandpiper, all of which reach south-east Australia, will be found also in New Zealand. Careful scrutiny of flocks of Wrybills in the harbours of Manukau and Kaipara and in the Firth of Thames has often led to the discovery of stray sandpipers and plovers which seem to seek the

---

[1] In America the Eskimo Curlew was shot virtually out of existence and the Hudsonian Godwit whose numbers sank dangerously low is still rare.

Waders classified according to size and breeding centre

New Zealand (a) Australia (b)	Size	Northern Asia, Siberia, north-west America
	Very big	Long-billed (Eastern) Curlew
		Bristle-thighed Curlew
S.I. Pied Oystercatcher (a)	Big	Asiatic Whimbrel
Variable Oystercatcher (a)		American Whimbrel
Black Oystercatcher (a)		Bar-tailed Godwit
Chatham Island Oystercatcher (a)		Hudsonian Godwit
Spur-winged Plover (a, b)		Asiatic Black-tailed Godwit
Pied Stilt (a, b)		Greenshank
Black Stilt (a)		Greater Yellowlegs
Red-necked Avocet (b) (formerly (a)		
Red-breasted Dotterel (a)	Medium	Grey Plover
		Pacific Golden Plover
		Oriental Dotterel
		Little Whimbrel
		Marsh Sandpiper
		Wandering Tattler
		Grey-tailed Tattler
		Turnstone
		Japanese Snipe
		Knot
		Great Knot
		Oriental Pratincole
Banded Dotterel (a)	Small	Large Sand Dotterel
		Mongolian Dotterel
Red-capped Dotterel (b) (?a)		Terek Sandpiper
Black-fronted Dotterel (a, b)		Sharp-tailed Sandpiper
Shore Plover (a)		Pectoral Sandpiper
Wrybill (a)		Curlew Sandpiper
		Common Sandpiper
Southern Snipe (4 insular races) (a)		Sanderling
		Broad-billed Sandpiper
Chatham Island Snipe (a)		Grey Phalarope
		Red-necked Phalarope
	Very small	Red-necked Stint
		Least Sandpiper (Long-toed Stint)

sanctuary afforded by the Wrybills as they trustingly rest in compact groups.

One unusual experience which sometimes happens to the observer of shore-birds in New Zealand is that he is able at the same time to watch closely related species or subspecies, the southern limits of whose ranges overlap in New Zealand. Siberian and American Pectoral Sandpipers have been encountered together again and again at Lake Ellesmere, Manukau Harbour and the Firth of Thames and perhaps elsewhere. Two forms of the Black-tailed Godwit, Hudsonian and Asiatic, have been noted within a few yards of each other in Manukau. A dark-rumped American Whimbrel may yet be found making friends with its paler-rumped Asiatic congeners.

OYSTERCATCHERS: Haematopodidae

Oystercatchers are sturdily built waders, black or pied, with red or pinkish legs and strong orange-red bills (3″). Hence in some districts they are commonly called Redbills.

SOUTH ISLAND PIED OYSTERCATCHER *Haematopus finschi*

Other names: Redbill, Torea.

Description: 18″. The plumage of the South Island Pied Oystercatcher presents a strikingly clear-cut pattern of black and white, especially in flight. Head, neck, chest, upper back, wings and tail black; underparts, wing-bar and lower back vividly white. Females are slightly larger and have longer bills. Immature birds have bills with dusky tips and their legs are paler.

By far the most plentiful of the oystercatchers of New Zealand even in the North Island.

Voice: A shrill far-carrying *hu-eep* or *kleep*. Song, a long musical piping with considerable variation, commonly heard on breeding grounds and sometimes in northern winter-quarters; similar to the piping ceremony described by Huxley for the closely related European Oystercatcher (*ostralegus*), but needs studying in New Zealand.

Habitat and range: Breeds inland in the South Island only (not Stewart Island)—not common west of the Alps. When inland may feed on arable land. After nesting forms large flocks at estuaries

and on tidal flats. While the bulk of the population stays on the east and north coasts of the South Island in winter, some even going to Paterson Inlet in Stewart Island, many thousands move north to Auckland and Northland, a few annually reaching Parengarenga. The northward movement begins in December, reaches a peak January–February and continues till April. The southward movement starts in July. Flocks of immature non-breeders summer in the northern harbours.

A thriving race which appears still to be increasing. The size of wintering flocks near Auckland has shown a spectacular increase since 1940.

Breeding: A fairly early nester on river-beds and lake shores up to 3000 feet. Eggs September to November; clutch 2–3; incubation period 24–28 days.

VARIABLE OYSTERCATCHER *Haematopus reischeki*
Local name: Mud Pigeon.

BLACK OYSTERCATCHER *Haematopus unicolor*
Local name: Musselpicker.

Description: 19″. The plumage of the Northern Oystercatcher is very variable. Pied examples can usually be distinguished from *finschi* by their larger size—very marked in some individuals—less angular and

Variable Oystercatcher *Haematopus reischeki*

more " humped up " carriage and by the smudgy blurring of their markings. A few are almost as pied as *finschi*; but the contrasting pattern is not as clear-cut; and even in the most pied specimens the white recess on the " shoulder " which *finschi* shows so clearly when standing, is seldom present; nor are the wing-bar and lower back so conspicuously white. Some show only a trace of white on the belly; some are entirely black and virtually inseparable from *unicolor*. It has been stated that the black form of *reischeki* is a browny black and lacks the purple gloss of true *unicolor*, but this needs verification. The plumage of black oystercatchers breeding on the northern coast of the North Island can be distinctly glossy; and black oystercatchers seen in flocks on Stewart Island are not noticeably glossy. Females are usually larger and have longer and more pointed bills. Dull colouring of legs and bill distinguishes young birds in their first winter.

Voice: Very similar to that of *finschi*; call note *kee-eep* perhaps a little huskier and less piercing. Piping ceremony accompanies pair formations and courtship.

Habitat and range: A bird of the coast frequenting both sandy beaches and rocks. *Reischeki*, nowhere numerous, occurs most commonly near sandy estuaries among the extensive dunes of Northland. Some pairs appear to occupy their territory throughout the year; but there is some local wandering; small flocks may be formed and odd *reischeki* may be sometimes found among the big flocks of visiting *finschi*. On Coromandel and in the Bay of Plenty the pied form of *reischeki* is much outnumbered by the black. In the South Island *reischeki*-type oystercatchers occur as far south as Kaikoura and Fiordland but the dominant form is black. The oystercatchers which breed on the coast of Otago, Southland and Stewart Island are mostly typical *unicolor*.

Breeding: Rather a late nester even in the north. Eggs commonly December–January, stone-buff spotted and blotched with dark brown; normal clutch 3. Both sexes incubate. Where *reischeki*-type oystercatchers occur, it is not unusual for one of a breeding pair to be black and the other pied.

CHATHAM ISLAND OYSTERCATCHER *Haematopus chathamensis*

Description: 19″. A pied oystercatcher without any tendency to melanism although the distinctions—and these are constant—between this form and *finschi* are all additional dark elements—viz., the line of colour demarcation on the chest is less distinct; the area of white on rump and lower back is smaller; there is less white in the pattern of the wing. Important characteristics are its stouter short bill and larger feet correlated with the rock-dwelling habit.

In plumage and behaviour this form seems to be more closely related to *reischeki* than to *finschi*. It has also been linked with *longirostris* of Australia.

Habitat and range: Confined to the Chatham Islands where it is widely distributed around the coast. Sedentary, non-migratory and strongly territorial ; apparently not forming flocks.

Breeding: Does not appear to have been studied.

PLOVERS AND DOTTERELS: Charadriidae

SPUR-WINGED PLOVER *Lobibyx novaehollandiae*

Description: 15″. A true " lapwing " strikingly patterned, quite unlike any other plover in New Zealand. Suggestive of a small heron, as it rises or flies low with slow, deliberate beats of its rounded wings. Brown above, white below; crown and shoulders black; bill and face-wattles yellow; legs reddish. In flight the wings are seen to be whitish beneath with a dark band along the rear edge; rump white; tail white with black tip. Bony spur ($\frac{1}{2}$″) on wing at carpal flexure. Has a sedate walk and also a nimble, tiptoe run.

Voice: A noisy grating rattle variously interpreted as *kitter-kitter-kitter*, *rikka-rikka-rikka*, or *kerrick-kurrick*, also described as a long crackling call in a descending scale. This call is commonly used when a passing Harrier is being mobbed.

Habitat and range: A common breeding species of south-east Australia and Tasmania, which since *c.* 1940 has become firmly established in Southland and appears to be spreading slowly northwards. Outlying colonies are well-established near Arrowtown; at Makarora on Lake Wanaka; at Lake Tuakitoto; and in 1962 breeding pairs were found in the Waitaki river system, the Mackenzie country and especially up the Hakataramea valley.

Flocking takes place after nesting season, but no large-scale movements so far noted in New Zealand.

These plovers are still rare outside Southland, but breeding has now (1968) been recorded in most provinces of the South Island. Two straggled to Campbell Island (1945). A very rare vagrant in the North

Island, mainly to coasts of Taranaki and Wellington, but only once reported from northern districts, viz. Matata, Bay of Plenty, 1957.

In Southland these plovers may congregate in fields of root crops while Black-billed Gulls and Black-fronted Terns are hawking insects overhead. They also visit the seashore and have been seen feeding in a runnel among gulls of three species.

Breeding: An early nester in open country, sometimes on dry stony ground, usually near a swamp. Normal clutch 4. Young sometimes hatched by August, but some pairs still have eggs in December. Incubation period *c.* 28 days. Both sexes incubate.

PACIFIC (ASIATIC) GOLDEN PLOVER *Pluvialis dominica*
Pl. 11

Description: 10″. A medium-sized plover without any salient characteristics in juvenile or winter plumage; mottled brown and buff above with the golden suffusion showing more clearly as breeding dress is assumed; throat and breast grey and yellowish-buff; eyebrow pale buff; underparts buffy white; tail and rump like back showing no white; underwing and axillaries uniform grey. Summer and winter plumages are very different. In February some adults start to show black on the underparts and the moult into nuptial plumage is complete by April when they leave; forehead broadly white and line over eye extending down side of neck to white patch on breast white; lores, spot in front of eye, cheeks, middle of breast and abdomen black. Bill black; legs slaty grey; rump and tail appear dark in flight and there is no wing-bar. Adults may retain traces of nuptial black when they return to New Zealand. The flight is rapid with strong, regular wing-beats. An alert and shy species.

Voice: Described as a shrill but melodious double whistle, *tuill tuill* or a harsh whistled *queedle*.

Habitat and range: A summer visitor (subspecies *fulva*) from Northern Asia and perhaps Alaska, arriving from September onwards and frequenting certain favoured stretches of coast every year from Parengarenga to the Bluff; and on Kermadec and Norfolk Island. Small parties have reached the Auckland Islands. Flocks sometimes fly a short way inland to marshes, ploughland and pastures, where herbage is thin and short. In some districts frequently accompanied by Turnstones. Occurs usually in small parties, but in Manukau, the Firth of Thames and near Bluff flocks of more than 100 birds have occurred. Flocks resting at full-tide do not form compact groups but are usually in a straggling line, apart from other shore-birds.

GREY PLOVER *Pluvialis squatarola*   *Pl. 11*

Description: 11". Distinctly larger and lighter-coloured than a Pacific Golden Plover and with a robuster bill; but not always easily distinguishable on the ground. Upperparts brown dappled with white; tail barred white and brown with a *broad white band* across the upper tail; underparts white except the *black axillaries* which, in flight, are diagnostic; but if the bird is flying away from the observer, they are not easily seen; the white upper tail also is an important aid in identification; whitish wing-bar visible in flight; bill black; legs ash-grey. Grey Plovers seen in New Zealand are likely to be in the winter plumage described above. In very handsome summer plumage adults have back spangled silver and black, and underparts black. A bird of the tideline, unlikely to be found far from the seashore.

Voice: A rather melancholy trisyllabic *hee-oo-ee* or *hee-er-ee*.

Habitat and range: Perhaps the most cosmopolitan of the true plovers. A circumpolar breeder, migrating south; some birds reaching the tips of the southern continents. Rare in Tasmania. A straggler to Macquarie Island. Very few certainly identified in New Zealand; single birds at Firth of Thames 1948–9; Grassmere, Farewell Spit, mid-Kaipara 1961; and two at Farewell Spit still in nuptial dress, September 1962, Manukau 1968, probably also 1946, 1947, 1957, but these sight records not acceptable because the black axillaries were not seen.

BANDED DOTTEREL *Charadrius bicinctus*   *Pl. 11*

Other names: Double-banded Dotterel, Mountain Plover, Tuturi-whatu, Pohowera.

Description: 7″. A handsome small plover easily recognised in breeding dress, i.e. from May to January when both male and female have *two bands*—one black and narrow on the lower neck, the other chestnut and wider on the breast. Males are a little bigger and more showy than females, but the intensity of the colour and distinctness of the bands vary considerably. Forehead white, edged above with black; a black band from bill towards eye; some white above and below eye but facial markings show some variation. Upperparts brown; underparts white; bill black; legs dull greenish yellow or yellowish grey. In eclipse plumage, February to May, the bands disappear or are much reduced. Juveniles in their first autumn have upperparts sandy and speckled, are not so white underneath and lack the pectoral bands.

Occurs in flocks of some size from January to July scattered over tidal flats or short-cropped pastures near the sea.

Voice: An incisive *chip chip* or staccato high-pitched *pit pit* is commonly used by pairs on territory and by birds in flocks. Courting and breeding males trill excitedly—hence Maori name " tuturiwhatu." A rippling liquid *qreep* and a high-pitched whistling *twrip* have been described (Moon).

Habitat and range: The most numerous and widespread of the smaller plovers which breed in New Zealand. But comparatively few breed in northern districts, viz. doubtful if fifty pairs nest within fifty miles of Auckland city, though large flocks appear in autumn. Common also at the Chatham Islands. A few pairs breed on off-shore islands, e.g. Great Mercury, Kapiti. A larger race, apparently non-migratory, inhabits the Auckland Islands.

After nesting, these dotterels move down to the coast, form flocks and begin to move northwards but some winter in the South Island. In early January, flocks numbering hundreds appear in districts where few or none have bred. Many cross the Tasman to Australia where between February and August they occur on the south coast from Queensland to Swan River. The trans-Tasman migrations of the Banded Dotterel make it unique among waders. Nesting in Australia has never been proved, though some non-breeders remain throughout the normal nesting season. Occurs on passage at Norfolk and Lord Howe Islands. Straggler to Fiji.

Breeding: Some nest on ocean beaches but most nest inland on river-beds, beside lakes, sometimes on ploughed land, sometimes in arid or stony fields or on mountain slopes up to 3500 feet. Eggs August to January, pyriform, greyish or greenish, closely marked with dark brown and black spots or blotches. Normal clutch 3. Incubation period 25–30 days. Both sexes incubate.

BLACK-FRONTED DOTTEREL *Charadrius melanops*   *Pl. 11*

Description: 7″. A small distinctive plover whose plumage presents a sharp contrast of black, white, tawny and red. Upperparts brown; forehead, eye-line and *V-shaped breast-band* black; eye with bright red orbital ring; a white line passes above the eye and round the back of the head; throat white; *shoulders deep chestnut red*; wing-tips black; broad white wing-bar visible in flight; *bill bright red, tipped black*; *legs thin, red*. Does not change into an eclipse plumage. On wing most un-dotterel-like. Flight jerky and dipping, recalling that of a short-tailed passerine. Runs very fast. Seems to feed mostly at water's edge.

Voice: A high-pitched metallic whistle or soft *tink tink* of a considerably higher pitch than that of a Banded Dotterel. Also a fast clicking *tik-tik-tik-tik*.

Habitat and range: Widely distributed and plentiful in Australia, where it is a bird of the inland rarely seen on estuaries or sea beaches. River shingle and the dried caked mud at the edges of lagoons are favoured resorts. Often forms small flocks in winter. Uncommon in Tasmania.

First recorded in New Zealand in 1954, near Napier, the Black-fronted Dotterel is now strongly established in Hawke's Bay, where breeding was suspected in 1958 and proved in 1961 (several pairs). In spring 1962 over 100, mostly in breeding pairs, were located on the shingle river-beds of the Tutaekuri, Ngaruroro and Tukituki associating without friction with the many Banded Dotterels which also breed along these rivers. The population had trebled by 1967.

Elsewhere reported from Manawatu and Ruamahunga river-beds and in the South Island at Leithfield (1956), Waimatuku (1963) and Oamaru.

Breeding: Nests seen in Hawke's Bay have been on river-shingle usually a few yards from the water's edge. The nest may be well formed of small pebbles carefully collected. Eggs September to January, pyriform, heavily marked; but rather variable, occasionally yellowish. Typical clutch 3.

RED-CAPPED DOTTEREL *Charadrius ruficapillus*   Pl. 11

Description: 6". An obvious dotterel, distinctly smaller than the common Banded Dotterel. Upperparts light greyish-brown; outer tail-coverts white, centre dark-brown; *crown of head and nape rusty red*: forehead broadly white, bordered above by a narrow black line; lores black; underparts white; a black and rufous patch at the sides of the neck; bill and legs black. Females lack the reddish head and are generally duller.

Voice: Call note a faint *wit-wit-wit* or *twink-twink*.

Habitat and range: The commonest of the small Australian dotterels, usually treated as a race of the very widely distributed Kentish Plover (*C. alexandrinus*). A very rare wanderer to New Zealand.

Breeding: On the Ashley river-bed (1947-9) it appears that a female mated with a male Banded Dotterel and young were reared showing characters clearly derived from both parents.

RED-BREASTED (NEW ZEALAND) DOTTEREL

Charadrius obscurus Pl. 11

Description: 10½″. A squat, broad-winged dotterel with a robust bill. Sexes in winter similar. Upperparts brown, feathers with paler edges; forehead and superciliary streak white; dark line through eye, thinning or fading towards bill; underparts whitish or unevenly rufous. Males in breeding dress, June to December, have red breasts and bellies, the red varying in extent and in intensity from dark chestnut to a pale cinnamon. (Latham's name, " Dusky Plover," is evidently based on a darkly red-breasted male.) Females, too, may show some red, but some breeding pairs show very little colour on the underparts at all. Bill black; legs grey.

Voice: The common call is a cricket-like *krik* or *kriki*. Breeding birds in flight make a variety of sharp calls, *weet, huit, rit, turr* or *torrt* with the rr emphasised. When they have young, an excited screaming may accompany the " rodent run " during distraction display.

Habitat and range: A bird of very curious distribution, apparently with two breeding populations separated by about 700 miles and living under very different climatic conditions, one in the north from the Aotea harbour and Bay of Plenty to Spirits Bay, with a few pairs on off-shore islands, e.g. Waiheke, Great Mercury, Great Barrier, Cavallis; the other on Stewart Island and the coast of Southland, with no known breeding pairs in between these populations. Frequents both ocean beaches and also sandy flats in harbours and estuaries, sometimes in winter visiting grassy paddocks near the sea. Formerly said to have occurred high in the mountains and has been reported recently from the top of Stewart Island at 3200 feet.

Rather a sedentary species, but first-year birds are known to wander locally. No evidence that southern birds move north. Forms small flocks in late summer; but one recorded gathering of 218+ in late May at Old Neck, Stewart Island, may represent the normal winter flocking of the southern population.

Breeding: In the north, breeds among coastal dunes preferably not far from running water or on sandy spits at estuaries, sometimes on pebbly beaches or shell-banks. Eggs August to February, buff or olive, heavily blotched with black and dark brown. Normal clutch 3. Incubation period 28–31 days. Both sexes will sit on the eggs; but does the male really incubate?

ORIENTAL DOTTEREL *Charadrius veredus*   *Pl. 11*

Description: 10″. About the same size as a Red-breasted Dotterel or Pacific Golden Plover, but the *upright carriage* and *longer legs* are distinctive. Upperparts smooth greyish-brown; underparts off-white or very pale buff; forehead and eyebrow line dull white or pale brown; crown and sides of face dark brown; throat whitish; breast sandy buff or washed grey; abdomen whitish; no white on tail. A dark line shows along the edge of the primaries; legs dull yellow and rather

Plate 11

HEADS OF DOTTERELS

Plate 12

WADERS

long; bill brown and slender. In nuptial dress, the breast-band is chestnut and black and the legs become a clear yellow.

The head is held high and bobbed when the bird is alarmed. Runs and feeds actively.

Voice: A piping *klink* heard as a flock rises.

Habitat and range: Seldom seen on sea-beaches, preferring dried mud and sandy wastes near lagoons. A very rare summer migrant to New Zealand from northern Asia, reported Raoul Island 1908 (1), Firth of Thames 1954-5 (flock of 10), Parengarenga 1955 (1) and 1968 (1). Should be looked for loosely attached to flocks of other species of dotterels or plovers.

LARGE SAND DOTTEREL (GEOFFROY'S SAND PLOVER)   *Charadrius leschenaulti Pl. 11*

Description: $8\frac{1}{2}''$. Rather larger and leggier than a Banded Dotterel with a conspicuously white forehead and a *stout black bill* (1''), a *blackish patch in front of and around eye*; lores grey; pale superciliary stripe; upperparts brownish grey, markedly greyer than those of Banded Dotterel; underparts white with a *grey wash at sides of foreneck*. In breeding dress this becomes a collar of a rich tawny or rufous colour, traces of which may remain till November—a useful aid to identification. Legs grey-green or greyish-brown. In flight, it is a distinctly larger bird than a Banded Dotterel with broader wings and a slow, buoyant wing-beat over short distances.

Voice: Rather a silent bird. A quiet *treep* or *tir-rip* slowly repeated three or four times, quite distinct from any note of Banded or Red-breasted Dotterel. Also described are a musical *peeph* and a melodious trill.

Habitat and range: First recorded in 1943, this dotterel has now been found during several summer seasons in the Firth of Thames, Manukau and Kaipara Harbours and occasionally in winter. Though rare, it may be a regular summer visitor from northern Asia. Its winter quarters extend from South Africa to the islands of the south-west Pacific.

In New Zealand Large Sand Dotterels have usually been associating with Wrybills or Banded Dotterels near their high-tide roosts; once with Pacific Golden Plovers on ploughed marshland. Also noted in winter feeding near Turnstones and Red-breasted Dotterels on a shelly beach and among Banded Dotterels on close-cropped pasture.

MONGOLIAN DOTTEREL *Charadrius mongolus*   *Pl. 11*
Other name: Lesser Sandplover.

Description: $7\frac{1}{2}''$. About the size of a male *bicinctus*, but with a longer and deeper bill ($\frac{3}{4}''$) with a strong dertrum—not however as heavy as the bill of *leschenaulti*. In juvenile or eclipse plumage, in which this "difficult" species is most likely to be seen in New Zealand, closely resembles *bicinctus* and *only separable with very great care*. Conspicuously white-faced; upperparts *greyer* lacking rufous tone; *dark patch below and behind eye* tapering forwards towards bill; underparts white with narrow grey band faintly visible at sides of lower breast; legs slate grey; rather upright stance and proportions reminiscent of an undersized *obscurus*. In nuptial dress, which might be seen in April or early May, crown and breast are brilliantly brick-red.

In eclipse plumage this is a rather nondescript and featureless dotterel. Among flocks of moulting or juvenile *bicinctus* it could easily escape notice.

Voice: One at Farewell Spit uttered a clear *trik* and a soft *tikit*, less incisive than the typical note of *bicinctus* and lacking its carrying quality. Also described are a clear penetrating *drrriiit* or sharp plaintive whistle, a chittering tern-like note uttered in flight, and a soft melodious trill.

Habitat and range: Breeds in eastern Asia, migrating south and annually reaching south-east Australia in some numbers. Very seldom recorded in New Zealand. One at Farewell Spit in January 1961 fed near Banded Dotterels, but tended to keep apart and returned again and again to the same green oasis of closely grazed saltmarsh among the sand-dunes. One at Karaka in Manukau Harbour, January to March 1963, was loosely attached to Banded Dotterels and Wrybills, both for feeding and for roosting. Three on Farewell Spit, January 1967.

SHORE PLOVER *Thinornis novaeseelandiae*

Maori name: Tuturuatu.

Description: 8″. In flight recalls a Turnstone, " the wing pattern, glistening white breast, dark collar, orange legs and general manner of flight being remarkably similar " (Fleming).

Forehead, cheeks, throat, forepart of neck and narrow nuchal collar black in males, brownish in females; crown and hind part of head greyish brown, separated from the dark area by a band of white which passes from the top of the forehead above the eye to the nape; rest of upper surface greyish brown; wing-coverts tipped with white; primaries dark brown with central white streak; underparts white. Bill orange-red with dark tip; in females the dark tip is more extensive; legs pinkish orange. Sexes are readily distinguishable by their plumage and soft parts. Though the measurements of males average slightly larger, in life females appear heavier.

Voice: A high-pitched *peep*. Agitated adults with downy young pipe in chorus.

Habitat and range: Former distribution and movements ill-documented and rather puzzling. Now apparently confined to South-east Island in the Chathams, where in 1937 the population was estimated at about 70 pairs, most densely distributed over the salt meadow in the bays, but with a few pairs on the top of the island. Feeds mainly in salt and brackish rock pools. Wind-blown stragglers may sometimes reach other islands.

Breeding: Mated pairs indulge in " pursuit flights " following a zigzag course together with perfect co-ordination. The nest, quite a bulky structure, is generally in a sort of horizontal tunnel, rarely open to the

sky. Nest sites are commonly a hole or crevice among boulders, but may be a mutton bird burrow, a hollow log, a tunnel in thick bidi-bidi, under buttress roots of a shrub. Eggs, November to February, 2–3, vary considerably in shape, colour and markings. Both sexes incubate.
Note: *Thinornis rossi* described from a unique specimen said to have been collected by the *Erebus* and *Terror* Expedition (1841) at the Auckland Islands, may be a vagrant *T. novaeseelandiae* in sub-adult plumage.

WRYBILL   *Anarhynchus frontalis*   *Pl. 12*
Other names: Wry-billed Plover, Crook-bill Plover, Ngutu-parore.
Description: 8″. A small grey and white plover about the size of a Banded Dotterel, but with a longer bill (slightly over 1″) which is unique because the *tip turns to the right*. Adults in breeding dress (June to January) have a clear cut pectoral band; forehead white edged above with a thin blackish line more pronounced in male; whitish superciliary streak. Except in breeding season, a bird of the open seashore, sometimes sheltering among low vegetation such as glasswort, to avoid wind. Runs fast with head tucked closely in to the body. Often rests on one leg and hops without untucking the other leg. In its winter-quarters usually tame and approachable.
Voice: " A high-pitched staccato whistle " (Stead). A shrill reedy *weet* or *peep*. A flock may keep up a thin soft chattering *wik-a-wik* or *chitter-chitter*. *Skürr, skürr* may denote anger: *zwee, zwee zweep* almost a trill, may be the start of a courtship song: *wee-te-ti* also recorded. A subdued bubbling trill *quit-würr* repeated denotes sexual excitement.
Habitat and range: Known to breed only on some of the larger river-beds of Canterbury and North Otago up to the mountains. After breeding small flocks have been noted on the Canterbury coast, but elsewhere in the South Island it is rarely reported, though a few may regularly pass along Farewell Spit. A few are now being recorded annually on the Southland coast. Apparently from late December onwards the whole population quickly moves northwards in small flocks; some pausing on the south-west and south-east coasts of the North Island, to winter-quarters mainly in the Firth of Thames, Manukau and Kaipara. Small numbers annually reach Parengarenga. The only inland localities from which passing migrants have been reported are Lake Rotorua and Lake Hatuma. In 1960 the total population, based on counts of wintering flocks, was conservatively estimated at about 5000.
    Small flocks of immature non-breeders summer in the north where they are joined by the first of the returning migrants about Christmas-time. The southward movement begins in July, reaches a peak in August and may continue till October. Infected by pre-migration excitement towards the end of winter, large flocks in the Firth of Thames perform lengthy and complicated aerial evolutions, a superb display of controlled flying *en masse*.
Breeding: Breeding pairs reappear on Canterbury river-beds in August.

Nests are near water in wide areas of clean shingle where the stones are rather large and clear of all growths and drift. Eggs, September–November; normal clutch 2, pyriform, pale grey faintly tinged with blue or green, closely and evenly peppered with minute dark and pale blotches, spots and lines.

CURLEWS, GODWITS, SNIPE AND SANDPIPERS: Scolopacidae

LONG-BILLED (EASTERN) CURLEW *Numenius madagascariensis*

Description: 24″. The largest of the arctic waders which visit New Zealand, easily recognised by its size, *long down-curved bill* (7½″) and distinctive call. Streaked brown and buff, both above and below, the underparts being lighter; pale eyebrow line; back and rump much the same shade of brown as wings and tail. Legs bluish-grey.

Voice: A tuneful *croo-lee*, a husky *kérr-eep* or *keep* and a harsher *ker-woik*. Also a rather husky *ker-kerup*. Often curiously silent; but when calling, audible a long way off.

Habitat and range: Breeds in north-eastern Siberia, migrating south and widely distributed on the coast of Australia. A few regularly reach New Zealand. Tired migrants may drop in on almost any stretch of coast, more often the west; but soon move to estuaries and harbours much frequented by other waders. A bird of the tide-line, associating with godwits and oystercatchers at high-tide roosts; but an uneasy mixer tending to keep apart and so easily noticed. May rest and feed among and sometimes actually under low-growing (3–4 ft.) mangroves. Godwits tend to resent stray curlews and have been seen to mob and chase them. As in Australia immature non-breeders may stay over the southern winter.

Observations over twenty years in Manukau and the Firth of Thames seem to show that these large curlews are occurring more frequently in New Zealand. Many reports are of single birds; but small flocks also are noted, e.g. 7 at Awarua Bay, May 1952, and 16 at Waituna, Southland, in January 1963; 37 on Farewell Spit in September 1962 and 35 during January 1963; 16 in the Firth of Thames, January 1959, where 10 had spent the previous winter, and 18 in January and 26 in December 1961; 4 at Karaka during winter 1958 and 5 in March 1959.

ASIATIC WHIMBREL *Numenius variegatus*   *Pl. 12*
AMERICAN WHIMBREL (Hudsonian Curlew) *Numenius hudsonicus*

Description: 16″. About the same size as a Bar-tailed Godwit but generally looks darker and robuster with a distinctly *decurved bill* (3½″). Smaller size and boldly streaked crown *with pale median stripe* and *voice* (q.v.) distinguish the whimbrels from the true curlews. A *whitish* *rump*—white feathers boldly barred with brown—distinguishes the Asiatic from the American Whimbrel in which the rump is of a uniform warm brown with mantle and tail. When a whimbrel is seen in flight, the "*pale blaze pointed up the lower back*" should be looked for, as it is the only means of separating in the field the two forms which occur in New Zealand. Females are rather larger than males and in a flock obvious differences in size, especially in the bill, may be noted. Legs bluish. At high tide among other resting waders, a whimbrel often remains alert and holds its head aloft.

Voice: An even rippling whistle of about seven notes. Hence its Scottish names "Titterel" and "Seven Whistler." The tittering call *ti-ti-ti-ti-ti-ti-ti* can be the first indication that there is a Whimbrel with a passing flock of godwits. The ordinary calls of Asiatic and American Whimbrels are indistinguishable. Sometimes whimbrels call repeatedly; sometimes they are curiously silent.

Habitat and range: A few Asiatic Whimbrels reach New Zealand annually from September onwards; and immature non-breeders may remain over the following winter. Single birds or small flocks make their landfall almost anywhere along the coast, but soon move to tidal estuaries and harbours, where small flocks are sometimes reported, e.g. 10 in January 1956 in the Firth of Thames; 8 in December 1956 in Kaipara; 6 in November 1958 in Manukau; 21 during January 1961 and 26 during January 1967 on Farewell Spit. Although the first whimbrel to be collected in New Zealand (1874) was of the American race, it has been recorded only rarely since. Most whimbrels which reach New Zealand are of the pale-rumped Asiatic form; but the dark-rumped American Whimbrel may occur more often than the few records suggest.

LITTLE WHIMBREL *Numenius minutus*

Description: 13″. Looks rather like a Golden Plover in size, shape and colour, except that in flight the wings appear longer and the *primaries blackish*, but easily recognised as a miniature curlew or small whimbrel by its strongly decurved bill (1¾″). Crown dark brown with *median streak of buff*; eyebrow conspicuously light buff; upperparts variegated dark and light brown; upper tail-coverts brown with light grey crossbars not showing noticeably pale in flight; tail grey-brown with dark bars; throat and abdomen dull white, breast streaked with brown. Legs dull bluish-grey.

Voice: A flock feeding busily may keep up a soft not unmusical chatter *te-te-te*. Alarm notes are a rather harsh *tchew-tchew-tchew*.

Habitat and range: Breeds in north-east Siberia and winters mainly in north-east Australia. A very rare visitor to New Zealand which has been reported from Lake Ellesmere at scattered intervals since 1900 and at Farewell Spit in 1961, and five times from the North Island. Napier, 1952; Manukau, Firth of Thames, Himatangi, 1964. In Queensland, where large flocks occur in autumn, said to prefer grasslands to the seashore; but freely associates with Sharptailed Sandpipers. In New Zealand Little Whimbrels should be looked for in grassy paddocks which are visited by dotterels and plovers as high tides force them off the flats.

Note: Some taxonomists make the Little Whimbrel conspecific with the very similar Eskimo Curlew, now probably extinct. If this view is correct, the Little Whimbrel must be treated as the Asiatic race of *Numenius borealis*.

EASTERN (PACIFIC) BAR-TAILED GODWIT *Limosa lapponica* Pl. 12

Local names: Godwit, Kuaka. (Also, quite incorrectly, " Snipe " and " Curlew.")

Description: 16″. Colour, proportions, long legs and long slightly upturned bill (3½″), readily distinguish godwits from other shore birds, e.g. stilts and oystercatchers, with which they commonly associate. Upperparts mottled brown and grey; lower back, rump and tail barred white and brown; underparts dull white, clouded with grey. The assumption of breeding dress starts in January and by the end of February many males have bright brick-red underparts; females show a buffy tinge on breast and some fine barring on the flanks. Traces of nuptial red are still visible in the plumage of some adults when they return to New Zealand in September. Females are distinctly larger than males, the difference in size being especially noticeable in the bills. Flight fast and direct; no wing-bar. Flocks commonly fly in long lines or chevrons.

Voice: A clear excited double note *kew-kew* is commonly used. A soft *kit-kit-kit-kit* is heard from passing flocks. Roosting flocks, if uneasy, may keep up a steady conversational chatter.

Habitat and range: Breeds in north-eastern Siberia and north-western America (possibly two subspecies), migrating south to Australia and New Zealand, the bulk of the population apparently coming to New Zealand, where it is by far the commonest of the migratory arctic waders. Plentiful, October-March, in all suitable harbours and estuaries from Parengarenga to Paterson Inlet, Stewart Island; flocks in a few favoured localities containing thousands of birds. A regular visitor to Kermadec and Norfolk Islands. A regular migrant to Chatham Island and a straggler to Campbell, Auckland and Macquarie Islands.

Feeds mostly on tidal flats; also visits marshes and pastures near the sea at spring tides or during very wet weather. Seldom reported inland. Some thousands of non-breeding juveniles over-winter, especially in the big harbours of northern New Zealand.

HUDSONIAN (AMERICAN BLACK-TAILED) GODWIT
Limosa haemastica Pl. 12

Description: 15″. About the same size as a male Bar-tailed Godwit, but upperparts greyer and less speckled; breast distinctly washed grey. Can be satisfactorily identified on the ground only if it raises its wings; or in flight when the *clear white upper tail-coverts strongly contrast with the sooty black tail* with its narrow white tip. A narrow white wing-bar is not always very noticeable; nor at certain angles are the *sooty axillaries and underwing linings* by which alone in the field the American can be distinguished from the Asiatic Black-tailed Godwit (q.v.). Most Hudsonian Godwits seen in New Zealand are in the grey and white plumage of juveniles or adults in winter; but some adults have been seen in late April with underparts reddish, finely barred with black and the white superciliary stripe much more definite than in winter. Bill flesh-coloured or yellowish, darkening towards the tip. Legs greyish-blue. Females are rather larger than males. Some males look curiously small and dusky, especially in flight.

Voice: Flight call a low double *ta-it* or a sharp, but not far-carrying *kit-keet*.

Habitat and range: A rare but possibly regular migrant from arctic America, where in autumn strays may be caught up in the southbound stream of Bar-tailed Godwits. So far all records in New Zealand are of single birds, usually attached to flocks of Bar-tailed Godwits and seldom inclined to leave them to join other waders in shallow waters away from the tideline. But tired migrants, just arrived, have been found among flocks of non-breeding Pied Stilts. Most frequently recorded from Lake Ellesmere and Manukau Harbour; also from Manawatu and Heathcote-Avon and Invercargill estuaries.

ASIATIC BLACK-TAILED GODWIT *Limosa melanuroides* Pl. 12

Description: 15″. About the same size as a male Bar-tailed Godwit, from which it cannot with certainty be distinguished on the ground unless it raises its wings, though generally it looks slimmer and more elegant; and with birds in winter plumage the uniform smooth grey of the breast is a useful pointer. In flight its salient characteristics are *pure white upper tail-coverts* contrasting with *broad black terminal band of tail*, *conspicuous white wing-bar* and *gleaming white underwing* narrowly edged with black. Bill long, pinkish, darkening towards the tip, straight or very slightly upward-curved. Legs greenish-grey. Breeding dress, with deep orange rufous underparts partly barred with black and with the brown-grey of the upperparts darkening, is assumed in March and April. Traces of this may still be seen on adults in September–October. Adult males in full breeding dress are richly coloured, females are slightly larger than males and less showy.

Voice: Rather a silent bird in its southern winter quarters. Feeding birds sometimes utter a single *kuk* or *kik*. The flight call has been described as a loud clear *wicka-wicka-wicka* or *gritto-gritto*.

Habitat and range: A rare migrant from northern Asia recorded only from the Firth of Thames and Manukau Harbour till January 1963, when one was seen at Enderby Island, nearly 1000 miles farther south (B. D. Bell). May be looked for wherever Bar-tailed Godwits occur; although, unlike the Hudsonian Godwit, it may often desert the tidal flats to join Pied Stilts on flooded grassland and freshwater pools. First recorded in New Zealand in 1952; but may be coming more frequently, even occurring in small flocks which may stay for some months in localities which obviously suit them, viz. 4 at Puketutu and

6 at Miranda in 1959. Single birds have now been reported from Kerikeri (1963) and Ahuriri estuary, Napier (1964). Immature non-breeders have wintered.

Note: The only feature by which the Asiatic Black-tailed Godwit can be separated with certainty in the field from the Hudsonian Godwit is by its *white underwing* as against the *sooty underwing* of its American counterpart.

GREENSHANK   *Tringa nebularia*

Description: 13″. About the same size as a male Bar-tailed Godwit. Upperparts grey, lightly flecked with white, with *white lower back and rump*; tail feathers so lightly barred as to appear almost white; wings blackish; underparts white. *Legs grey-green*; bill (2″) bluish-grey, slightly upcurved.

In flight the Greenshank looks to be an almost black and white bird, the blackish wings contrasting with the *inverted V of white up the back*. Often calls as it rises.

Voice: A musical ringing *tchew*, *tlooi* or *chewey*, sometimes single, more often repeated. Three which flew high over Manukau Harbour calling were audible at more than a mile on a calm day in May 1954.

Habitat and range: Though a regular summer visitor from the northern hemisphere to southern Australia and Tasmania, where some also spend the winter, very few seem to straggle to New Zealand. Southland lagoons (1) 1956 and (1) 1963; Otago (1) 1874; Gisborne (1) 1952; Manukau almost annually since 1953. Also reported from Manawatu estuary, Farewell Spit, Ellesmere and Washdyke. Shows a marked liking for the company of Pied Stilts, avoiding the big packs of Godwits and Knots. A wader of muddy creeks and lagoons rather than of the open shore. Most untypical of New Zealand were three Greenshanks and a Little Egret sharing the top of a small mudbank at full-tide in Manukau on 14/10/53.

GREATER YELLOWLEGS   *Tringa melanoleuca*

Description: 14″. A graceful wader, very like a Greenshank in size and shape, but with *vividly orange-yellow legs* and the back and upper wing-surface much more spotted. Underparts white irregularly barred with crescentic spots. In flight appears a dark-winged bird with whitish rump and tail. Bill (2¼″) relatively stout and slightly upturned, whereas the bill of the Lesser Yellowlegs (*T. flavipes*) is shorter (1½″), slender and straight.

On the average, females are slightly larger than males.

Voice: A loud, clear, forceful whistle usually of three or four syllables, *wheu-wheu-wheu*, very like a Greenshank's (q.v.), or *tleu-tleu-tleu*, having a melodious labial quality.

Habitat and range: Breeds across North America from Newfoundland to Alaska, migrating south as far as the straits of Magellan; occasionally straggling west to Hawaii. More plentiful on the west coast of North America than the Lesser Yellowlegs. One[1] on a shallow brackish

[1] This identification of the Porirua Yellowlegs has since been questioned. In 1964 an obvious Yellowlegs at Lake Ellesmere was tentatively but not conclusively, identified as *flavipes*.

pool at Porirua, November 1962, is the only record for the south-west Pacific. Prefers to feed in shallow water, often wading up to its breast and even swimming.

MARSH SANDPIPER *Tringa stagnatilis*

Other name: Little Greenshank.

Description: 10″. An elegant wader resembling a small Greenshank, except that its *legs are disproportionately long* or, in flight, a miniature stilt with legs projecting well beyond the tail. Upperparts dark grey, underparts white; forehead and face white; lower back and rump white, showing clearly as bird flies away from observer; tail so lightly barred that it appears almost white; thin grey flecking on throat and breast is a mark of breeding dress; legs greenish; bill (1½″) fine and straight.

Voice: A single *tew, teeoo* or *kewip*, not very loud; reminiscent of Greenshank's *tchew*.

Habitat and range: A palaearctic species wintering from Africa through southern Asia to Australia, only recently discovered in New Zealand. One in Manukau Harbour (1959) associated closely with Pied Stilts from March to May, wading up to its belly and feeding off the surface of the water. Essentially a wader of fresh and brackish pools, not of the tideline. One in Firth of Thames on 28/4/63 rested inland with Pied Stilts at full tide and later flew with them to feed on the exposed mudflats. Presumably the same bird after wintering appeared at Miranda, where it was frequently seen between September and December. Another which visited a farm-pond near Hawera, Taranaki, on 1/11/63 was identified from colour photographs. One near Westpoint, May 1968, is the first South Island record.

TEREK SANDPIPER *Tringa cinerea*   *Pl. 12*

Description: 9″. Long, thin, *distinctly upcurved bill* (1¾″) (hence the appropriate name, Avocet Sandpiper) and *orange* or *bright yellow legs* distinguish this from other small sandpipers, none of which at all resemble it. Crown and upperparts brownish-grey; underparts white; faint streaks on neck and breast varying according to the season. In flight the white-tipped secondaries forming a *white rear-edge to the rather dark wings* show up clearly. Runs actively and bobs tail.

Voice: A pleasant musical trill *weeta-weeta-weet*; also interpreted as a fluty *du-du-du-du* or a melodious *tiririr*. Often calls when it rises; sometimes on the ground, as it runs.

Habitat and range: A northern palaearctic breeder wintering in Africa, Asia and Australia. Now recorded almost annually in the Firth of Thames, where it was first discovered in New Zealand in 1951. Since then this unique sandpiper has been seen often enough to suggest that a few stragglers may be reaching New Zealand every year. Records from Kaipara, Manukau, Gisborne, Napier, Manawatu and once from South Island, Kaikoura (1966). A bird of the wide tidal flats, often in company with Wrybills. In the hot summer days when these are drowsing at their high-tide roosts, a Terek Sandpiper will remain alert; and one has been seen to run from one end of a dozing flock to another.

the one moving bird in a gathering of hundreds. In mid-winter two Terek Sandpipers edged away from a big close flock of Wrybills soon after the tide began to fall and fed eagerly while the Wrybills continued to rest. In flight with Wrybills, often takes the lead. The over-wintering of immature non-breeders first proved in 1952 is now known to be not exceptional.

GREY-TAILED (SIBERIAN) TATTLER *Tringa brevipes*
Other name: Grey-rumped Sandpiper.
Description: 10″. A slim, graceful wader. Upperparts almost uniformly slate-grey, the evenness of the grey especially noticeable in flight, but some fine white barring on the rump may be visible at close range; underparts white except for some finely pencilled barring on breast. Dark line through eye, clear white superciliary stripe. Bill straight and long (1½″); *legs yellowish* becoming yellower about April. *Nasal groove* extending *half length of bill*. In breeding plumage barring on underparts develops, but *under tail-coverts remain white*. A typical *Tringa* when alerted, bobbing its head, tipping its tail and perhaps running to and fro. Inclined to be solitary; and, when disturbed, to fly low across water, sometimes without calling.
Voice: Usual call a sharp, high-pitched, double whistle *twhéet* or *toowéet* resembling the call of a Pacific Golden Plover but less melodious. Also described as *whew-rit* or *whewew-réet*, the final syllable being emphasised and higher in pitch. Also a soft trill of three or four notes, *ter-wee*, repeated in fluty tones. Apparently less vocal than Wandering Tattler.
Habitat and range: Breeds in alpine zone of eastern Siberia, migrating south, reaching south-eastern Australia and Tasmania. Rare but possibly regular migrant to New Zealand, especially Parengarenga; also recorded recently from Manukau, Napier, Waikanae, Farewell Spit, Heathcote-Avon estuary, Ellesmere, Otago Harbour, Lake Tuakitoto. Tattlers may stay some months or even years in some estuary or on a stretch of shore which clearly satisfies their requirements, frequently resorting to a favourite perch on a post, a piece of driftwood or an isolated rock. What was evidently the same individual used the same distinctive resting places for more than four years on the Karaka coast of Manukau.

Several instances of over-wintering seem to indicate that most of the tattlers which reach New Zealand are first-year birds.

WANDERING (ALASKAN) TATTLER *Tringa incana*
Description: 11″. In winter plumage only separable with extreme care from *T. brevipes* (with which some authors consider it conspecific); but slightly larger, of a darker grey and looks robuster. In breeding plumage the underparts *including under tail-coverts* are heavily barred. Relatively *longer nasal groove, extending two-thirds* of bill, is visible in a good light with a strong telescope. One at Kawakawa Bay assumed

breeding plumage in February and March (1949) but remained through-out the following winter.

Voice: A clear sweet whistle or rippling trill of 6–10 notes with the accent on the second note, the following notes diminishing a little in volume and given more rapidly than the first two or three.

The quite distinct calls of the two forms of tattler are perhaps the safest guide to correct identification, especially when tattlers are in winter plumage as they usually are in New Zealand.

Habitat and range: Breeds along mountain streams in Alaska. Winter range includes the islands of the central Pacific and Polynesia south to Fiji and Tonga, occasionally straggling to south-eastern Australia and New Zealand. Recorded from Raoul Island in Kermadecs, Portland Island and Kawakawa Bay, where for more than a year one frequented the vicinity of a ridged shingle reef; and C. Kidnappers. Unspecified tattlers perhaps belonging to this form have been reported on the east coast from Napier, Gisborne, Kuaotunu, Port Jackson; and from Chatham Island.

TURNSTONE *Arenaria interpres*   Pl. 12

Description: 9″. Distinguished at all seasons from other waders by its shape, the contrast of black and white and " tortoise-shell " in its markings and its *orange* legs. Upperparts dark-brown, mottled black and chestnut; lower back white with second white band curving across upper tail; throat and abdomen white; upper breast broadly black. Bill blackish, robust, slightly tip-tilted. White wing-bar conspicuous in flight. The amount of white on face and head varies considerably, some adults in breeding plumage becoming almost white-headed. Dusky heads and duller colouring easily distinguish young birds when they first arrive.

Voice: A metallic rattle or twittering *kitititit* is heard most commonly. In large mixed flocks of passing waders a ringing *kee-oo* draws attention to Turnstones. A noisy excited version of these notes has been heard from two birds just before they leave for their breeding grounds. It accompanied a swift darting and twisting flight concerned with pair-formation or courtship.

Habitat and range: A holarctic breeder, migrating south. The third most numerous of the arctic waders which regularly reach New Zealand occurring in flocks from Parengarenga to Bluff in favoured coastal localities. Tends to avoid smooth sandy beaches and open mudflats, preferring to feed on a shelly or stony foreshore or among rockpools (e.g. Kaikoura). Small flocks of immature non-breeders over-winter mostly in the northern harbours. A marked association of Turnstones with Pacific Golden Plovers has frequently been noticed, the two species together visiting rough ploughland near the sea or even dried out pastures a mile or more inland. An active feeder deftly flicking over stones and tide-wrack with its bill. Stray Turnstones readily join groups of other small waders.

SUB-ANTARCTIC SNIPE   *Coenocorypha aucklandica*

Maori name: Tutukiwi.

Description: 9″. Small primitive snipe-like birds—Seebohm's semi-Woodcocks—with long sensitive bill (2″), short wings, striped head and richly variegated upper-surface. Legs yellowish-brown. Females rather larger.

Voice: A low hoarse double croak on Big South Cape (Guthrie-Smith); also a repeated double-whistle, usually given in flight just after dusk (Bell).

On Snares a repeated whistle as in *C. pusilla* (Fleming).

Habitat and range: These snipe have been aptly described as living fossils, which belong, strictly speaking, to a past geological period. They may be the relic of an ancient stock which at one time had a more northerly or more general distribution and from which the present-day woodcocks and snipe arose. They have survived because of the long isolation of certain islands and the consequent freedom from ground predators. Four well-marked insular races at (*a*) Auckland Islands (Ewing and Adams Island) (*aucklandica*) paler, only flanks

barred, not abdomen; (*b*) Antipodes Island (*meinertzhagenae*) darker above, underparts yellower; (*c*) Snares (*huegeli*) undersurface barred throughout; (*d*) islands off Stewart Island, e.g. Big South Cape, possibly others (*iredalei*), rather more rufous, lower abdomen and flanks barred, throat spotted.

By day they tend to avoid the open, preferring the shelter of bush or scrub. At the Snares they frequent the fringes of the penguin colonies. If disturbed they can fly short distances; but apparently they take wing more readily at night with a swift and woodcock-like flight.

Breeding: Often quite a substantial structure, e.g. deep cup of fine grass (Snares); pile of moss, lichen and twigs (Big South Cape). Eggs, October–December. Clutch 2, not gallinagine in either shape or colouring; but bluntly ovoid, closely resembling woodcock eggs; markings rather variable, but basically pale brown with dark spots or blotches. Both parents sit. Apparently only one young is reared.

CHATHAM ISLAND SNIPE   *Coenocorypha pusilla*

Description: 8″. Similar to *C. aucklandica* of which it is sometimes treated as a strong subspecies, but distinctly smaller and with lower breast unbarred and abdomen buffy white. Males and females readily distinguishable, the males being smaller in body and bill, and darker in the plumage of the back and more strikingly patterned on the upper-surface. Usually in pairs. Flight, when suddenly alarmed, fast and fairly strong with a characteristic whirring beat.

Voice: Alarm note a drawn out *cheep* (Bell). A feeding male "chir-ruped" softly. The typical call, which is heard more frequently in the evening than in the day-time, begins as "soft, low, sibilant chirrups" and quickly works up to "a series of sharp, tuneful, whistles on high B, repeated eight or ten times in about five seconds." At every whistle the bird's cheeks and throat were seen to vibrate. Two males some distance apart sometimes called at each other and the cries then reach an excited pitch (Fleming). Note of female is pitched lower.

Habitat and range: Now confined to South-east Island, where it feeds on the rich moist leaf-mould of the forest floor, among rank grasses and on spongy seepages above the rock-fringe.

Breeding: Reported to nest among the roots and buttresses of trees or under fallen logs. Clutch 3. Eggs, similar to those of *C. aucklandica*, but slightly smaller. Downy plumage of young is uniformly umber-brown.

JAPANESE SNIPE *Gallinago hardwicki*

Description: 13". An obvious snipe with long bill (3") and short legs. Upperparts heavily marked brown and black; crown prominently streaked with a buff stripe down the centre; throat and sides of face buffy white; underparts buffy; flanks barred; chestnut band on tail; bill long and black; legs brown and short. Rises suddenly at feet of observer, with a whirr of wings, usually uttering a harsh note, *kek*. Rapid twisting flight.

Habitat and range: Breeds in Japan, migrating to eastern Australia and Tasmania where it is not uncommon from late August to March. Seldom reported from New Zealand but has occurred in widely separated districts in both islands. Easily overlooked because of its lurking habits. Feeds by probing the soft mud among short vegetation along the edges of reedy or grassy swamps.

EASTERN KNOT *Callidris canutus*

Maori name: Huahou.

Description: 10". A compact short-legged rather nondescript shore-bird, often in very large flocks; and of the arctic waders which migrate to New Zealand, easily the most numerous after the Godwit. Some-times big flights of "godwits" over the northern harbours are more than 50% Knots.

In winter plumage the upperparts are grey, lightly speckled; eye-stripe whitish; rump barred white and dark brown showing pale in flight; rather indefinite white wing-bar; underparts pale grey or off-white. The moult into red summer plumage begins in February. Head, neck and breast become richly rufous and the black and silver speckling of the mantle more intense. Females are less resplendent than males. By April adults are in full breeding dress. Rather curiously, it is not unusual for flocks of red Knots to remain in New Zealand throughout the winter. Bill (1¼″) robust and straight; legs dull green.

Voice: A throaty *knut knut*. Flocks feeding or flying along the tideline often keep up a subdued not unmusical chatter, with higher-pitched notes *too-it-wit* or *quik-ik* interspersed.

Habitat and range: Breeds in eastern Siberia, migrating south; the bulk of the population of the eastern race (*rogersi*) evidently coming to New Zealand, where very large flocks occur annually in Kaipara, Firth of Thames, Manukau and at Farewell Spit, while smaller numbers visit most suitable harbours and estuaries as far south as Paterson Inlet. Occasionally at the Chathams. Has straggled to Macquarie. Very much a bird of the tideline, commonly consorting with Godwits; and with them sometimes visiting salt-marshes and coastal pastures to feed where the vegetation is short and the ground wet. Sometimes Knots may be found apart in large unmixed flocks forming a solid grey carpet on sandy flats.

The Great Knot (*Calidris tenuirostris*) (11½″) a rare and rather unknown bird which breeds in the alpine zone of Siberia and reaches south-eastern Australia at the southern limit of its migration, was first recorded in New Zealand in 1966, 3 at Manawatu estuary. It is larger and leggier than *canutus*, with a *longer bill* (1½″), *striped crown*, some irregular markings on the breast and a *white rump*. Unlike *canutus*, it does not assume a red nuptial plumage.

PECTORAL SANDPIPER *Calidris melanotos*

Description: 8½″. Closely resembles the Sharp-tailed Sandpiper and only separable after close and careful scrutiny. Breast densely spotted and streaked, the markings forming a *solid gorget which ends abruptly* and contrasts sharply with the white underparts. In breeding dress does *not* develop crescentic spots on flanks. Superciliary stripe variable. Bill dark, *yellowish at base;* legs usually yellower than in *C. acuminata*. In flight a pale wing-bar shows indistinctly. On the ground has a habit of stretching its neck.

Voice: Rather silent; but call-note, an incisive *kreek* audible at some distance, is very helpful as a mean of confirming identification when Sharp-tailed Sandpipers are also present.

Habitat and range: Breeds across Arctic America and Siberia west to about Taimyr peninsula its Siberian breeding range being more extensive than that of the Sharp-tailed Sandpiper. Main migration is to Central and South America; but a few evidently come directly south. Very rarely reported in Australia. Probably regular in very small numbers in New Zealand, where it has been reported from numerous estuaries and coastal lagoons from Kerikeri to Foveaux Strait.

Prefers shallow pools with vegetation to open shore-line. Will feed snipe-like in grassy marshes and can easily escape notice among water plants. In the Firth of Thames and Manukau, where it has frequently

Plate 13
GULLS

Plate 14
TERNS

been observed on the same pools as parties of Sharp-tailed Sandpipers, it tends to keep near them but apart on the fringe.[1]

SHARP-TAILED (SIBERIAN PECTORAL) SANDPIPER
Calidris acuminata   Pl. 12

Description: 8½″. A brown, richly speckled sandpiper, which never looks really grey. Crown, chestnut streaked black; superciliary stripe whitish and varying in clarity; upperparts dark-brown, striped darker; rump and pointed tail dark brown with white sides; breast mottled grey or buffish with irregular streaks, fading to white on abdomen; but *with no sharp line of demarcation.* Young birds when they arrive in October look tawny and have bright chestnut crowns. In complete eclipse plumage the throat and breast are often quite unspotted. In breeding dress a warm buffy tone suffuses the plumage, the breast becomes more heavily spotted and *crescentic streaks " little boomerangs" develop on the flanks.* Bill (1″) very slightly decurved; legs yellowish-green. Faint wing-bar shows in flight. When these sandpipers are in flocks, it can be seen that they may vary considerably not only in appearance, depending on age and state of moult, but also in size. Their brownness makes them conspicuous when they roost among Wrybills as they often do in Firth of Thames and Manukau.

Voice: Rather silent. A flock, when flushed, may utter some soft *pleeps* or *pips.*

Habitat and range: Breeds in a rather restricted area of north-east Siberia from lower Lena in west to Kolyma delta in east; migrating south mainly to Australia where it is one of the commonest of the arctic waders. A regular migrant to New Zealand, where though not common, it is the most numerous of the smaller sandpipers; occurring in small flocks with some regularity, Firth of Thames, near Napier, Wellington west coast, Lake Ellesmere and near Invercargill. So far the largest number seen together in the North Island is 28 at Miranda; in the South Island 35 at Waituna. Will forage on open mudflats with Knots, but prefers shallow brackish lagoons, and may feed effectively hidden among *Salicornia, Cotula,* etc. As in Australia, only rarely do any of these sandpipers stay over the winter.

CURLEW SANDPIPER *Calidris ferruginea*   *Pl. 12*

Description: 8½″. A small sandpiper about the same size as a Wrybill but with a *slender distinctly decurved bill.* In flight a narrow white wing-bar and white *upper tail-coverts* show clearly. The Curlew Sandpiper is one of those waders in which there is a striking difference between red summer and pale winter plumage. Curlew Sandpipers seen in New Zealand are usually brownish-grey and white juveniles or adults in eclipse; but some adults when they arrive in September

---

[1] Our Pectoral Sandpipers do not necessarily come from America. The range of this bird extends into Siberia, actually farther westwards than the rather restricted range of the Siberian Pectoral or Sharp-tailed Sandpiper, whose breeding range in fact is enclosed within that of the American Pectoral.

retain traces of rufous nuptial plumage which is quickly lost, though an exceptionally red bird was seen in Manukau late in October 1959. Some adults begin to redden in January and by the end of March are in rich rufous breeding dress. In summer often feeds on the tideline among Knots where it is difficult to detect.

Voice: A distinct liquid *chirrip*. A fast-flying, swerving flock of 8 in the Firth of Thames on 27/11/60 kept up a musical twittering, *tirri-tirri-tirri*.

Habitat and range: Breeds in arctic Asia. A few annually reach New Zealand from early September onwards and stay till March–April. Occasionally non-breeding juveniles are reported in winter, when they tend to join flocks of Wrybills among which they can easily escape notice. A bird of tidal flats and shallow brackish pools. Most recent records come from the large harbours of northern New Zealand. Stead found them several times at Lake Ellesmere; but few, e.g. 2 on Farewell Spit in January 1961 and 7 in April 1965, have since been reported from the South Island. Typical flocks recently recorded are Firth of Thames, 12, February–March 1948; 9, January 1960; 10, January 1961. Manukau, 9, March 1959.

RED-NECKED STINT *Calidris ruficollis*

Description: 6″. The smallest of the arctic waders which visit New Zealand regularly, dwarfed even by Wrybills and Banded Dotterels, with which it habitually associates on the seashore. Adults when they arrive about October may still retain traces of rufous feathering on the neck; but in New Zealand this very small sandpiper is usually a predominantly grey and white bird; the head and sides of neck shaded grey; the back and wings mottled and the underparts white. Bill and *legs black*. Wing-bar just visible in flight. Before leaving for their arctic breeding grounds in April, adults assume nuptial plumage, most noticeable in the reddening of the feathers of the neck. The colour spreads upwards till the head seems to be wearing a red balaclava, while the mottling of the back and wings deepens and becomes a richer brown. First-year birds retain their grey and white plumage and may stay behind in New Zealand often attached to flocks of wintering Wrybills. A voracious feeder with a sewing-machine action.

Voice: When rising it sometimes utters a weak *chit, tit* or *wik*, repeated two or three times.

Habitat and range: Breeds in north-eastern Siberia. Though said to be the most numerous of the arctic waders which visit Australia, only small numbers annually reach New Zealand. Most frequently recorded from the harbours and estuaries of the north. Possibly a regular visitor to Lake Ellesmere and the Southland lagoons. Two at Enderby Island, January 1963 (B. D. Bell). The biggest flocks so far recorded are of 26 at Miranda, Firth of Thames, during the summer of 1958–9, after an exceptional flock of 20 had wintered; 57 near Bluff and 38 on Farewell Spit, 1968.

Note: The Long-toed Stint or Least Sandpiper (*Calidris minutilla*) has twice been reported in New Zealand. It is very similar to the Red-necked Stint but has *greenish yellow legs*, is a little browner above and has a *spotted greyish band across the lower throat*. It is said to have a shrill piping cry, uttered as it rises and also when running about on the sand. The colour of the legs of all stints should be critically examined.

SANDERLING   *Calidris alba*

Description: 8″. An active, small, plump, short-legged sandpiper, very white about the head showing *a small dark patch at the bend of the wing* and in flight a prominent white wing-bar. Upperparts pale grey faintly marked; underparts white; dark tail has white sides; in winter plumage the *palest of the sandpipers* resembling a Wrybill; but in April upperparts, head and breast become pale chestnut speckled with black. Bill and legs black. Bill straight and stout. Hind toe entirely absent.

Voice: Flight note a shrill but liquid *twick twick*.

Habitat and range: Breeds mostly in the high arctic; migrating south, small numbers regularly reaching the south-eastern coast of Australia. Recorded from Parengarenga, Bay of Plenty, Waikanae, Farewell Spit, Waimakariri estuary, Lake Ellesmere, Invercargill. Usually single birds reported, but small flocks do occur. Mainly frequents sandy beaches, where it always seems to be in a hurry as it feeds busily close to the tideline.

BROAD-BILLED SANDPIPER   *Limicola falcinellus*

Description: 7″. One of the smallest sandpipers, larger than a Red-necked Stint and smaller than a Wrybill; and with rather snipe-like proportions. Upperparts brown-grey, mottled; feathers of wing-coverts with darker centres and pale margins; *head prominently streaked* with a dark-grey central panel, below which whitish stripes converge on the bill; underparts whitish; chest faintly spotted; tail blackish with white at sides. Bill long (1¼″), robust and black, distinctly *dipping downward near the tip*: legs short, dull-green or olive-grey. In flight a narrow pale wing-bar becomes visible.

Voice: Sometimes trills *pürrr*, as it rises. Flight-note also described as a dry *chr-r-r-reet*.

Habitat and range: Breeds in remote arctic regions; migrating south, a few reaching south-eastern Australia. A very scarce visitor first recorded Firth of Thames, January to March 1960, when one freely associated with other small waders both on the tideline and also at a roost on reclaimed saltmarsh sown with turnips; Karaka, 1/12/63, when one was present among summering Wrybills at a high-tide roost. In its winter-quarters from Africa to Australia, this is a notoriously elusive species. In New Zealand the likeliest way of adding to our scanty knowledge of it may be by close examination of flocks of Wrybills in the northern harbours. Two near Miranda, February 1968.

STILTS AND AVOCETS
Recurvirostridae

PIED STILT *Himantopus leucocephalus*   *Pl. 12*
  Other names: Stilt, Barker, Poaka, White-headed Stilt, Daddy Long-legs, Torea (Rotorua), Pip (Kaipara).
  Description: 15″. A black and white wader with very long pink legs (10″) which in flight trail far behind the tail. Noisy and gregarious, often breeding in colonies, but isolated pairs may occupy small swamps. Wings, back and hind neck black; head and underparts white. A not uncommon variant has a complete black collar round the lower neck. Most first-year birds have traces of grey on head and lack the black hind neck; but some have almost pure white heads and necks. Bill (2⅛″) black, fine and straight.
  Voice: A puppy-like yapping *yep yep*. The call of the young is a shriller *kip kip*. Stilts call frequently when migrating by night.
  Habitat and range: This is evidently one of the birds which has benefited from pakeha methods of farming in the North and South Islands. In the middle of the nineteenth century it seems to have been relatively rare; but now it is the commonest of the larger waders which breed in New Zealand and it is still seeking new breeding grounds, especially in the north where it hitherto has been a rare and local breeder. After nesting there is a general movement from inland breeding grounds to the coast. Some winter in the South Island; but large numbers move north, though evidence is needed for the crossing of Cook Strait. After midsummer many thousands pour into the great harbours of the north and stay till about July, when the southward migration starts. By the end of August those remaining are the local breeders and immature non-breeders. Most Pied Stilts winter on the coast; but inland some are attracted by the shallows of Lake Rotorua.
  Casual visitor to some off-shore islands, e.g. Little Barrier; breeds on Kapiti, Great Barrier, Ruapuke, and has bred on Waiheke. First recorded Stewart Island, 1956, and at Chatham Islands, 1961, when a pair bred.

Breeding: A successful coloniser because of its wide range of breeding habitats among which are the seashore, boulder banks, saline lagoons, swampy paddocks, river beds and lakesides up to more than 2500 ft. Breeding season, June to February (Auckland). Eggs buff or olive heavily blotched with black and dark brown spots and streaks; normal clutch four, occasionally five; incubation period 23–7 days; fledging 27–37 days. Incubation shared by both sexes.

BLACK STILT *Himantopus novaezealandiae*

Maori name: Kaki.

Description: 15″. Plumage entirely black with a greenish gloss on upper surface. Bright red eye. Bill (2¾″) black; legs pink. With its longer bill and shorter tarsus it is a bird of different proportions from the Pied Stilt. Both on the ground and in flight, it looks more compact and robust.

Voice: Described as louder and deeper in pitch than that of the Pied Stilt.

Habitat and range: Formerly widespread; now rare but persisting in at least four scattered inland colonies in South Canterbury and North Otago. Winter behaviour not known, but some evidence points to a northward dispersal, as small flocks (the largest of 14 birds) have been reported several winters in Kawhia Harbour and odd birds usually reappear in autumn on the Auckland isthmus.

Breeding: Nests both on dry shingle-beds and also on adjacent swamps. Eggs, September to December; similar to those of Pied Stilt, but " the difference they exhibit is very manifest to the eye, although not easily described " (Buller); normal clutch, 4. Both sexes incubate.

Note: Sometimes, perhaps as a result of crossing with the Pied Stilt, almost, but not entirely, black stilts are seen. In these a little smudgy white usually shows on the face and lower abdomen. Alternatively, there is some evidence to suggest that such birds may be Black Stilts in immature plumage.

RED-NECKED AVOCET *Recurvirostra novaehollandiae*

Description: 18″. White with *chestnut head and neck*; two black lines on mantle; wings brownish-black with broad white band across middle; bill long (3½″) *upcurved*; legs greenish-blue. In flight legs are stretched out straight behind. Feeds with scythe-like sweep of the bill from side to side.

Habitat and range: An Australian species, but rare in Tasmania and the south-east; apparently tenuously established in New Zealand between 1859 and 1878, perhaps till 1892. Said to have bred in a few localities and reported in small flocks, mainly South Island; only twice North Island, viz. Wellington west coast and Whangarei. The only acceptable twentieth-century records are of one shot at Ellesmere in 1912 and one near Westport in 1968. Typically a bird of shallow saline lakes and lagoons. Should Australian Avocets again attempt to establish themselves in New Zealand, there would not seem to be a lack of suitable breeding habitats.

PHALAROPES : Phalaropodidae

A small anomalous family (3 species) of sandpiper-like birds, in which *the females are larger and brighter than the males*. Two species are circumpolar, breeding in arctic and sub-arctic latitudes and migrating south to certain definite areas of the equatorial and southern oceans. In winter they are truly pelagic, living on the surface of the open sea and swimming buoyantly, sometimes in very large flocks.

At sea they feed on plankton. Hence they are sometimes known as " whalebirds " or " mackerel-birds " to sailors who believe that flocks of phalaropes indicate the presence of crustacea-eating whales and fish. As an adaptation to aquatic life their feet are partially webbed (lobed) and their under-plumage is thick.

GREY (RED) PHALAROPE *Phalaropus fulicarius*

Description: 8″. Females in breeding plumage with rich red under-parts, white cheeks and dark crown are unmistakable. Males are paler. Upperparts boldly striated; broad white wing-bar conspicuous in flight. In winter fairly uniform blue-grey above, with white head and underparts, rather like a Sanderling, but with a dark mark through the eye. *Bill relatively heavy and broad, yellow* with dark tip. *Legs yellowish.* Appears a stockier and thicker-necked bird than the Red-necked Phalarope.

Habitat and range: Breeding range more northerly than that of the other phalaropes. The only known wintering ground in the Pacific is off the west coast of Central and South America to about Lat. 50° S., especially on the off-shore border of the Humboldt current. A rare wanderer to New Zealand. Rather curiously, the three specimens collected here have all been females in breeding dress from the east coast, Waimate South (1883), Lake Ellesmere (1925), Hastings (1934). Continuous gales may drive phalaropes to seek the shelter of coastal lagoons.

RED-NECKED (NORTHERN) PHALAROPE *Phalaropus lobatus*

Description: 7½″. Similar in habits to Grey Phalarope, but perhaps more dainty and graceful. Easily recognisable in breeding plumage by white throat and underparts and *orange patch down sides of neck*. Bill black *slender and needle-like; legs blackish*. In winter the darker grey back, conspicuously streaked and the darker wings on which by contrast the white wing-bar is shown up more vividly, are useful field characters. As in the Grey Phalarope there is a dark eye-to-ear patch.

Flight rapid and often erratic. Swims jerkily and may "pirouette" when feeding among surface weeds on shallow water. Appears long-bodied as compared with a Sanderling. Notably approachable and indifferent to man.

Habitat and range: Breeding range less northerly than that of the Grey Phalarope. Known wintering grounds in the Pacific are in the seas adjacent to Borneo and to the north of New Guinea; also with Grey Phalaropes along Humboldt current (*v. supra*).

A rare wanderer to New Zealand recorded from Lake Ellesmere (1929), Wanganui estuary (1935), Washdyke (1961).

PRATINCOLES: Glareolidae

Short decurved bill, forked tail and swallow-like flight in pursuit of insects set the pratincoles or swallow-plovers apart from other waders.

ORIENTAL COLLARED PRATINCOLE *Glareola maldivarum*

Description: 9″. Looks unusual either in flight or on the ground. Upperparts olive-brown, darker on head; *rump white*, tail white with dark tip, *deeply forked*; throat buff, enclosed by a black line (less distinct in juveniles), which passes up the side of the neck to join the dark lores; breast rufous buff; abdomen white. Legs black and short; bill short ($\frac{1}{2}$″) and curved with a *scarlet margin to the gape*. Wings long, dark and pointed; *axillaries chestnut*. During the aerial hawking of insects, shape and action suggest a big brown swallow. On the ground has an almost tiptoe stance; walks or runs rapidly.

Voice: A soft plover-like note *towheet towheet* uttered as the bird rises has been described. Flocks of the typical race *G. pratincola* are noisy in flight making a sharp rippling call *kikki kirrik* with variants; and also a simpler *kik kik kik*.

Habitat and range: Breeds widely in Asia in paddy plains, desert places and the drier areas of marshes; migrating south to Australia, but only occasionally in the south-east. A very rare straggler to New Zealand recorded Westport (1898), a flock of at least five on the beach; Appleby, one, May 1959; Port Adventure, Stewart Island, one, April 1963.

SKUAS: Stercorariidae

Skuas, sometimes called Jaegers, are strong-flying pelagic birds allied to the gulls, with hooked beaks and piratical habits. In New Zealand waters they are most frequently seen pursuing terns and forcing them to drop or disgorge their food. They also attack gulls and other seabirds and will feed on offal.

Of the four species which occur in New Zealand one (*lönnbergi*) breeds commonly in the sub-antarctic region; one (*maccormicki*) is a very rare wanderer from the antarctic continent; two (*parasiticus* and *pomarinus*) are summer visitors from the arctic, the one common and the other rare. The adults of these two species are dimorphic, having light and dark phases; the plumage of immature birds shows a bewildering range of variations.

SOUTHERN SKUA *Catharacta lönnbergi*

Other names: Sea-hawk, Hakoakoa.

Description: 25″. Mainly dark-brown; superficially resembling a young Black-backed Gull in the brown plumage of its first autumn; but with conspicuous white patches in the wings at the base of the primaries and with some yellow showing in the feathering of the neck.

Wings broad and rounded, not so angled and pointed as in the two northern skuas. Bill and feet black. Females are slightly larger than males.

Voice: Noisy at nesting site only, where there is a loud display call *charr-charr-charr*; single or double clucking notes and a thin wheezy call made with the beak open.

Habitat and range: Breeds sparingly in Fiordland; abundantly on Stewart Island and outliers and most sub-antarctic islands, north to the Chathams, south to Macquarie, usually in the vicinity of penguin or petrel colonies. Breeding grounds are deserted June–August, when it ceases to be a shore scavenger and becomes an ocean raider, reaching northern waters of New Zealand, but seldom reported near land except after persistent gales. Verification of flocks in Otago coastal waters in late summer is needed. Little known of its winter habits. Prions may be its main prey. One caught in a hawk trap on Awhitu peninsula. **Breeding:** Some adults return to breeding grounds in August; most in September. Eggs dark stone colour with irregular blotches of dark brown, laid late October–early November. Incubation period about 27 days. Normal clutch 2, but usually only one chick reared. Chicks in down are uniformly cinnamon brown. Three adults often reported in attendance at one nest.

ANTARCTIC SKUA *Catharacta maccormicki*

Description: 21″. Similar to Southern Skua but smaller and lighter in colour. Adults, but not first winter young birds, have feathers of neck conspicuously streaked with yellow.

Voice: A similar range of notes to that recorded for *lönnbergi*.

Habitat and range: The skua of the coast of Antarctica and the pack-ice; has been found farther south than any other bird in the world. Occasionally wanders north in autumn and winter to New Zealand waters, but so far only four recorded, all wrecked on the long west coast of the North Island.

These skuas may visit and pass through New Zealand seas more often than is suspected, as they appear every May off the coast of Japan where they constantly attack shearwaters especially *P. tenuirostris* during the northern summer.

Breeding: The nest is commonly a mere scrape near a large breeding colony of penguins, petrels or seals. Eggs slightly paler in ground colour than those of *lönnbergi*; clutch 2. Down of nestlings is pale grey with a faint buffy tinge.

ARCTIC SKUA   *Stercorarius parasiticus*

Description: 17″ (without projecting tail-feathers). A dimorphic species about the size of a Red-billed Gull. Light phase—upperparts sooty-brown, sides of head and neck yellowish, underparts whitish, white patch in wings at base of primaries. Dark phase—almost entirely dark brown, with a little white usually visible at the base of the primaries, but sometimes difficult to see. Tail wedge-shaped with the central feathers elongated to a point in the adults. These develop about April. (It does not seem to be easy in New Zealand to see adults with these tail feathers fully elongated.) Immature birds in mottled plumage of different shades are very variable. Wings sharply pointed and angled. Before and after a dashing attack on terns, skuas usually fly low. Often hunts in pairs, but gatherings of up to fifty birds have been reported.

Habitat and range: Summer visitor to New Zealand from arctic regions where it is a circumpolar breeder. Easily the most numerous skua off the coasts of the North and South Islands south to Banks Peninsula and Okarito. Commonly seen near breeding colonies of White-fronted Terns; rarely attacks Caspian Terns. Some immature birds remain over the winter, when they have been seen to harry Red-billed Gulls and to pursue a small passerine. These skuas are seldom on or over land; but occasionally one will settle on a beach near terns or gulls.

POMARINE SKUA *Stercorarius pomarinus*

Description: 19″ (without projecting tail feathers which, when present, are paddle-shaped and curiously twisted). A dimorphic species similar to Arctic Skua but bigger and more powerful. Easily distinguished if the central tail feathers are developed. Otherwise not easily separable from the Arctic Skua; but size, larger extent of white in the wings, and, *in immature birds, the pale rump*—upper tail-coverts white or black barred white—are useful pointers.

Habitat and range: Breeds mainly within the Arctic Circle. Scarce but probably regular summer visitor to New Zealand south to Cook Strait, especially Farewell Spit, where they haunt the gull and tern colonies and appear to molest the big flocks of waders. Fairly common off the eastern and south-east coasts of Australia, where it habitually follows ships.

GULLS, TERNS AND NODDIES:
Laridae

Three species of gull are among the familiar birds of New Zealand. Two of them are conspicuous at most ports and along the popular beaches. In some districts the three occur together. The least plentiful is the endemic Black-billed Gull, which is primarily a bird of the South Island, where over large areas it replaces the Red-billed. All three species may be found well inland and the two smaller gulls readily follow the plough. Considerable skill is sometimes needed in differentiating between Red-billed and Black-billed Gulls. When they are in first-year or sub-adult plumage, before the colours of bills and legs have become fixed, the surest and safest guide to identification is the shape of the wings, and the pattern of the primaries as seen in flight.

In view of the great variety of climates and biotopes in the New Zealand region, it is not surprising that the terns and noddies are strongly represented. Fifteen species are known to occur, of which nine breed; three are scarce but possibly regular migrants from the northern hemisphere; and three are unusual stragglers from Australia or the tropical south-west Pacific.

The Sooty Tern and three small kinds of noddy nest at the sub-tropical Kermadecs. Caspian and White-fronted Terns frequent the coasts of the main islands. The Fairy Tern seems to be confined for nesting to a single stretch of sandy coast in Northland. The marsh-terns are represented by the Black-fronted Tern, which breeds widely in the South Island east of the Alps. The Antarctic Tern has colonies at all the truly sub-antarctic groups and reaches the northern limit of its breeding range at Stewart Island.

Little difficulty will be experienced in identifying most New Zealand terns when they are in breeding dress; but adults of the several black-capped species, both resident and migratory, in eclipse, when the black cap is lost or recedes and the colour of the bill is dulled, and young birds in first-year plumage, can be very hard to determine, even when closely seen and carefully observed.

SOUTHERN BLACK-BACKED GULL *Larus dominicanus Pl. 13*
Maori name: Karoro, Ngoiro (imm.).
Description: Length, 24″. A large gull, with head, neck, upper tail-coverts, tail, and all underparts including under wing, white. Back and wings above are black, but tertials and secondaries are broadly tipped with white forming two bands when the wings are closed. The four outer primaries are also white-tipped and the outermost has a second sub-terminal patch of white, sometimes repeated on a smaller scale on the next. Bill yellow, with a splash of red at the angle of the gonys: gape and eyelid orange: iris pale hazel; feet mustard yellow or olive-green according to age or season: female smaller and more slender than the male. This plumage is not attained until the bird's third winter. In first winter plumage the general tone is dark clove-brown all over, varied with buff-edged feathers dorsally, mottled beneath and barred brown and white on rump and tail-coverts above and below. Flight feathers and tail are uniformly brown, bill blackish, eye brown, feet grey. As most of the body feathers are basally dull white the plumage rapidly becomes paler with wear. The first moult produces some dark scapulars and more white on the body, and the progress to maturity is accompanied by colour change in bill, iris and feet. The rate of change is not uniform and birds of the same age often appear superficially older or younger.
Voice: A wide range of calls used in varying circumstances has been fully described by Fordham (*Notornis* x, 5, 1963).
Habitat and range: Although as a species it has a circumpolar distribution in the Southern Hemisphere this gull is sedentary and not pelagic. It frequents estuaries, harbours and open coastline, outlying and off-shore islands, river systems, lakes and alpine tarns. Scavenging and predation enable it to survive in non-marine localities, but its numbers are greatest near supplies of offal and smallest where it depends on shellfish and other sea-food. Rare straggler to the Kermadecs and Norfolk Islands.
Breeding: Colonies are found on coastal sand dunes, rocky islands, grassy seaward slopes, river-beds well inland and even on the mountains up to 5000 feet. Isolated pairs may rest on rock stacks. Nests are well formed, and may have a depression nearly as deep as the short diameter of the egg; eggs, normally three to a clutch, are greenish-bluish or buff in ground colour with purple or brown spots and blotches. Incubation period, 24–25 days. Downy chicks are mainly stone grey broadly spotted blackish on head and back, shading to greyish white on belly. Bill and feet leaden colour.

RED-BILLED GULL   *Larus scopulinus*   *Pl. 13*
Other names: Tarapunga, Mackerel Gull, Jackie (Chathams).
Description: 14½″. A small gull related closely to the Silver Gull (*Larus novaehollandiae*) of Australia. New Zealand populations are by

no means uniform, the sub-antarctic race having a shorter, stouter bill and slightly darker plumage. The entire plumage of head, neck, underparts and tail is white. The mantle, back and wing-coverts are uniformly pale pearly grey as are the under wing-coverts. The primaries are mainly black but all are white-tipped in fresh plumage having hidden basal patches of white, and the two outermost have broad sub-terminal white bands on both webs. Bill, eyelids and feet are scarlet; the iris silvery white; males are larger and more robust than females. In the first immature plumage the feathers of the mantle have pale buffy tips and a dark band on the wing is formed by brownish patches on the secondaries. There is much less white on the primaries in this plumage. Bills are dark brownish black; eyes brown and feet purplish brown. The nestling down is warm greyish buff mottled with darker spots on the upper surface and paling to white on the abdomen. **Voice:** A strident and tremulous scream is the usual alarm note associated with a short sharp cry as well as a variety of skirling calls and softer notes associated with the elaborate display in the breeding season. **Habitat and range:** In the main an inhabitant of coasts and off-shore islands, these gulls are also found in small numbers inland on the larger lakes. Densely packed nesting colonies occur on many rock stacks and cliffs, but large colonies are also known from sandbanks and flat areas near the mouths of rivers. A small colony in Hokianga occurs on piles of an old jetty. Although fairly successful as predators on small post-larval fish, these gulls are also scavengers and have a wide range of diet including earthworms, insects and occasionally berries. Rare straggler to the Kermadecs and Norfolk Islands. **Breeding:** In the situations already mentioned the nest is usually well formed of grass and other adaptable material. The usual clutch is two eggs, sometimes three, of variable ground colour, but mainly brownish-ochre, with the dark spotting and blotching characteristic of gulls' eggs generally. Incubation period *c.* 21 days. The sub-antarctic forms, already mentioned as distinguishable, have also a distinctive nesting habit, the nests being found in caves and cavities and rarely exposed in the open. Both sexes incubate.

BLACK-BILLED GULL *Larus bulleri*   *Pl. 13*
Other name: Buller's Gull.
Description: 14½″. Superficially similar to the Red-billed Gull this species has nevertheless the more delicate structure and characteristic wing pattern of the several Black-headed Gulls of the Northern Hemisphere. It resembles them also in its habitat preference. Entire plumage of the head, neck, underparts and tail is white. Mantle and upper wing-coverts are very pale pearly grey as are the under wing-coverts. *The pattern of black and white on the primaries is* the most conspicuous field character, the *outer primaries being mainly white* for the greater part of their length with a small sub-terminal area and border of black. As in most other gulls, they are white-tipped. Bill black with reddish gape and interior; feet dark reddish black; eyelid

dark red; iris white. In immature plumage there are buffy tips to
most of the mantle feathers. Sometimes a trace of black in the tail
and brown patches sub-terminal in the secondaries. In very young
birds the bills are pale pinkish brown and the feet about the same colour;
iris brown. However, the first stage of change in bill and feet is in the
direction of red which becomes quite bright in the second year and is
a field character causing some confusion with the Red-billed Gull, as
in fact the immature brownish-black bill of the latter causes it to be
sometimes misidentified as a Black-billed Gull. The downy plumage
of chicks is pale buff, sometimes almost pinkish, with a light blotching
of darker tufts. Belly down is whitish.

Voice: Very similar to that of the Red-billed Gull, but more high-
pitched and less powerful.

Habitat and range: This is essentially an inland gull of the larger river
systems and inland lakes of the South Island, although it moves to the
coast in winter, when fair numbers drift northwards and cross Cook
Strait. Many colonies in association with Red-billed Gulls occur near
the mouths of the larger rivers. In the North Island the only known
regular breeding colony was at Rotorua; but up to 15 pairs now nest
near Gisborne annually. Non-breeders are the dominant small gull at
Hawke's Bay estuaries in summer. A flock of some hundreds winters
on the Miranda coast of the Firth of Thames; and smaller numbers
occur at Bay of Plenty estuaries.

Aquatic and terrestrial insects form much of its diet but it also feeds
in flocks over farmland and obtains a good deal of marine food from
estuaries and shallow coasts. Less inclined than the Red-billed Gull
to become parasitic on man. Not known from any of the off-shore or
outlying islands.

Nesting: Nesting habits except its preference for river-beds well inland
are very similar to those recorded for the Red-billed Gull. The eggs
are usually somewhat lighter in colour and have less intensity of
spotting and blotching. In the mixed colony at Rotorua, Black-billed
Gulls lay two or three weeks later than the Red-billed. Clutch, normally 2. Incubation period, 20–24 days. Chicks are covered with a
streaky grey, brown and white down. Both sexes incubate.

GULL-BILLED TERN *Gelochelidon nilotica*

Description: 17″. An obvious tern, but distinguished from the typical
terns by its *thick black gull-like bill*, less forked tail and longish legs.
Upperparts greyish-white; crown and forehead black; underparts
white; outer webs of outermost primaries slate-grey; legs black. In
winter plumage head is nearly white. Long tarsus (1½″) gives rather
high stance.

Voice: The calls of the typical race have been described as a " throaty
rasping *za-za-sa* or *kayweek*." Those of the Australian race have been
recorded as *kuh-wuk kuh-wuk* repeated several times; and a *che-ah*.

Habitat and range: Mainly a freshwater tern, which commonly feeds
over pasture, marsh and still water. An almost cosmopolitan species,

represented in Australia by *macrotarsa*; but not common in south-east Australia or Tasmania.

Two were found associating with gulls and waders on the short turf of Invercargill airport in May 1955 and were reported still present two months later. One near Woodend in the same estuary, December, 1944.

BLACK-FRONTED TERN   *Chlidonias albostriatus*   *Pl. 14*
Other names: Tara, Sea Martin, Ploughboy, Inland Tern, Riverbed Tern.

Description: 12″. The common inland tern of the South Island; rather dusky and markedly smaller and greyer than the White-fronted Tern with which it sometimes associates at river mouths and on sea beaches. Adults in breeding dress are dapper and colourful. Top of head and nape deep velvety black; broad white sub-ocular stripe; mantle, upper surface, tail and underparts a delicate blue-grey; *rump white particularly noticeable in flight*; bill and *feet bright orange-red*. During the post-nuptial moult the black cap is lost and the top of head and nape are a very pale grey. Many adults have assumed their distinctive breeding dress by the end of May.

Young resemble adults in eclipse; but show some brown speckling on the upper surface, have a white throat and paler breast; bill yellowish with dark tip and legs dull yellow.

Voice: The common call is " a high-pitched, staccato, whistling note given at intervals " (Stead). Variations of this sharp *ki-kit* include *ki-ki-kit*, *ki-ki-ki-ki-kit* and sometimes a single *kit*. Intruders near the nest are assaulted with a harsh angry *yark*; and an additional call when disturbed is a *curr* like protest note of the White-fronted Tern.

Habitat and range: Now known to breed only in the South Island east of the main range, on river-beds and lake shores up to the foot of the glaciers, from Marlborough to Southland. Almost unknown in Westland. Formerly bred in the North Island " far up the course of the Whangaehu River " near the south-east base of Ruapehu, and may yet be discovered breeding on some river-beds of Hawke's Bay, where some are found every winter at the estuaries.

In autumn there is a general movement from the breeding grounds down to the coast. Some go south to Stewart Island and some hundreds cross Cook Strait to winter on the Wellington coast especially at Waikanae, where biggest flock recently recorded in North Island was *c.* 320 on 18/5/58; and Palliser Bay. On the west stragglers and even small flocks may reach Auckland, the northernmost records coming from Kaipara.

Another regular wintering ground is in the Bay of Plenty from Whakatane to Matata, especially the estuaries of the Rangitaiki and Tarawera, where in 1952 over 120 were present. The provenance of these birds is unknown.

Inland these terns habitually hawk insects over rivers, lakes, swamps, and damp pastures, and even growing crops; and they will follow the plough. In winter commonly feeds offshore.

Found only in New Zealand, the Black-fronted Tern is sometimes treated as a strong subspecies of the Whiskered Tern (*C. hybrida*).
Breeding: Breeds in loose colonies on shingly river-beds often in association with Black-billed Gulls. Nest a scrape in silt or sand among large round stones. Eggs, late September–January; dark stone copiously marked with light and dark brown blotches. Clutch 1–3, typically 2. Incubation period *c.* 21 days. Both sexes incubate.

WHITE-WINGED BLACK TERN *Chlidonias leucopterus* *Pl. 14*
Description: 9". In breeding dress which is strikingly smart and distinctive, head and body black; *tail conspicuously white* and only slightly forked; wings black, white and grey, the fore-edge above (shoulder) being white and beneath black, thus showing a quite diagnostic pattern; bill small and reddish; legs red. Breeding dress is assumed between January and April; but these terns in full or almost full breeding dress have been observed in New Zealand in every month of the year.

Adults in eclipse are mainly grey and white; but a black band passes from behind eyes over the back of the crown and joins a club-shaped area of black on the nape. First-year birds resemble adults in winter; but have upperparts variably mottled with brown. The plumage changes of the White-winged Black Tern are notoriously puzzling.
Voice: Rather a silent tern. One in Manukau was once heard to utter an incisive *keevit* and a sharp *keet*.
Habitat and range: A typical marsh-tern, breeding across the temperate palaearctic from eastern Europe to eastern Asia. Reported to have bred in Africa south of the equator. Birds from eastern Asia migrate south, to winter especially in Borneo and north-eastern Australia; but juveniles are particularly prone to be over-carried and may reach New Zealand where the same bird may frequent a suitable habitat for several months or even years. Reported from Kaipara to Invercargill, mainly at coastal lagoons, estuaries and marshes; once on a subalpine tarn at 2500 feet in the Mackenzie country. A few seem to reach New Zealand annually.

Shallow pools which attract Pied Stilts are likely to suit wandering White-winged Black Terns. They are largely insectivorous and have been seen to walk round on muddy ground, snapping up flies. The flight is swift, agile and buoyant. In cold blustery weather they seem tireless, and for hours on end they will hawk insects over a pool dipping down to the water but not breaking the surface; flying low they work their way upwind till they reach the edge of the pool; then they swing back to the lee shore and begin the circuit over again. To rest they will settle quite fearlessly among Pied Stilts or other species of terns and on the edge of flocks of waders.

CASPIAN TERN *Hydroprogne caspia*
Maori name: Taranui.
Description: 19"–22". The largest of the terns with a wing span of

Plate 15

DUCKS

4½ ft. Upperparts pale grey; underparts white. Forehead, cap and nape of adults black in breeding dress; cap greyish, almost white in winter; but many adults have assumed breeding dress by mid-July. Bill (2¾″) massive orange-red, dusky towards tip which is yellow; legs black. Juveniles have top of head more or less streaked; upperparts at first spotted with black and brown; bill duller and feet dusky yellowish.

In flight the *wing-tips* are seen to be *black on the underside* and the tail not deeply forked.

A tern of shallow coastal waters, over which it fishes often hovering characteristically with head pointing downwards; seldom seen far out to sea.

Voice: Commonly a harsh grating corvine *kaah* or *karh-kaa*; also a slow gruff *kuk-kuk*; a faster *kak-kak-kak* and a scolding *yakketi-yak*. Several months after fledging young birds will still badger adults with a peevish mewing or high pitched squeaky whistle *queea-queea*.

Habitat and range: Widely but unevenly distributed in tropic and temperate zones. Fairly plentiful around the coasts of the North and South Islands; most numerous in the north, but becoming scarce south of Canterbury and Westland, though recorded as breeding near Bluff. Not yet reported from Stewart or Chatham Islands.

Commonly frequents estuaries and penetrates rivers especially in the North Island to inland lakes. Regular at Rotorua where a few pairs breed at 900 ft. a.s.l. and winter roosting flock may number 50. In autumn the large shallow harbours of the north receive an influx; and it is quite normal to see groups of 100–200 resting on shellbanks at high tide among waders. There is growing evidence that birds from the south tend to move north for the winter. Banding has shown that there is considerable local movement in the province of Auckland, and one bird banded in Northland has been recovered in the South Island.

Breeding: Mainly a colonial nester on shingle banks, beaches and sand-dunes. A normal colony has 5–20 pairs; but at least two in the north have more than 100 pairs. Sometimes isolated pairs will breed on promontories or rocky islets. Inland nesting occurs at Rotorua, near or in the colony of Red-billed and Black-billed Gulls. Eggs, September–January, light stone or pale blue-green thickly sprinkled with dark brown spots and blotches; clutch 1–3, most frequently 2. Incubation *c*. 21 days; fledging at least four weeks. Inopportune gales with high tides or blown sand cause many casualties among eggs and chicks. Both sexes incubate.

CRESTED TERN *Sterna bergii*
Description: 18½″. Markedly larger than a White-fronted tern and

with much greyer upperparts. *Forehead white*; crown and nape black with elongated feathers which can be raised to form a crest; underparts snow-white. Bill (2½″) powerful, *greenish-yellow*; feet dull red or brownish black. Juveniles and adults in eclipse have crown streaked or mottled black and white.

Voice: A throaty dissyllable variously recorded as *kurrik, kyark, kair-rik, kārruk.*

Habitat and range: In the Indian Ocean and south-west Pacific, a common and widespread species, of which the form *cristata* is plentiful on the coasts of Australia and Tasmania, habitually fishing in estuaries and penetrating rivers. A very rare straggler to New Zealand, only thrice recorded: Raoul Island (April 1910); Spirits Bay, one ashore dead (March 1951); Farewell Spit, one among White-fronted Terns (January 1960). In Australian waters often feeds well out to sea, e.g. among shearwaters.

ANTARCTIC TERN   *Sterna vittata*   *Pl. 14*

Description: 16″. Rather smaller than a White-fronted Tern. Forehead, crown, nape black; a broad streak of white from gape below eye to nape; upper surface a soft shade of light bluish grey; outerwebs of outermost primaries blackish; rump and tail white, only the outer webs of the tail feathers being pale grey; underparts, including throat, greyish white; but under tail-coverts white. Bill vermilion or coral red; legs orange-red. Tail deeply forked, white. In eclipse April to October forehead and crown are white; bill and feet dusky red. In their first winter young birds closely resemble adults in eclipse, but have pure white underparts.

Flight undulating. Boldly attacks Southern Skuas, if they pass near the nest.

Voice: Shrill and high-pitched.

Habitat and range: Circumpolar, represented in New Zealand by the subspecies *bethunei*, which breeds in all groups of the sub-antarctic islands from Macquarie to the Snares and South Cape Islands. No evidence of migration in the New Zealand region.

Breeding: Nest a shallow scratching with some protection usually afforded by vegetation on rocks near the sea and on cliffs up to 400 ft. a.s.l. Eggs, November to January, dark green, olive or olive-brown with spots of black or dark brown and underlying markings of grey. Clutch 1–2.

ARCTIC TERN   *Sterna macrura*

Description: 15″. Distinctly smaller than a White-fronted Tern. The salient features of breeding dress are: black cap, contrasting with white streak below; bill blood-red, without dark tip; legs coral red; tail deeply forked with long streamers projecting a little beyond wing-tips, when perched; throat, breast and abdomen pale grey. It is just possible that a northward bound Arctic Tern, showing these characteristics, in April, might pause on the coast.

However, most Arctic Terns in New Zealand seas are likely to be in eclipse, immature (first winter) or sub-adult plumage with bill and legs blackish; forehead and crown white or streaked black and white; under surface white, not grey.

In breeding dress Antarctic and Arctic Terns would be almost indistinguishable in the field; but where the two species occur together in the southern oceans, Antarctic Terns are generally in nuptial plumage, whereas Arctic Terns are not and are without their long tail streamers; but sub-adult non-breeding Antarctic Terns complicate an already difficult problem of field identification. The following guide to distinguishing the two species in the Antarctic has been proposed by M. C. Downes (*Emu* 1952, 307).

Arctic Tern	*Antarctic Tern*
slighter build	bigger body
shorter wings and tail	longer new feathers
dives up and down frequently	dives more decisively
straight flight	undulating flight
black bill and feet	red bill and feet
white or slightly grey underparts	deeper grey underparts
sometimes brown patchy mantle and back of wings	even grey on mantle wings
dark cubital band	no cubital band

The *very short tarsus* of the Arctic Terns is a useful aid to identification, if they are seen perched. The narrow grey band on the inner web next to the shaft of the outermost primaries and the dark grey outer webs of the outside tail feathers are hardly field characters; but are pointers to establishing the identity of a bird in the hand.

Voice: A high whistling note *kee-kee* rising in pitch is said to be characteristic.

Habitat and range: In the course of a year an Arctic Tern enjoys more daylight than any other bird. In the northern autumn these terns set out for Antarctica, migrating mainly by two routes, one down the eastern side of the Atlantic, the other down the eastern side of the Pacific. Those that reach antarctic and sub-antarctic seas south of New Zealand probably do so by the Atlantic route and are swept eastwards by the prevailing westerlies.

They are certainly more numerous in the New Zealand region than the few records suggest.

Probably a regular visitor to our sub-antarctic islands where they have been reported from Macquarie, Auckland and Campbell Islands. Very rarely recorded from the main islands, mostly west coast of North Island as northbound migrants, possibly off course, since there is some evidence to show that these terns keep well out to sea on their long journeys to and from Antarctica.

Note: The dark-billed Eastern Common Tern (*S. hirundo longipennis*) may reach the Tasman Sea at the southern limit of its migration. It has been recorded several times from Lord Howe Island and the south-

eastern coast of Australia. Its claim to be on the New Zealand list
depends on the fragmentary remains of a single bird found at Karekare
on the Auckland west coast on 23/8/59.

FAIRY TERN *Sterna nereis*   *Pl. 14*

Description: 10". The smallest and rarest of the terns which breed in
New Zealand. Very pale grey above, white below, with crown of head
and nape black and a black band extending forward from eye, *ending
about a quarter of an inch from bill*; forehead white. Bill yellow,
without dark tip; legs orange. Though the tails of breeding birds are
forked, the outer tail feathers are not markedly elongated. Immature
birds have dusky legs and bills and are said to be inseparable in the
field from *S. albifrons*.

Voice: Call note a high-pitched rasping *zwit* or *zewit*. If disturbed
near nest the protest note is a repeated *tee-tee*, followed by the rasping
zwit.

Habitat and range: Primarily an Australian species, breeding commonly
on the south and west coasts, but not in eastern Australia or Tasmania
where it is replaced by *S. albifrons*. Now known as a breeding bird
in New Zealand only from Northland, where probably fewer than ten
pairs attempt to nest. A hundred years ago it is said to have been
more widespread and even to have bred inland on the river-beds of
the South Island. This small tern is not a colonial nester, the few pairs
being scattered over many miles of open sandhills. For some months
in winter apparently the breeding area is deserted and it is not known
where the few New Zealand Fairy Terns go.

Breeding: Fairy Terns reappear at breeding grounds in September and
begin to make trial nest scrapes in the sand. Eggs, November to
January; clutch usually 2; pale buff blotched and spotted with
black, dark grey and brown. Incubation at least 18 days; fledging
c. 24 days. Both sexes incubate.

LITTLE TERN *Sterna albifrons*   *Pl. 14*

Description: 10". Separable in the field from *S. nereis* only in breeding
plumage by colour of bill, *yellow with black tip*, and pattern of black
and white on head, viz. a black narrowing streak from eye *forward to
bill*; black crown well forward and white recess below forming *an
acute angle* above eye, not rounded as in *S. nereis*. Immature birds,
with blackish patch on shoulder of wing, and adults with crown mostly
white, bill and legs dusky, appear in spring, especially November, in
the Firth of Thames, in small flocks and stay over the summer, the
adults assuming breeding dress between February and April when they
disappear; a few presumably immature birds have been seen in winter.
The tail which, over most of the summer, is so short as to be stumpy, is
well forked by April.

Voice: A sharp *kweek* or a rasping *zweek* which seemed to be a note
of alarm was made by each of seven as they rose from among Wrybills.
While hovering an urgent *peep-peep-peep* may be often repeated.

A lively pleasant chattering *chi-chi-chi-chi* or an excited chittering may accompany what appears to be pair formation or courtship flights.

Habitat and range: An almost cosmopolitan species, represented in the western Pacific by *sinensis*, which breeds from China and Japan to eastern Australia and Tasmania. Small terns adjudged to be *sinensis* regularly associate with the big mixed flocks of waders in summer feeding over the shallows in Kaipara and Manukau Harbours and the Firth of Thames. In the South Island small dark-billed, short-tailed terns have recently been reported from the estuaries of Taramakau and Wairau (Blenheim), Lake Ellesmere, Otago Harbour and the Southland lagoons. States of plumage, times of moult and seasonal behaviour of most of these small terns postulate an origin in the northern hemisphere. The largest number so far seen together in New Zealand is 35 in the Firth of Thames, December 1962.

WHITE-FRONTED TERN *Sterna striata*   *Pl. 14*

Other names: Sea-swallow, Kahawai Bird, Tara, Blackcap, Grenadier, Swallowtail, Noddy (Chathams), Tikkitak (Stewart Is.).

Description: 16½″. A typical sea-swallow and by far the commonest tern around the New Zealand coast. *Forehead* and *lores white*; crown and nape black; upperparts pearl grey; outer web of first primary brownish black; underparts white; breast sometimes showing a transient pink. Bill black; legs dusky or dull red. Some adults assume breeding dress, as indicated by *narrow white forehead* and long tail-streamers by midwinter. Adults in eclipse have more white on forehead and a mottled crown; sub-adults (second year birds) are similar, but above the *high white forehead* are black on the crown. First winter birds have crown and nape streaked with black white and buff; mantle barred and mottled, a blackish wash on the shoulders of the wings, and a dusky edging to fork of tail. Tail, white in adults, deeply forked, the depth of the fork varying according to the season.

Voice: Call note a high-pitched *siet*, *tsit* or *zitt*, frequently used in flight either by day or night or e.g. when " working " over a shoal of fish. When molested the protest note is a rasping *kee-eet* or harsh *keark*, or *keh*, *keeahk*, *keeakh*.

Habitat and range: Breeds only in New Zealand (not Three Kings), from Cavallis and adjacent mainland south to Chatham and Auckland Islands. In autumn large numbers, especially young birds, migrate to south-eastern Australia, where widespread May–November on coasts of New South Wales, Victoria and Tasmania, a few ranging west to Southern Australia or north to Queensland.

The annual trans-Tasman migrations of this tern give it a certain unique distinction. Ringing has shown that birds from both Lake Ellesmere and the Firth of Thames may cross to Australia. Many, however, remain in New Zealand throughout the winter.

Said to be completely absent from Chatham Islands from about end of March to mid-August.

Rarely reported inland; but has visited Taupo and Rotorua. Feeds mainly in coastal waters, sometimes a few miles out to sea, forming great " swirls " over shoaling fish with gannets and shearwaters; in autumn especially a few may fish up tidal creeks and rivers.

Breeding: Breeds in colonies among sand-dunes, at estuaries on shingle-banks, rock-stacks and cliffs; many colonies in inshore waters containing hundreds of pairs; others, especially on the outer off-shore islands of the north, only a few, 10–20 pairs. Notoriously capricious; a site successfully used one year may not be used the next; or else a few pairs will return, lay a few eggs in a rather desultory way and then abandon the site for the rest of the season.

In the north these terns start revisiting nesting grounds in August; but the first eggs do not appear until mid-October. Some young are on the wing before Christmas. Casualties are heavy and egg-laying may continue into January, but, more often than not, the young which are hatched from late eggs are abandoned before they can fly. Eggs, almost indescribably variable; clutch commonly 1, sometimes 2. Incubation *c.* 24 days; fledging *c.* 4 weeks. Both sexes incubate.

SOOTY TERN *Sterna fuscata*

Other name: Wideawake.

Description: 18″. Entirely dark brownish black above, except for *white forehead*, and *white recess above the eye* from which a narrowing black stripe runs forward to beak. White below, *including underwing.* Tail deeply forked, the outer tail feathers having the appearance of streamers, though their length and the depth of the fork varies considerably. The outer edge of the longest tail feathers is white. Bill and legs black. Flying low at a distance, this tern looks jet black till the white underparts become visible.

Voice: Not unlike the word *wideawake* spoken in a squeaky voice or with a twang, the accent being on the first and last syllables. A protest note at the nest *go-ak*.

Habitat and range: Ranges over most tropical and sub-tropical seas. Though it breeds abundantly at Lord Howe, Norfolk and Kermadec Islands, it is seldom reported from New Zealand proper. The recorded occurrences form an interesting pattern, 7 for February–April, following northerly gales; 6, late July–August when New Zealand waters are at their coldest. Sooty Terns are sometimes blown inland. The three most southerly records are from the Wellington west coast.

Breeding: The first Wideawakes return to Raoul about mid-August. Most eggs are laid between mid-October and the end of December. Clutch 1. Incubation *c*. 24 days. Some young are on the wing in mid-February. By the end of April the breeding grounds are almost deserted.

COMMON NODDY *Anous stolidus*

Other names: Noddy Tern, Brown Noddy.

Description: 15½". Forehead almost white, top of head pale grey; lores black, sharply contrasting with whitish forehead; plumage otherwise dark brown, with primaries and tail nearly black; underwing and throat greyer. Bill stout (1¾"), black; feet brownish-black with yellowish webs. Tail rounded, not forked.

Voice: A harsh corvine *kar-r-rk* or *kwok-kwok*.

Habitat and range: Tropical and sub-tropical waters of the Atlantic and Pacific. The subspecies *pileatus* ranges throughout the south-west Pacific, its southernmost breeding stations being at Lord Howe and Norfolk Islands. Rather anomalously this noddy has not been reported from the Kermadecs and its claim to be on the New Zealand list is based on two rather unsatisfactory nineteenth-century reports. It is curious that it should be so scarce in New Zealand waters, for in the Atlantic it breeds as far south as Tristan da Cunha, in the same latitude as Auckland.

WHITE-CAPPED NODDY *Anous minutus*

Other names: Lesser Noddy, Black Noddy.

Description: 13½". Forehead and top of head silvery white; plumage otherwise black, but not uniformly; wings very dark; tail brownish-black; lores, band through eye and throat jet black. Bill slender (1⅔"), black; feet dark brown.

Habitat and range: Several subspecies have been described from tropical seas. The form *minutus*, which breeds at Norfolk and Kermadec Islands, ranges from New Guinea and Queensland to the Tuamotu Archipelago. From New Zealand proper it is seldom reported. An exhausted bird flew into a tree at South Kaipara Heads during a north-westerly gale (October 1953); another was seen sitting among White-fronted Terns on Farewell Spit and then flying strongly out to sea (January 1961). Others have since occurred in Northland after tropical storms.

Breeding: On Meyer Islet a nest of forest debris occasionally with some seaweed is built in a tree, karaka, ngaio or pohutukawa. On Macauley Is., in the almost complete absence of woody plants, the nest is placed on rock ledges and in caves. Laying begins in October. Clutch 1. Incubation 35 days; fledging *c*. 51 days. Most young are on the wing by the end of March.

WHITE TERN *Gygis alba*

Other names: White Noddy, Love Tern, Fairy Tern.

Description: 12½". The most ethereal of seabirds. Ivory white, with a narrow black ring round the eye and usually dusky shafts to the primaries and tail feathers. Bill (1½") rather stout, black, blue at base; feet black or bluish with yellowish webs. Juveniles have a black spot behind the eye, darker shafts to the wing-quills and tail feathers; and the feathers of the mantle are tipped with rusty brown. Against the sunlight the wings and forked tail of these elfin-like terns appear translucent. Flight swift and erratic.

Voice: Of the Atlantic form, Murphy remarks, " They have a way of fluttering just in front of one's face, not attacking, but merely staring, hovering like overgrown mosquitoes, and wheezing in a way to suggest the buzz of some such noxious insect."

Habitat and range: Six subspecies have been described from tropical seas. The race *royana* breeds at Norfolk and Kermadec Islands. Though it is the sort of seabird that might be expected in New Zealand coastal waters after a northerly blow, there are only three recorded occurrences: Waipu (1885), Ettrick, Otago (March 1945), Bethells (May 1960).

Breeding: White Terns begin to return to Raoul Island early in September and most have left the island by the end of April. Eggs may be found from mid-October to the end of January. The single egg is laid usually on a tree preferably at a considerable height. Eggs are described as being more uniformly elliptical than those of most terns and decidedly blunt at both ends.

GREY TERNLET *Procelsterna albivitta*

Other names: Little Blue Petrel (Norfolk Island), Grey Noddy, Blue Billy (Lord Howe).

Description: 11". A small predominantly grey tern with rather long legs and large feet. Head and underparts greyish white; upperparts and undertail feathers ash-grey; underwing white; a ring around the eye is black in front and white behind. Bill (1¼") short and weak, black; feet black with yellow webs.

Voice: A noisy scream comes from birds on the wing at the breeding cliffs. Birds sitting on the rocks seem to be more curious than alarmed and keep up a kind of purring note like *cror-r-r-r*.

Habitat and range: Sub-tropical south-west Pacific, breeding at Lord Howe, Norfolk, Kermadec and Friendly Islands, occasionally wandering to the coast of Northland, south to Bay of Islands, in summer. The great gale of mid-April 1968 swept one down to Banks Peninsula.

Breeding: At the Kermadecs nesting starts in August. The nest is invariably in the shade on a niche in a cliff or under vegetation or boulders. Clutch 1. Fledging *c*. 36 days. Double-brooded. At Phillip and Nepean Islands in the Norfolk Group the eggs are usually placed in niches on inaccessible cliffs.

PIGEONS AND DOVES: Columbidae

The New Zealand Pigeon belongs to one of several subfamilies that feed largely on fruit and berries: subfamily Treroninae (S.E. Asia, Malaya and Africa).

NEW ZEALAND PIGEON   *Hemiphaga novaeseelandiae*   *Pl. 16*

Maori names: Kereru, kuku, kukupa.

Description: 20″. Can generally be seen at close quarters on a reasonably cautious approach, when the rich coloration of the back and purplish-crimson bill and feet are prominent; forehead, face, throat and upper breast metallic green with purple reflections; back of head, nape, scapulars and lesser wing-coverts deep purple with blue-grey sheen; a zone of bronze reflections between purple of head and neck, and green of throat and breast; lower back pale green with grey sheen; wing quills and greater coverts green (bronze reflections), with grey to pale grey centres; tail quills above dark brown with metallic green edges at base, below silvery grey, broad dark brown band towards tip; *underparts* from the line of green breast *white*. At some angles the light may produce a mainly grey appearance on the back; the white underparts and pale grey-green lower back distinctive in flight; pale grey at base of primaries also shows in flight. Iris crimson, eyelids purplish crimson; bill tip yellowish; legs and feet dark blood red

Soft swish of wings, sometimes including wing-clapping, is a distinctive feature; there is also much flapping as the birds move about the branches feeding on foliage and fruits giving an indication of their presence before they are seen.

In juvenal under tail-coverts pale buff.

Voice: A single soft, but occasionally quite penetrating, *ku*; also low scarcely audible variant of the same note or a soft moan. Further variants given at the nest are a growl, faint whistle and a " double sound of a grunt and whistle " (Guthrie-Smith).

Habitat and range: Throughout in forests at European settlement and, after a period of decrease throughout the early settlement period, now well established and probably increasing in the remaining forest areas and residual forest remnants. From native vegetation now freely transfers feeding activity to exotic trees, e.g. poplar, willow, orchard trees, but these in the main do not supply the frugivorous part of its diet.

Food comprises a large proportion of young leaves, and fruits of trees and shrubs of which some species are available practically throughout the year: although few fruits are available in late winter and spring. Fruits of the following trees or shrubs taken: konini (fuchsia), puriri, mangeao, makomako (wineberry), tawa, taraire, matai, miro, kahikatea, titoki, maire, hinau, porokaiwhiria (pigeonwood), mahoe, supplejack, poroporo, five-finger, karamu, nikau, cabbage-tree and karaka; also the introduced holly, cherry, rowan and sweetbriar. In addition to the leaves of a wide range of native trees or shrubs (especially kowhai, wineberry, and the common liane, *Parsonsia*), it has been known to eat foliage of various introduced species: willow, poplar, tree lucerne, apple, laburnum. It will freely descend to the ground for clover. Flowers of kowhai and of introduced shrubs (broom, tree lucerne, laburnum) form an important element in its diet.

Restriction on the shooting of Pigeons was found necessary as early as 1864; total protection since 1921 has probably been the most important factor restoring populations to a high level.

The Chatham Island Pigeon (subspecies *chathamensis*) has purple head and breast with bronze and green reflections; pale grey lower back (*cf.* grey-green); greenish-grey greater wing-coverts and extensive grey bases to the primaries; bronze-green under tail-coverts. Rapidly decreased on the main island of the group with European settlement, persisting in fair numbers until recently on Pitt Island, but its status on the main island and even on Pitt Island is now evidently precarious; originally occurred also on Mangare Island but absent from other outlying islands.

Breeding: Nest a flimsy structure of twigs and sticks supported on several smaller branches, at 10–30 feet from the ground, even lower on off-shore islands; sometimes overhanging a cliff. Breeding November–March (occasionally September); possibly double-brooded as eggs recorded as late as June–July; one egg, white. Incubation period *c.* 30 days. Down yellowish-white, sparse; bare on abdomen and round eye. Fledging 6–7 weeks.

ROCK PIGEON *Columba livia*
Other name: Blue Rock Dove.
Description: 13″. From the wild Rock Pigeon have been derived more than 200 breeds of dovecote and racing pigeons, many of which have gone " wild." Hence the motley assortment of pigeons which may now be seen in many public parks and squares. In the wild form, the plumage is mainly blue-grey; *rump whitish*; *two prominent black bars across the wings*; sides of neck glossy green and purple; tail broadly tipped black; *underwing white*; bill leaden; feet pinkish. When the many domestic strains are crossed, the original type tends to emerge.
Voice: *our-roo-cooo* and variants.
Habitat and range: Introduced in the early days of settlement and now established in many towns, breeding on ledges or in niches on buildings. In some districts, notably Auckland west coast, Hawke's Bay and Banks Peninsula, the Rock Pigeon has gone truly feral and reverted to its traditional habitat, breeding in caves on sea-cliffs and inland cliffs.

SPOTTED DOVE *Streptopelia chinensis*
Other names: Turtle Dove, Laceneck, Spotted-necked Dove.
Description: 12″. Upperparts pinkish-brown with darker markings; hindneck and upper back black finely spotted with white; outer tail-feathers black, broadly tipped with white, conspicuous when the tail is fanned; underparts greyish pink, paler on the throat; under tail-coverts whitish. Bill black; legs pink. Has a swift, direct, level flight.
Voice: A cooing call of two, three or four notes varying in rhythm and emphasis, e.g. *croo-croo*; *cuck-croo-cuck*; *cu-cu-croo-crook*. Cooing occurs at all seasons, with apparent peak periods in autumn and spring.
Habitat and range: Introduced from Asia as a cage-bird and now

breeding wild in the suburbs of Auckland from Albany—not common on the North Shore—south to Papakura. Prefers well-treed gardens and parks. Somewhat elusive; but perches openly on roof-tops and commonly feeds on the ground, expecially on lawns.

Breeding: Has an extended breeding-season. Increased cooing in autumn may indicate pair-formation. A spectacular part of display is a steep upward flight and a downward glide with wings and tail stiffly spread. Nest a flimsy platform of twigs, well concealed in a big, thick tree. Eggs two, white. Probably more than one brood a year.

PARROTS AND PARAKEETS:
Psittacidae

KAKAPO   *Strigops habroptilus*   *Pl. 2*

Description: 23″–26″. Colours mainly *moss-green* (bluish sheen in strong light) *above, greenish-yellow below*; forehead and face below eyes yellowish-brown, faintly streaked paler, and throat yellowish white; tail and wing quills barred brown and dull yellow. More or less distinct yellow eyebrow-stripe divides the brownish face from the green crown. The feathers of the back with dark brown and yellow crossbars inside the green tip, and this results in a somewhat irregular mottled effect where brown and yellow coloration shows under green; the dorsal feathers also have irregular central longitudinal stripes which may be visible as yellow streaks. A similar barred and streaked effect on the yellowish underparts, the longitudinal streaks tending to be especially noticeable on the upper breast. Cere pale brown; bill yellowish white, with a varying area of brown at base of upper mandible and generally brown along the fluting of lower mandible; feet brownish grey. The abundant stiff, brownish bristles round the base of the bill are characteristic; this, together with the brown facial disc and strongly arched bill, give an owl-like appearance (hence the old colonial name of " Owl-parrot "). Male averages larger than female, generally with distinctly larger bill.

Voice: The most characteristic call is a series of bittern-like booms heard during the breeding season: other calls are hisses, croaks, screams and mewings (Williams).

Habitat and range: Now one of New Zealand's rarest birds, the only population known with certainty being that discovered in February 1958 by officers of the Wildlife Branch, Department of Internal Affairs in the Cleddau watershed, Fiordland. Early explorers' accounts and ornithological writings, however, give a fairly satisfactory picture of its original range: this was apparently almost exclusively the beech forests of the North and South Islands, more especially in mountain districts although in some areas (especially Fiordland) extending down to sea-level. G. R. Williams, in a survey of its pre- and post-European distribution, considers that its range and numbers had been shrinking before the effects of man—European and Polynesian—were felt; still abundant in certain localities of western South Island up to *c.* 1900 after which it decreased rapidly. Occurred in the North Island at the time of European discovery only in small numbers mainly in the central mountain ranges. On Stewart Island occurs in mixed rain-forest (recent records). The kakapo's habitat extends above the forest into the subalpine and alpine zone: this proximity of herbaceous and shrubby vegetation may well have been a factor limiting its distribution as fruits of subalpine shrubs, and leaves and roots of grassland species formed an important food source. In grassland the blades of tussock grasses are chewed and fibrous material is left hanging in loose balls on the plant. The latter become bleached by sun and rain, providing an indicator of the presence of the species in any area; various types of fibrous plant matter, in addition to tussock, may be chewed in this way. Other items of diet recorded include ferns, mosses, fungi, lizards. The Kakapos recently kept in captivity by the Department of Internal Affairs in an attempt to establish a breeding stock have shown a strong liking for sweet substances, obtainable in the wild by chewing nectar-bearing flowers.

Early accounts make special mention of the tracks cleared by the Kakapo through low vegetation, especially on ridges and spurs; shallow depressions beside the tracks are believed to be dusting bowls. As this species is entirely flightless, it progresses by walking along these tracks, or clambering up leaning trunks and branches; the wings are large and with these the bird can perform a downward glide of as much as 100 yards. It is closely nocturnal, spending the day in natural crevices or excavated burrows.

Three subspecies described (one from North Island, two South Island) are still not satisfactorily defined.

Breeding: Nest in a hollow amongst tree roots, a crevice or excavated burrow, extending back as far as nine feet; the eggs placed on powdered wood with the addition of some feathers. Breeding December–February (records also for May, suggesting sometimes a second brood); eggs 2–4, white. The female is said to be responsible for incubation. Downy young white. The claim (by Richard Henry, caretaker of Resolution Island sanctuary) that all birds bred only in alternate years would, as pointed out by G. R. Williams, be very surprising if true; Henry based this view on the incidence of " booming " (or " drumming "), which he maintained was produced only by the males throughout the breeding season, and on his lack of any evidence of nesting when no birds were heard drumming. Sometimes more than one year was missed, and on one occasion the Kakapos drummed in two succeeding years.

KAKA *Nestor meridionalis* Pl. 2
Description: 17″–19″. Harsh call is often heard before the bird is seen. Large size in comparison with other forest species (except pigeon), and heavy bill, together with dark coloration are characteristic when

amongst foliage: predominating colours seen closely are olive browns or dull greens (see description of subspecies below) and reds; *crimson rump and abdomen*; *grey to greyish- or greenish-white crown*; *tawny-orange patch below eye*; *underwing scarlet*. In flight the head is prominent owing to size of bill; scarlet underwing (coverts and axillaries) conspicuous in suitable light. Bill of adult male more arched than in female, upper mandible being distinctly longer. Cere brown; bill dark brown to dark steel grey; feet dark grey.

Voice: Common call a harsh *ka-aa*; also ringing, musical whistle *u-wiia* (both calls commonly in flight); a musical subsong to the chicks sometimes delivered at the nest; a call, perhaps also given to the young, *chock, chock, chock* is described by Guthrie-Smith.

Habitat and range: More or less continuous native forest tracts form the present habitat of this species; a decrease even in such areas on mainland is likely, as early accounts suggest that it was present in great numbers. Unlike various native forest species, the Kaka has shown only a very limited tendency to spread into exotic plantations or settled districts, exceptions being individuals attracted to nectar-bearing trees and shrubs—Kakas have under these circumstances been known to appear in city gardens. On sanctuaries (Little Barrier and Kapiti) orchard fruits readily taken. Mainly a fruit and insect eater; tears up decaying wood to obtain insect larvæ, especially the grubs of wood-boring beetles. Also eats leaves and obtains nectar from the flowers of rata (*Metrosideros* spp.) and other forest trees or shrubs.

Flight powerful when travelling any distance; small flocks of up to 10, probably family parties, may be seen above the forest. Often heard at night, and is possibly to some extent nocturnal.

The North Island (*septentrionalis*) subspecies is of smaller average size and duller plumage (olive brown above, feathers with darker crescentic tips, and the collar somewhat obscurely mottled with crimson and gold feathers; crown grey to greyish-white): distribution of this subspecies includes native forest areas of the North Island, and larger coastal islands—Hen and Chickens Islands, Great and Little Barrier, Fanal, Mayor, Kapiti. South Island (*meridionalis*) subspecies of more vivid coloration (greenish brown above, the green brighter in male; crimson collar of gold-tipped feathers prominent in male, less distinct in female; crimson underparts exceptionally extend over the whole breast in the male; crown much paler than in *septentrionalis*—greyish-or greenish-white): found throughout the South Island, Stewart Island, and on islands of the latter area.

Breeding: In a large hollow tree, a site being used year after year and probably by successive pairs; entrance generally a hole 10–30 ft. from the ground; opening often widened in either dead or living wood by the birds; eggs laid on powdered wood. Breeding, October–February; eggs 4–5, white. Incubation period *c.* 21 days. Down of chicks pale grey; bill and facial skin lemon-yellow. Fledging 10 weeks (J. R. Jackson).

KEA *Nestor notabilis*   *Pl. 2*

Description: 18″–19″. *Olive-green above and below*, underparts a little fainter green; *scarlet underwing* (coverts and axillaries); *dull scarlet rump*; *blue outer margins wing quills*; feathers of body plumage and wing-coverts all with dark crescentic tips. Tail quills blue-green with a subterminal black band, and a series of orange-yellow bars on the inner web of each feather. Brown patch below eye. Adult: cere dark brown; bill dark brown; feet dark grey. In young birds cere, eyelids and base lower mandible are yellow, feet yellowish; this colour lost finally at the end of the second year in the female and at end of third year in male (J. R. Jackson). In juvenal plumage crown yellowish.

The Kea has a considerably more slender bill than the Kaka; in female upper mandible comparatively little arched, but longer and prominently arched in the male.

When Kea is seen in forest, where it may be confused with Kaka, the presence of much green in the plumage is a reliable field marking; both species have scarlet underwing patches.

Voice: Call *keaa* is delivered mainly in flight; has a variety of softer and conversational calls. It lacks the musical whistle of the Kaka but has a similar subsong at the nest (J. R. Jackson).

Habitat and range: Restricted to the South Island mountain area; up to *c.* 1870 only in southern districts (S. of Hurunui River), including Fiordland, but has subsequently extended into high country of Nelson and Marlborough. Despite this habitat, the Kea is not limited to the alpine zone: recent field studies by J. R. Jackson have shown that it obtains much of its food (leaves, buds and fruits together with insects) in the forests clothing mountain valleys, and, further, nests in high-level forests or near the forest edge. Ranges widely to the alpine grassland and subalpine scrub for the fruits abundant in autumn; commonly feeds also on the open river flats. Takes nectar when available.

The Kea has received wide publicity as an inveterate sheep-killer: while Keas certainly feed on dead sheep and carrion, they can at most be accused of only the occasional killing of healthy animals. J. R. Jackson, after assessing all the evidence available on the subject, states: " It is credible that Keas do attack sheep trapped in snow, sick sheep, sheep injured by falls or sheep they mistake as dead. When such a sheep reacted they would take flight, but return when it relaxed. If such occurs, the evidence suggests it must be very rarely." (*Notornis*, 10, 33–8: 1962.)

Breeding: Nests on the ground in a hole or crevice between rocks, sometimes in a hollow log; twigs, leaves, etc., are used as nesting material, although in a hollow log only powdered wood may be used. Site is commonly at the base of a rocky outcrop breaking through forest canopy. Breeding July–January (peak of laying in October); eggs 2–4, white. Incubation period over 21 days; mainly by female. Down of chicks is pale grey; bill and facial skin a vivid orange-yellow. Fledged in 13–14 weeks (J. R. Jackson).

Plate 16

HONEYEATERS, WATTLE-BIRDS, THRUSH AND PIGEON

RED-CROWNED PARAKEET *Cyanoramphus novaezelandiae*
Maori name: Kakariki. *Pl. 2*
Description: 10½″–12″ (male), 9″–10½″ (female). Although male is larger, and difference in size between the sexes is clearly seen in fresh plumage, note that this may be less distinct in the field when tail worn or moulted; the larger head and heavier bill of male is distinctive when pair seen together. Green above, yellowish green below; *crimson forehead and crown*, extending back to a little behind the eye; *crimson stripe forehead to eye*; *crimson patch* (larger in male) *immediately behind the eye*; outer webs of inner portion of wing quills and primary coverts *violet-blue*, visible when wings slightly spread or in flight; a *crimson patch on each side of rump*. Upper mandible pale steel blue, tip black, lower mandible blue-grey, darker at tip; feet greyish brown. The plumage is notably cryptic in effect amongst foliage, the bird being commonly located only by movement or call. Note that size of male of yellow-crowned species is equal to that of red-crowned female: it is not safe to distinguish these species on size alone. Yellow-crowned and Orange-fronted Parakeets lack red patch behind the eye.

Flight is direct and rapid, sometimes with side-slipping through the trees, and trailing tail is generally a useful guide to identification. The broad, graduated tail is spread as the bird swoops up to alight.
Voice: A rapid chatter is commonly given in flight, *ki-ki-ki-ki* (enables the bird to be located *after* it has taken flight). When perching this call may be given as a more relaxed, conversational chattering (often abbreviated); also a shriller one- to three-syllable call when perching, which is commonly rendered as " pretty dick," " do-be-quick," etc.; and a soft musical *tu-tu-tu-tu*, as well as a variety of conversational notes.
Habitat and range: Both Red-crowned and Yellow-crowned Parakeets were apparently birds of the mainland forest at all altitudes when European settlement began: subsequently after a brief period when they were reported in plague numbers in orchards and on crops, and seemed likely to have a potential as injurious species, both greatly decreased. The Red-crowned Parakeet is now very rare on the mainland, found only in larger forest tracts (cf. present distribution of Yellow-crowned Parakeet, below). It occurred on nearly all coastal islands, and was widespread (see subspecies) on New Zealand's outlying islands; most of the island populations remain in a flourishing state. Food consists of an extremely wide variety of vegetable matter ranging from fruits and seeds to leaves and buds. Commonly observed where abundant on islands obtaining such food as seeds of biddybid (*Acaena*), centres of ice-plant flowers, on the ground.

Coastal islands on which it occurs include Three Kings, Poor Knights, Hen and Chickens, Great and Little Barrier Islands, Moko-hinau, Mercuries, Aldermen, Kapiti, and Stewart Island with its numerous outliers. The Auckland Islands population cannot be separated from *novaezelandiae* of the mainland. Subspecies occupy: (*a*) Kermadec Islands—distinguished by the greater amount of blue on

wings and bluish green tail (*cyanurus*); (*b*) Chatham Islands—larger
size, emerald green facial area (*chathamensis*); (*c*) Antipodes Island—
larger size, plumage distinctly yellower above and below, blue on wings
more faint, orange-red (rather than crimson) crown, eye-stripe and
rump spots (*hochstetteri*); Macquarie Island—characters as for the
Antipodes I. subspecies (*erythrotis*) (extinct). Also extralimital subspecies of the Red-crowned Parakeet on Lord Howe Island (extinct),
Norfolk Island and New Caledonia.
Breeding: In hollow tree, eggs on powdered wood; on islands commonly in rock crevices. Breeding October–March; eggs 5–9, white.
Laying interval 24–48 hours, incubation starting with second egg;
incubation period 18–20 days; performed entirely by female (M. E.
FitzGerald) (in captivity). Chicks grey down. Fledging 5–6 weeks;
male assists in feeding chicks (food mainly transferred to female, but
male feeds chicks if female absent).

YELLOW-CROWNED PARAKEET *Cyanoramphus auriceps*
Maori name: Kakariki.   *Pl. 2*
Description: 9″–10½″ (male), 8″–9½″ (female). Differs from preceding
species in smaller size (size range of male overlaps female of Red-
crowned: note under Red-crowned Parakeet) and *absence of red patch
behind eye*; *crimson forehead* and *golden-yellow crown* (to a little behind
eye); crimson stripe from forehead to eye; *crimson patch on each side
of rump*. *Violet-blue* on wings. Bill and feet as in Red-crowned.
Voice: The same range of calls as in Red-crowned. Calls tend to be
higher pitched and weaker, and flight call *ki-ki-ki-ki* is noticeably so.
Habitat and range: As noted under Red-crowned Parakeet, both
species were originally widely distributed on the mainland; after a
period of decrease there has apparently been a fairly recent expansion
of this species which reports suggest is now moderately common in
larger forest tracts in both North and South Island (central mountain
chain of North, mountains from Nelson to Fiordland in the South
Island). Food, as far as known, the same as in the Red-crowned
Parakeet, but observations on islands where it occurs suggest that it is
less dependent on ground plants.
   Occurs on Three Kings, Hen, Big Chicken, Little Barrier, Kapiti,
and Stewart Island and surrounding smaller islands. On Solander and
Auckland Islands the mainland sub-species (*auriceps*) occurs. The
Chatham Island subspecies (*forbesi*) was originally found on Pitt, Mangare, Little Mangare Islands of this group, but is now represented only
by *c.* 100 birds on Little Mangare: larger size, and brighter generally,
with more yellowish underparts and emerald green on sides of face.
Breeding: As for Red-crowned; breeding recorded August–April;
eggs 5–9, white. Incubation 18–20 days; fledging 5–6 weeks (in
captivity).

Pl. 2
ORANGE-FRONTED PARAKEET *Cyanoramphus malherbi*
Description: 8″–9″ (male), 7½″–8½″ (female). Like Yellow-crowned

parakeet, but smaller with comparatively weak bill; rich green and yellowish-green of the two previous species is lacking, plumage being distinctly less yellowish ("cold pure green," Buller); *forehead bright orange* and *paler orange stripe forehead to eye*; *pale yellow crown* (to a little behind eye); *orange patch on each side of rump*; no patch behind eye. *Violet-blue* on wings. Bill and feet as in Red-crowned.

Voice: Apparently closely resembling Red- and Yellow-crowned.

Habitat and range: South Island only (records claimed from Hen and Little Barrier Islands unacceptable). Probably, as suggested by Buller, a species of higher altitude forest and scrub; recorded throughout the South Island mountain area from Nelson to Fiordland. According to Buller (1888) it was " by no means uncommon in the wooded hills surrounding Nelson "; recorded in the Nelson district recently.

Breeding: General breeding habits probably like the above species, but nothing yet recorded.

Pl. 2

ANTIPODES ISLAND PARAKEET *Cyanoramphus unicolor*

Description: 12"–13" (male), 11"–12" (female). The two species of parakeet occurring on Antipodes Island may be distinguished without difficulty: the present species is the largest of the New Zealand parakeets, and lacks prominent red or yellow markings. Body plumage slightly yellowish green above, strongly yellowish below—the yellow element is approximately as strong as in the Antipodes Red-crowned Parakeet (*C.n. hochstetteri*). Wing quills and primary coverts violet-blue as in other species. *Crown* to immediately behind eye and *whole facial area a brilliant emerald green* which shows prominently in the field and may have a bluish sheen. Head and bill massive as compared with Red-crowned, and the pale basal portion (blue-grey or bluish-white) of the bill is prominent in the field; the bill is comparatively broad and blunt. Feet stouter than in Red-crowned, greyish brown.

Voice: All calls the same as in Red-crowned, although conversational notes seemed softer and deeper (E. G. T.).

Habitat and range: Antipodes Island consists of steep seaward slopes rising to a tableland, the highest point, Mount Galloway, reaching 1320 feet. In area the island is approximately 24 square miles. The slopes and plateau are uniformly clothed in tussock, with extensive areas of prickly-fern (*Polystichum*); a little low scrub comprises various species of *Coprosma*. Both parakeets occur throughout on slopes and tableland; considerable portions of the slopes are invaded by penguins in October–May, and the colonies are freely entered by the present species. Observations on a visit in November 1950 (E. G. T.) suggested that *unicolor* depended to a considerable extent on food derived from the penguin colonies: skins and carcasses of dead penguins which had been eaten by skuas were constantly investigated for fat and probably fragments of flesh; older dried skins seemed to be especially attractive to the parakeets; eggs broken by skuas were also examined for remains of yolk and albumen. Observations of *hochstetteri* in November 1950 were all of leaf- and seed-feeding, but Oliver records this species as feeding on broken eggs. The diet of *unicolor* must be largely vegetable for part of the year, and probably includes leaves, seeds, and fruits of *Coprosma*, as for *hochstetteri*.

This species flies quite strongly.

Breeding: In holes in ground, or in bases of taller tussocks. Eggs white.

ROSELLA   *Platycercus eximius*   Pl. 2

Description: 13". Larger and more gaily coloured than any of the native parakeets. Head, neck and breast red; cheeks and lower throat white; " shoulders " blue; back black and yellow; *rump pale green*, very noticeable as bird flies away; abdomen yellow and green; under tail-coverts scarlet; tail tipped pale blue.

Often feeds on the ground. Where plentiful, gregarious after the nesting season.

Voice: A crisp, ringing *kwink*, sometimes single, sometimes rapidly reiterated.

Habitat and range: An Australian species, which became naturalised when caged birds escaped into the Waitakeres; now strongly established between Manukau Harbour and Houhora; rare south of Auckland but still extending its range northwards. There appear to be expanding pockets near Raglan and north of Wellington. Prefers open or lightly timbered country, but will enter denser forest. Disliked by orchardists.

In the South Island a small population surviving in the hills near Dunedin is said to include hybrids between Eastern (*P. eximius*) and Crimson Rosellas (*P. elegans*), which were released from a ship off Otago Heads about 1910.[1]

Breeding: Not studied in New Zealand, though the bird has clearly been breeding very successfully in the north.

WHITE (SULPHUR-CRESTED) COCKATOO   *Kakatoe*
galerita

Description: 20". White with a bright yellow crest; and a yellow tinge on underwing and under tail-coverts. Bill and feet black.

Flies strongly on broad rounded wings. Often feeds on the ground. Gregarious outside the breeding season. Very alert.

Voice: A raucous screech.

Habitat and range: A familiar Australian species, now well established in the North Island in two localities (*a*) the limestone country between the lower Waikato and Raglan; (*b*) the watersheds of the Turakina and Rangitikei. Also a small colony Wainuiomata Valley, Wellington. The hundreds of these cockatoos now wild in New Zealand are said to be sprung from escaped caged-birds, but some may be self-introduced. It is curious that the two main populations are near the west coast, where wind-blown stragglers might make a landfall; and it may be significant that in May 1959 after three days of strong westerlies a White Cockatoo was seen at South Kaipara Heads, so tired that it could fly only downwind.

[1] Feral Crimson Rosellas now appear to be breeding near Wellington (1964).

Breeding: Little recorded in New Zealand. Said to nest in a hole high in a big tree; perhaps also in limestone cliffs; but one of the few nests found in New Zealand was on the top of a pile of hay-bales close under the roof of a barn. Eggs 2–3, glossy white.

CUCKOOS: Cuculidae

The many species of true cuckoos (subfamily Cuculinae) which inhabit the Old World have few diagnostic features in common except that they lay their eggs in the nests of other birds. They have long been a byword for parasitism and general rascality.

Six members of this subfamily are known from New Zealand. The two which are essentially Neo-zelanic, namely the Shining and Long-tailed Cuckoos, are not at all alike in size, shape, colouring or voice. Both have achieved a certain distincton because of the very long oceanic crossings which their migrations entail before and after a breeding season spent in New Zealand.

The flying ability of cuckoos must be deceptively strong, as four other species reach New Zealand, despite its far isolation, as casual strays. Of these, three breed in Australia and Tasmania, two commonly, one rather more sparingly; the fourth breeds in eastern Asia and, like its European near relative, migrates south towards the end of the northern summer.

ORIENTAL CUCKOO *Cuculus saturatus*
Description: 13″. Closely resembles the famous cuckoo (*Cuculus canorus*) of the Old World. Head and back blue-grey; tail slaty-black spotted and tipped with white; wing-surface dark brown spotted white on the inner webs of the outer primaries; throat pale grey; *breast and abdomen closely barred black and white.* Eyelids yellow. Bill blackish above, greenish below; yellow round the gape. Legs and feet yellow. Juveniles are browner. This cuckoo like *C. canorus* has a rufous or " hepatic " phase.
Voice: " Four dull booming notes on a monotonous *hoo-hoo-hoo-hoo* not unlike the call of a " Hoopoe " or " a mellow triple hoot, *hoop, hoop-hoop.*" (Smithies)—not likely to be heard in New Zealand.
Habitat and range: Breeds in eastern Asia and migrates southwards, some reaching south-east Australia. A surprising number have been taken at Lord Howe Island. At least five recorded in New Zealand during summer months, one being as far south as Winton. One at Whangaroa perched on posts from which it dived to the ground to take worms.

PALLID CUCKOO *Cuculus pallidus.*
Description: 12″. Paler and slightly smaller than *C. saturatus,* and

without the abdominal barring. Upperparts a light uniform brownish-grey with white spotting on the wings and outer tail-feathers and a small white patch on the fore-edge of the wing; underparts light grey, the under wing being grey-brown barred with white. Females differ in being copiously marked with chestnut and buff on the head and back and the spotting on wings and tail is buff rather than white. Eyelids yellow. Glides like a hawk and often mobbed by small birds. Habitually perches on fence-posts.

Voice: " At times it seems to endeavour to run up a chromatic scale; so it is called the Scale Bird. At other times after three running notes, it repeats one note strongly. So persistent is the call that it is named in places the Brain-fever Bird." (Leach.) Often calls at night. The female's call is a hoarse single-noted *cheer* or *kheer*.

Habitat and range: The commonest and best-known cuckoo in Australia, where it is a migrant from the north arriving in Tasmania early in the spring. A very rare straggler to New Zealand recorded from Craig Flat (1941), Okarito (1941) and Greymouth (1942). In Australia honeyeaters are favoured as foster parents, but many other passerines are also victimised.

FAN-TAILED CUCKOO *Cacomantis pyrrhophanus*

Description: 10″. Head and upperparts dark blue-grey except for a white patch on the fore-edge of the wing below the shoulder; throat light-grey; breast rust-red, abdomen paler; tail dusky with white spots; eyelids yellow; legs and feet yellowish brown. Habitually raises and lowers its tail several times before and after flight.

Voice: A loud plaintive call often heard at night; or a shrill trisyllabic whistle; also a murmuring note, a melancholy *coo-coo* slurred. In Tasmania the first calls are heard in July.

Habitat and range: A common Australian species only partly migratory; some wintering even in Tasmania; but nomadic after the breeding season. Parasitic on a wide variety of small song-birds. Only once so far recorded from New Zealand; Governor's Bay, Canterbury, 1960.

SHINING CUCKOO *Chalcites lucidus*   *Pl. 17*

Other names: Pipiwharauroa, Whistler.

Description: 6½″. A small cuckoo, much more often heard than seen; about the size of a sparrow. Its true colours can only be appreciated in a good light. Upper surface metallic green with a golden or coppery glint; sides of face and underparts white, finely barred with glossy green, which may look black; lateral tail-feathers barred with white. Females similar but crown and nape more purplish bronze and the abdominal bars more bronzy. Bill black, rather broad. Feet black with yellowish soles. Young birds have prominent stripes on flanks; but barring on throat and breast is obscure.

Voice: " A series of double notes," upward slurs, several times repeated, followed by fewer downward slurs, the whole in a musical whistle with ventriloquistic effects " (Oliver). The full summer song is represented in Maori as *kui, kui, whiti-whiti ora, tio-o*. The call note, a clear *tsee-ew* or *tsiu*, may be heard from Shining Cuckoos as they pass in the night; and is much used at any time of the day when several of these cuckoos gather in a tall tree and fly in and out, chasing and calling excitedly.

Habitat and range: A summer migrant arriving from mid-August onwards but not widely distributed till October. Parasitic mainly on the Grey Warbler and so found throughout main islands south to Stewart and up to *c.* 4000 ft. a.s.l. Feeds mainly on insects, especially on the black hairy caterpillars of the Magpie Moth and often killed by cats among the cinerarias. Often also a casualty from flying into windows.

Singing ceases early in February and these cuckoos slip unobtrusively away to their winter quarters which extend over the Solomon Islands and Bismarck Archipelago. The New Zealand subspecies (*lucidus*) occurs irregularly on migration on Lord Howe and Norfolk Islands; and as a straggler in eastern Australia. Sometimes reported as wintering, especially in the north of the North Island.

Breeding: Needs intensive study. Courtship feeding occurs. Average number of eggs laid by one female in a season is quite unknown. Eggs greenish or bluish white to olive brown or dark greenish brown. Incubation period *c.* 12 days. The Grey Warbler is the usual foster-parent; but eggs have also been found in nests of Fantail, Tomtit, Silvereye and some of the smaller introduced passerines. In the Chatham Islands victimises the endemic warbler.

LONG-TAILED CUCKOO *Eudynamis taitensis*   *Pl. 17*

Maori names: Koekoea, Kawekawea, Kohoperoa.

Description: 16″. More often heard than seen; but voice and flight silhouette with very long tail are diagnostic. Upperparts dark brown, barred and spotted rufous, with white spots on head, back and wings; underparts white with dark longitudinal streaks. Females more rufous and slightly smaller. In juveniles the underparts are rufous; throat has broad dark stripes or irregular spots; and the white spots on back and wings are larger and much more conspicuous. Legs greenish-yellow.

Voice: A harsh, piercing, long drawn out screech *zzwheesht*, unlike any other sound in the bush. This call is used at night by these cuckoos on migration and in northern New Zealand is often the only evidence of their landfall in October. Another call is a rapid, ringing, prolonged *zip-zip-zip-zip*; or a loud *rrrrp pe-pe-pe-pe-pe*. " The *rrrp* had a ringing quality and was sometimes uttered alone, without the series of sharp *pe-pe-pe* notes " (A. T. Edgar).

Habitat and range: Arrives mostly in October. Breeds from Little Barrier to Stewart Island, its distribution depending almost entirely on the presence of suitable foster parents, i.e. in the North Island, Whiteheads, which it has followed into the exotic pine forests; and in the South and Stewart Islands, Yellowheads and Brown Creepers. On

Kapiti has been watched hunting and catching sunbathing skinks. During February there is a steady, if not very noticeable, movement northward throughout the main islands. The winter range covers a vast arc of the Pacific from the Marquesas and Austral Islands in the east, north to the Marshall and Caroline Islands and west to New Guinea. Present at all seasons on Raoul.

Breeding: Comparatively unknown. The three typical fosterers are: Whitehead, Yellowhead and Brown Creeper. Other species known to have been victimised are: Tomtit, Robin, Silvereye, Fantail (once), Greenfinch, Song Thrush; but nesting Tuis are strongly hostile. Egg, variable, e.g. creamy white blotched all over with purplish brown and grey; or pale flesh prettily spotted with brownish red and vandyke brown.

CHANNEL-BILLED CUCKOO   *Scythrops novaehollandiae*

Description: 24″. The giant of the cuckoos with a massive yellowish bill (4½″) and a conspicuous patch of bare red skin round the eye. Head, neck and underparts light grey; back and wings brownish-grey with some blackish barring; flanks finely pencilled; tail large and fanlike with a broad black subterminal band and a white terminal band narrowest at the tip.

Voice: A loud call often heard as this cuckoo flies high during rainy weather; described by Gould as a " frightful scream "; but Sharland considers it " melodious, though certainly strange in its trumpeting quality."

Habitat and range: Migrates from Indonesia to breed in Australia where " it recruits the aid of magpies, crows and currawongs to rear its offspring; " rare in the south-east and Tasmania. Known to have straggled to New Zealand only once; Invercargill, 1924.

OWLS: Strigidae

MOREPORK   *Ninox novaeseelandiae*

Maori name: Ruru.

Description: 11½″. *Brown above* with scattered buff flecks on head and neck, whitish flecks on remainder of upperparts (flecks may form a collar on hindneck, and crown may lack spots or they may take the form of radiating stripes); white forehead and face at base of bill, the bristles black; wing quills spotted white or buff on upper and prominently barred white or buff on lower surface; tail dark brown with obscure paler brown bars; *feathers of under surface have brown centres, and prominent white spots or stripes on outer margin, giving a mottled pattern,* the whole under surface being more or less washed with orange-brown (age differences or local variation in pattern of the Morepork remain to be clarified); brown and white barred undertail coverts; tarsus (feathered) yellowish brown to reddish buff; toes yellow or brownish yellow, dark brown claws; bill varies from dark brown with white ridge on upper mandible to white or yellow with dark brown cutting edges on both mandibles; iris golden yellow.

Distinguished from the Little Owl by the much browner general coloration; also by larger size, comparatively long tail and the more rounded outline of the head.

Voice: Characteristic call a clear and individually variable *more-pork* (also rendered, probably more accurately, as *quor-coo*); a common variation is repetitive and often prolonged *more-pork-pork-pork...* Also a scream apparently used in hunting and a vibrating *cree-cree*, according to Moon, mainly heard in the breeding season.

Habitat and range: Settled districts throughout New Zealand, as well as in forest; early records show that it was one of the native forest birds which adopted modified and exotic vegetation in the earliest stages of settlement; also in larger exotic plantations.

Commonly seen at dusk when it begins to hawk for insects from a prominent perch, frequently mobbed by small birds in the day-time. Food largely insect, especially wetas, moths, beetles, spiders; pellets examined by Cunningham (in the urban area of Masterton) in nearly every month of the year yielded remains of a high proportion of moths, with spiders and beetles of lesser importance, and a few remains of other invertebrates; other food items lizards, small birds, especially House Sparrows, rats and mice (Cunningham recorded bird remains throughout the year). According to Moon flying insects such as moths and huhu beetles are caught with the talons before being transferred to the beak. On outlying islands diet includes smaller petrels; Kiore (*Rattus exulans*); Short-tailed Bat once recorded (Stead). Cunningham found that the time of ejection of pellets was generally mid-afternoon or late afternoon.

Distribution includes nearly all of the off-lying islands including Three Kings south to Stewart, but not Chathams or sub-antarctic islands. Present in the Christchurch urban area until some time in the 1930s but is reported to have begun to decrease at about the time of a marked increase of the Little Owl.

Other subspecies range from Australia, and Norfolk and Lord Howe Islands, to New Guinea. North Island Moreporks (*venatica*) have been separated from those of South Island (*novaeseelandiae*), but the distinction between these subspecies remains to be satisfactorily established.

Breeding: In hollow tree or dense clump of vegetation (especially *Astelia*); sometimes in the open on a platform provided by a fork, or even in a depression on top of an old Sparrow's nest (Stead); once in a nesting-box. Breeding October–November; eggs 2 (occasionally 3), white. Laying at two-day intervals, incubation starting with the first egg; incubation period 30–31 days; by female (Moon). Chicks have first coat of white down when newly-hatched, gradually replaced (beginning at 10 days old) by the second down which is dark smoky brown (Stead). The chicks leave the nest at about 5 weeks old, at which stage much of the second coat of down remains and shreds of the first down form a white " halo " on the crown and nape; young brooded during day by the female until well fledged, the male remaining hidden nearby. Moon found that the male at first transferred food to the female, but later fed the chicks himself.

LAUGHING OWL *Sceloglaux albifacies*
Maori name: Whekau.

Description: 15″. A large owl with *yellowish-brown plumage striped with brown*; white stripes on scapulars (sometimes also feathers edged white rather than yellowish-brown on hindneck and mantle); *face white behind and below eyes, greyish towards the centre*, the feathers with brown shaft-lines; wings and tail brown with brownish-white bars; tarsus (feathered) yellowish to reddish-buff; toes " fleshy brown " or " pale-yellow " (Buller), dark brown claws; bill horn-colour, black at base; iris " dark reddish brown " (Buller).

Apart from size, the Laughing Owl differs from the Morepork in proportions, the tail being comparatively short.

Voice: According to early accounts the call from which this species received its name is heard mainly on dark nights accompanied by rain or drizzle, or before rain: it is " a loud cry made up of a series of dismal shrieks frequently repeated " (Potts). Buller records " a peculiar barking noise . . . just like the yelping of a young dog "; a melancholy hooting (or " cooeying ") note; also various whistling, chuckling and mewing notes (Buller's observations were on birds in captivity).

Habitat and range: Apparently, from early accounts and localities of specimens, inhabited mainly the low-rainfall districts of the South Island (Nelson, Canterbury and Otago), but penetrated deeply into the mountains of the central chain; also probably into Fiordland. Stewart Island, specimens obtained *c*. 1880. Buller thought from his observations of captive birds that it fed much on the ground, and notes that the legs are long for an owl; most of the early specimens were obtained from fissures in rocky areas.

It was plentiful during the first 40 years of colonisation, but by 1880 was extremely rare; no fully substantiated record since July 1914 (specimen found at Blue Cliffs, South Canterbury, by Mrs. A. E.

Woodhouse), but occasionally claimed, localities including South Canterbury (Hakataramea and adjacent districts), Wanaka and Te Anau.

The Laughing Owl occurred according to Maori tradition in the Urewera, but only two specimens have been collected (both in forest districts) in the North Island (Mt. Egmont, *c.* 1856; Wairarapa, *c.* 1868), the second forming the basis of Buller's description of the North Island subspecies (*S.a. rufifacies*). Sight records from Porirua and Te Karaka.

Food as shown by pellets included beetles, rats and mice (W. W. Smith), and all of these items were eaten in captivity; raw meat and lizards also readily taken.

Breeding: Amongst rocks, nest being lined with dry grass. Breeding, September–October; eggs 2, white. W. W. Smith who observed the breeding habits of several pairs in captivity found that incubation was carried out by the female. Nestling when freshly hatched covered with coarse yellowish-white down (Buller).

LITTLE OWL *Athene noctua*
Local name: German Owl.
Description: 9″. Upperparts dark brown liberally flecked with white; underparts whitish broadly streaked with dark brown; tail brown crossed by four whitish bands and tipped white. Flat-topped skull, low forehead and yellow eyes produce a stern frowning look. Distinguishable from Morepork by much smaller size, whitish face, broad band across throat and whitish boldly streaked undersurface; generally greyer. Female slightly bigger than male. Flight dipping.

Less nocturnal than Morepork. May often be seen on the wing by day and will feed on carrion, e.g. a car-killed rabbit in strong sunlight. Sometimes also seems deliberately to choose a perch where it can bask in the sun. Walks freely on ground.

Voice: Some calls are soft and plaintive; others louder and more strident. The call heard at any season is a clear arresting *kiewick* or terse whistled *whíu* or *kíew*. A slower, more rounded, rather melancholy *pee-ou* or *pāw-ut* is used at dusk in the breeding season.

Habitat and range: Between 1906 and 1910 several shipments were liberated in Otago whence other districts were stocked. Now established in the South Island east of the main range from Southland (Puysegur Point) to Marlborough and Golden Bay; more recently Westland, where probably increasing. Some were transferred to the North Island, where its status is uncertain, since a number of reported sightings have not been confirmed. Hunts mostly over open country, taking much of its prey on the ground; even digging for earthworms.

Breeding: Nest-site is usually a hole in an old building, tree or bank, e.g. rabbit burrow. Eggs 2–5, near Queenstown, normally 3; white, rounded. Incubation period 28 days; fledging *c.* 26 days.

AUSTRALIAN BARN OWL   *Tyto alba*

Other names: White Owl, Screech Owl.

Description: 13½″. Upperparts a beautiful soft light greyish brown tinged yellow, finely spotted blackish brown and white; underparts white; facial disc heart-shaped, large and prominent, white with buff margins; tail grey barred with buff. Flight soft, silent and buoyant. " Lovely are the curves of the white owl sweeping, Wavy in the dusk lit by one large star." (George Meredith.)

Voice: A menacing, long-drawn *skiirrr*, sometimes uttered during hunting-flight. Young in nest hiss and snore.

Habitat and range: The Barn Owl is the most widely distributed landbird that exists. Three specimens of the Australian race (*delicatula*) have been found in Westland, at Barrytown (1947), Haast (1955), Runanga (1960). There is no evidence that this useful rodent-eater has bred in New Zealand, but it could become established through wind-drifted strays from Australia.

SWIFTS: Apodidae

Somewhat swallow-like in appearance and behaviour, but with very long narrow scythe-like wings and short tails. Structurally quite distinct, especially the feet, of which the toes are directed forward. Hence swifts do not perch like swallows but, for rest, cling to the sides of trees, rocks or walls. In fine weather swifts generally fly high and fast and so escape notice, but depressions may force them to fly low over open water where insects are abundant.

Two species which breed in north and east Asia commonly migrate to Australia. Only rarely are they reported in New Zealand.

FORKED-TAILED SWIFT *Apus pacificus*
Description: 7″. Upperparts brownish black with greenish gloss; *rump white*; *tail strongly forked*; chin and throat whitish; underparts obscurely barred. Wings long and slim with a span of 16″. In Australia has been noted hawking insects in company with Tree-martins, which by comparison look diminutive.

Habitats and range: Breeds in eastern Asia, migrating south and sometimes straggling to New Zealand, viz. Taranaki, December 1884; Karamea 1952; South Westland 1957; Southland 1960.

SPINE-TAILED SWIFT *Chaetura caudacuta*
Description: 8″. At first glance very dark, with swept-back wings. Larger than Fork-tailed Swift; forehead, chin, throat and *under-tail coverts white*, the white passing up the flanks to lower back; chest, abdomen and back brown; crown, wings and tail shiny gun-metal blue; tail short and squarish with feather-shafts protruding as fine spines, but not likely to be seen in a bird flying free.

Habitat and range: Breeds in north-eastern Asia, migrating south, regularly to Tasmania but in varying numbers. Has straggled to Macquarie. From time to time considerable invasions occur, the most notable being in 1942–3 when, between November and March, strays were widely reported from Whangarei to Stewart Island and flocks appeared in Westland. In New Zealand these powerful swifts have been noted circling a hill top, e.g. Rangitoto on 19/4/58; and a small island, e.g. Stephen Island on 19/11/58.

KINGFISHERS: Alcedinidae

Forest kingfishers (subfamily Daceloninae)—including both the New Zealand Kingfisher and the Kookaburra—are an Old World group, differing from the fishing kingfishers (subfamily Alcedininae) in their broader, more flattened bills and more varied habits; the subfamily includes a number of species which never go near water, and others living on both aquatic and terrestrial foods.

KINGFISHER   *Halcyon sancta*   *Pl. 2*
Maori name: Kotare.
Description: 9½″. Crown, mantle and scapulars *deep sea-green*, tinged with olive; back, rump and wing-coverts *ultramarine with green reflections*; *wing and tail quills cobalt*, brown inner webs; a broad band of black passing back from angle of mouth encircles the neck and below this is a buff or reddish-buff collar; crown edged with ultramarine (often a white or buff spot or band divides this from the black hindneck); a spot of buff or reddish-buff behind nostrils passes back as a faint stripe above the eye; under wing-coverts and axillaries buff; throat white to buffy-white; *breast buffy-white to deep reddish-buff* (the latter only strongly developed in the male, probably intensified with age); bill black, base of lower mandible pinkish-white; feet brown.

Immature plumage like adult, but feathers of breast and of pale collar are broadly margined with brown; successive plumages retain narrow brown margins, most adults showing some trace.
Voice: A penetrating *kik-kik-kik* is given occasionally throughout the year, but delivered repeatedly in spring and summer. For about a month before nesting begins, chasing and other mating displays are accompanied by a loud *kreel*, generally repeated from six to eight times, or by a scream; the scream is also given as an alarm note, especially when an intruder is near the nest.
Habitat and range: Occupies a remarkably wide range of habitats, and, as these include nearly all types of habitat associated with man, it has probably increased as the result of settlement: it is a bird of the more open portions of the forest, and of open country with scattered trees, lake shores, rivers and streams, and the coast (especially tidal estuaries). Commonly uses power and telephone wires as a perch and man-made excavations, including road cuttings, provide nesting sites.

Food items recorded are: worms, insects and spiders, crabs and other crustaceans, shell-fish, small fish, tadpoles, lizards, mice and occasionally small birds, even ducklings. Prey is captured by a sudden dash from a prominent perch; killed by beating against the perch before swallowing. Stead found that flies and other insects were caught in his garden at flowering shrubs in winter, the Kingfishers either taking the insect off the flower in passing, or diving straight on to the foliage, stopping themselves from penetrating too far by keeping their wings spread. According to Stead's observations, when diving for fish or water insects the Kingfisher may " flop " into the water with out-stretched neck, so that its body is barely submerged; sometimes, however, it dives into the water " going in with bill, neck and body in a straight line, and wings clapped tight to the sides, after the manner of a Gannet."

Moon states that a Kingfisher was seen bathing from an overhanging branch: it splashed clumsily into the water several times in succession, each time giving a few wing-beats in the water before flying back to its perch, and finally began to preen.

There are numerous observations of a seasonal change in distribu-tion, although possibly increased numbers, e.g. on coastal estuaries in winter, result from a local dispersal to a new food supply rather than migration; some are always present throughout the year in inland districts.

The New Zealand Kingfisher (*H. s. vagans*) is found throughout New Zealand and on most off-lying islands from Kermadecs and Three Kings south to Stewart but not at Chathams or sub-antarctic islands. Very common in northern districts, ranging up to *c.* 2500 ft. a.s.l. in the centre of the North Island; rather scarce over much of the South Island, especially inland. The species ranges from the Loyalty Islands to New Caledonia, Australia, Norfolk Island and Lord Howe Island. **Breeding:** In holes bored in a rotting tree or bank; tunnelling is started by perching opposite the site and flying straight at the selected spot; the birds strike with some force and drive the bill into the wood or earth; finally when the hole is some inches deep they sit in it and begin to peck at the material. Tunnel is inclined slightly upwards, length 4–9 inches; the nest-chamber 6–8 inches in diameter. The same tunnel may be occupied year after year. Eggs placed on earth or wood without nesting material. Breeding October–January; eggs 4–5, white. Incubation period *c.* 18 days (Moon). Chicks naked when hatched, but soon sprout spiny pin-feathers and these break out to reveal the juvenal plumage; food remains and excrement are allowed to accumulate in the nesting tunnel. Moon found that the chicks were fed (by both parents) at intervals of 10–30 minutes; chicks have a characteristic rasping note and call frequently. Fledging *c.* 24 days.

KOOKABURRA *Dacelo gigas*
Other name: Laughing Jackass.
Description: 18″. A giant kingfisher, not highly coloured, which escapes notice by sitting still on top of a pole or stump. Head, neck and underparts buffy-white; crown streaked brown; dark stripe through eye; back and wings brown; *pale blue spots* on shoulder and *white patch* at base of wing quills, conspicuous in flight which is laboured and undulating; tail brown, barred with black and tipped white. Bill long (2½″) and heavy, black above and white below.

Voice: A loud raucous laugh, most often heard at dawn and sunset When one bird starts laughing, others in the vicinity will join in.

Habitat and range: Several small shipments from Australia were liberated between 1866 and 1880. The only district in which a small, but apparently fairly stable, population survives is along the western shore of the Hauraki Gulf among the creeks and islands between Cape Rodney and Whangaparaoa Peninsula. Wanderers sometimes reach Little Barrier, Auckland, Kaipara and Whangarei. Elsewhere Kookaburras have been reported in places and circumstances which strongly suggest that they were wind-blown strays from Australia.

Breeding: Nest in a hole in a tree or bank. Eggs 2–4, white, rounded. Little known about breeding in New Zealand. Apparently only one or two young are reared.

ROLLERS: Coraciidae

Rollers, so named from their spectacular aerial acrobatics, are found throughout the temperate and tropical countries of the Old World. One successful eastern species (*Eurystomus orientalis*) has numerous sub-species, one of which (*pacificus*) is a common summer migrant to eastern Australia from the tropics and an occasional visitor to New Zealand.

BROAD-BILLED ROLLER   *Eurystomus pacificus*

Other names: Australian Roller, Dollar-bird.

Description: 11½″. Head and neck dark brown; throat dark blue; upperparts brownish green; underparts pale green; wings blue and green with a *greenish white or silvery blue patch on the primaries*, conspicuous in flight; tail bluish green with black tip. Bill and feet red. Juveniles are less brightly coloured with greenish throat and dusky bill.

Flight strong and buoyant with slow, steady wing beats. Attention may be drawn to a Dollar-bird by its peculiar aerial antics as it hawks insects near trees or over open country.

Voice: A harsh grating chuckle or rough *treek treek* commonly uttered during swallow-like flight towards dusk, when these birds become more active.

Habitat and range: Dollar-birds arrive in south-eastern Australia from the tropics from late September onwards; and after breeding, leave between February and April. Though very rare in Tasmania, they have been recorded more than a dozen times in the North and South Islands between 1881 and 1956, mostly from districts near the west coast as far south as Ross, but also from as far east as Havelock North, Tikitiki and Great Barrier and as far south as Fortrose (1967). Some of the occurrences have been in spring, especially November, but most have been in late summer, when young birds on northward passage from south-eastern Australia may be drifted across the Tasman by adverse winds.

Plate 17

SOME BIRDS OF GARDEN, BUSH AND SCRUB

NEW ZEALAND WRENS:
Acanthisittidae

An endemic family, of doubtful relationships as affinity has been suggested both with the Old World pittas and South American antpipits.

RIFLEMAN *Acanthisitta chloris*   *Pl. 17*
  Other names: Titipounamu, Thumbie (Nelson).
  Description: 3″. A forest species generally located by very high-pitched " zipt " notes given by pairs or family groups passing through the trees. Sexes differ: *male* clear bright yellowish-green above, white (tinged buff) below; wing with *yellow bar and behind this a white spot*; yellow rump and flanks; faint dark eye-stripe and above this *distinct white eyebrow-stripe*; tail black tipped with buff; slightly upturned black bill; *female* striped dark and light brown above but otherwise like the male. In summer and autumn family parties include immatures, both sexes striped as in the female. The wholly white underparts provide the best distinguishing feature at a distance in the upper foliage. Distinctly smaller than the Grey Warbler and other small forest species but appears much smaller because of comparatively short tail. A distinctive feature is vigorous flicking movement of the wings when standing on a branch, not seen in any other bush bird.
  Voice: Irregular sharp, high-pitched *zipt-zipt-zipt-zipt*; sometimes a single *zipt* but often rapid bursts. When bursts heard two or more birds probably often call together. Fledged young *tsit-tsit* (Soper).
  Habitat and range: Now found throughout North Island (except northern third from a line approximately through Te Aroha), South Island and Stewart Island in all bush areas; also Great Barrier and Little Barrier Islands. Also readily occupies modified habitats with some native forest remnants. Feeds freely in exotic trees near native forest, and has been recorded in larger exotic plantations although it is not one of the abundant species in the latter (has been recorded in hedgerows in Taranaki, and gorse near Wellington). Its range now includes a high proportion of higher altitude beech forest on the mountain chains of both main islands but it was probably originally widely distributed in lowland mixed forest. Habits are to a large extent those of a tree-creeper, searching crevices in bark, and amongst epiphytic mosses and lichens, on trunks and branches of larger trees; also explores all portions of the tree as far as the twigs, both in the second storey and canopy. Only rarely feeds on the forest floor. May be seen arching neck to extract food items with the comparatively large bill, and hanging under a twig. Believed to be entirely insectivorous, mainly insects and spiders.
  The subspecies described for the North (*granti*) and South Island (*chloris*) are doubtfully distinct, the yellow rump being greenish in

granti. In Fiordland and mountain districts of Otago and Nelson specimens with brighter yellow rump and flanks have been obtained and distinguished subspecifically (*citrina*), but further field work and taxonomic study are needed.

Breeding: Nest ground-level to 60 ft. (average 10–20 ft.), generally in a hollow limb or crevice in bark; clay barks of old bush roads are often favoured; constructed of abundant material, loosely woven with lining of feathers, entrance at the side. Has nested in settled habitats in the neighbourhood of native vegetation, sites including stone walls, a hollow post and beneath corrugated iron roof. Records suggest generally double-brooded. Breeding recorded August–January; eggs 4–5, white. Both parents perform incubation and feed chicks. According to M. F. Soper, the young of the first brood sometimes assist in feeding second, and Soper's observations show that this species is frequently polygamous.

BUSH WREN *Xenicus longipes*   *Pl. 17*

Other names: Matuhi, Tom Thumb Bird (Stewart Is.).

Description: 3¾″. In comparison with Rifleman of generally stouter build. Dark brown head and face; dark green back and wings; *above eye prominent white stripe*; prominent *yellow patch surrounded by dark brown* at angle of wing; underparts *grey on breast and abdomen, yellowish-green sides and under tail*. Female duller. Slightly upturned bill. The Bush Wren shares with the next species, the Rock Wren, the habit of bobbing the whole body, a vigorous action repeated frequently on alighting.

Voice: Common call note a " subdued trill " (Buller); Guthrie-Smith records a " faint rasping sound " and a loud cheep for the Stewart Island Bush Wren.

Habitat and range: In remote forests, and of extremely limited range in North Island (in recent years observed only at Waikaremoana) and rare in the South Island. Formerly widespread (apparently not in northern North Island), although never as abundant as the Rifleman.

Little known of its habits, but it is apparently less creeper-like than the Rifleman; feeds less on trunks and more amongst foliage, and according to Buller only rarely on the ground. Entirely insectivorous as far as known

North Island (*stokesi*) and South Island (*longipes*) subspecies distinguished only by minor differences—mainly yellower sides in *stokesi* —have been described; a third and more distinctive subspecies on Stewart Island and its neighbouring islets (*variabilis*) has generally browner plumage and less distinct eyebrow-stripe.

Breeding: Nesting habits probably as in Rifleman, although little information on record. On the mainland it probably nests above ground level; on the outlying islets of Stewart Island the nest is commonly in an old petrel burrow, or other hollow in the ground, and sometimes in a prostrate log or clump of fern. Eggs, December (South Island); November–December (Stewart Island area), 2–3, white. Incubation by both parents, and young fed by both (Stewart Island Bush Wren).

ROCK WREN *Xenicus gilviventris* Pl. 17

Description: 3¾″. Habitat is distinctive, mainly open screes, moraines and fell-fields of mountains above the bushline; also enters the zone of subalpine scrub. In colour general shade browner than the preceding species, dull green above and grey-brown below, with a yellow wash on the sides; *creamy white stripe above eye; narrow pale yellow stripe* with *black surrounding patch* at the angle of the wing. The sexes differ slightly, the back being brown faintly washed with green in the female. The comparatively large feet and long hind toe form an additional distinguishing feature. Bobs the body vigorously on alighting; also a " bowing movement " (Soper).

Voice: Common call consists of three notes, the first being accentuated; also a thin pipe. Calls penetrating and may carry for some distance.

Habitat and range: Only in South Island, where it extends from Nelson to Fiordland. Found in Fiordland at lower altitudes in subalpine scrub: a subspecies described from Fiordland (*rineyi*), with brighter green upper surface and brighter yellow on the sides, is still of doubtful status.

Feeds actively on the ground amongst alpine vegetation, and in scattered shrubs or dense subalpine scrub; the latter also furnishes shelter and is probably often inhabited in bad weather. Can fly fairly strongly, but normally flies only 5–6 yards between rocks when feeding. Feeds on fruits of alpine plants as well as insects, spiders, etc.

Breeding: In rock crevices in comparable sites to those of the two arboreal wrens; nest bulky, with entrance at side, and lined with feathers; eggs, September–November, 2–3, white. Both parents feed the young: food observed at Homer Tunnel was Orthoptera, moths and beetles (Soper).

A fourth species of wren, the Stephen Island Wren (*Xenicus lyalli*) discovered in 1894, became extinct almost as soon as discovered, the population on the island at that time being destroyed by a cat. In colour this species was mottled brown above, and yellowish below; the bill was stouter than in the mainland wrens. Although weak flight is suggested by the short, rounded wings and soft plumage, there is no clear evidence of flightlessness. The only observations were those of the lighthouse keeper on the island, Lyall, who saw them but twice, on both occasions in the evening. They ran like a mouse and " did not fly at all " (Rothschild).

LARKS: Alaudidae

SKYLARK *Alauda arvensis*

Description: 7″. Upperparts brown heavily streaked with dark brown, especially on the crown, with a whitish eye-stripe and a crest which can be raised at will; underparts buffish white with breast boldly streaked;

outer tail feathers pure white, conspicuous as bird arises; when also greyish-white edging along rear of wings is revealed. Bill short; hind-toe furnished with a very long claw. Has a crouching walk. Flight strong and slightly undulating with alternate spells of wing beats and "shooting" with closed wings. Often takes dust baths on country roads.

Voice: Note a liquid *chirrup*. Song a torrent of trills and runs, fast, variable and sustained—sometimes for as long as 5 minutes—delivered as it soars steeply or while poised at a considerable height, head to wind, or as it drops earthwards. Sometimes sings on the ground. Song may be heard in all months, but at a minimum mid-February to mid-April.

Habitat and range: Imported by the hundreds and widely released from 1864 onwards, they quickly became established in all types of open country up to 5000 feet. Introduced to Chatham Islands; self-introduced to Auckland Islands and Kermadecs. Some flocking in autumn and local movement, but no evidence as yet in New Zealand of regular migration. In Auckland in spring loose flocks are still present in country where local birds are paired and males singing strongly on territory.

Breeding: Nest a neat grass-lined cup in a hollow of the ground, e.g. hoof-print, well concealed by grass. Eggs, October–January, 3–7, greyish white thickly speckled brown, frequently with a darker zone. Incubation period *c.* 11 days; fledging up to 20 days. Two or three broods.

SWALLOWS AND MARTINS:
Hirundinidae

WELCOME SWALLOW *Hirundo neoxena* *Pl. 18*

Description: 6″. Forehead, throat and chest rufous; head and back blue-black; wings and tail dark brown; abdomen and under wing greyish white; tail forked, outer feathers elongated, inner feathers having a subterminal row of white spots. Flight swift, darting and graceful.

Voice: A twittering *twsit, twsit, twsit.*

Habitat and range: The Welcome Swallow, now usually treated as a race of the widely distributed Pacific Swallow (*H. tahitica*) is common in Australia, but prior to 1958 was known only as a rare vagrant to New Zealand, reported Northland (1920), Auckland Islands (1943),

Stewart Island (1953), Farewell Spit (1955). In 1958 at least three pairs are known to have nested near Rangaunu Bay, and others perhaps near Kawakawa. The increase has been spectacular. Common throughout Northland, south to Kaipara. Elsewhere in North Island breeding widely, especially Bay of Plenty, Hawker Bay, lakes of lower Waikato and Manawatu. In South Island, reported all provinces; breeding at Lake Ellesmere since 1961; now also Nelson and Marlborough.

Breeding: Nest a mud cup, strengthened with grass and lined with feathers. Most nests so far found in New Zealand have been in man-made sites, e.g. under concrete and wooden bridges, concrete culverts, a ramshackle jetty, a neglected launch swinging at anchor. Long breeding season, 2 or 3 broods being raised. Eggs August–February, 3–5, white, variably freckled with brown, sometimes with a denser zone towards the upper end. Incubation period *c.* 15 days; fledging 17–22 days. For some time after flying young return to nest to roost.

AUSTRALIAN TREE-MARTIN   *Hylochelidon nigricans*

Other name: Tree Swallow.

Description: 5¼″. Upperparts steely black *except rump which is dull white*; forehead rust-red; throat and chest grey; rest of underparts dull white. Tail slightly forked. Viewed from below brown undertail-coverts contrast with white of the remainder of the underparts. Smaller than Welcome Swallow from which it is readily distinguishable by white rump, small amount of red on head, and tail not deeply forked.

Habitat and range: Widespread in Australia and a common summer visitor to Tasmania, forming large flocks before departure. From time to time vagrants and even small flocks reach New Zealand; rarely in spring, more often in autumn when wind-drifted migrants, probably from Tasmania, have occurred, especially in the province of Nelson or near Farewell Spit. Elsewhere in the North and South Islands widely reported from Hick's Bay to Oamaru; but rather anomalously,

not from Auckland or North-land. Reported as wintering Blenheim (1878) and Featherston (1946). A typical swallow in its feeding habits, hovering and dipping over rivers and lakes or hawking insects around trees.

Breeding: A pair is said to have nested successfully in a mill at Oamaru in 1893. In Australia normally nests in holes in trees, but sometimes uses ventilators and suitable cavities in buildings.

CUCKOO-SHRIKES: Campephagidae

BLACK-FACED CUCKOO-SHRIKE *Coracina novaehollandiae*
   Description: 13″. Mainly a uniform bluish dove-grey; but forehead, face, throat and primaries black; abdomen and *tip of tail white*, conspicuous in flight. Instead of a black face, young birds have a dark line through the eye and whitish underparts. Flight strong and undulating. Easily approachable.
   Voice: A curious soft churring call.
   Habitat and range: This is a highly successful species, of which there are nineteen accepted races extending over India, south-eastern China and Australasia. Common in Australia and Tasmania where it is a partial migrant. Recorded in New Zealand about a dozen times from Invercargill to Kaipara, mostly near the west coast. It appears that most of those which have reached New Zealand have been young birds, wind-drifted across the Tasman on their first northward migration. One at Pouto, near North Kaipara Heads, was present from June to September. Habitually chooses a conspicuous perch from which to swoop cuckoo-like upon its prey. Will feed on the ground on insects and worms. Also eats fruit, such as mulberries and boxthorn berries.

BULBULS: Pycnonotidae

Bulbuls are a large tropical family of Africa and Southern Asia. Some species are popular cage-birds and have become established as wild birds outside their normal range. Thus the Red-whiskered Bulbul (*Pycnonotus jocosus*) is now common in the suburbs of Sydney N.S.W.; and the Red-vented Bulbul (*P. cafer*) thrives in Fiji.

   In 1952 it was suspected that a species of bulbul was present in Auckland; but their identity as Red-vented Bulbuls was not established till 1954 when pairs were proved to have bred or to be breeding in at least three suburbs. The Department of Agriculture decided that they were undesirable aliens and a determined and apparently successful attempt was made to exterminate them. None has been reported since 1955.

RED-VENTED BULBUL *Pycnonotus cafer*
   Description: 8″. About the same size as a Starling, but slimmer and with a longer tail. Head and throat glossy black; breast dusky; back sooty brown with wavy grey lines. Rump white, noticeable in flight; tail black with white tip. Abdomen grey, under tail-coverts red. Bill and feet black. Sexes alike. An important field character is the triangular crest, " like a Roman helmet."
199

Voice: Described as " cheerful and attractive " though it has " only one or two call notes and no song " (Whistler). The most common call-note heard in Auckland was a low, scratchy, double croak *cark-cark*, but single notes of more musical quality were sometimes uttered. **Habitat and range:** The species has a wide range in India and south-eastern Asia with numerous races. Apparently about 1952 some (of the subspecies *bengalensis*) escaped or were released from a ship in the Auckland harbour and adapted themselves to a new climate and environment. None seems to have survived the order for their suppression.

FLYCATCHERS: Muscicapidae

In this large Old World family (distribution: Europe, Africa, Asia together with many Pacific Islands) the bill is typically broad at the base surrounded by abundant bristles. A habit almost universal in the family (except in the whistlers) is to capture insects in the air with short flights from a prominent perch; flight when hawking erratic. The characteristics mentioned so far apply to the fantails (Pacific, Australia, New Zealand) which constitute a subfamily—Rhipidurinae. In the genus *Petroica* (Pacific, Australia and New Zealand) facial bristles are sparse, and the legs comparatively long (especially long in the New Zealand Robin): birds of this genus obtain insects by searching in foliage and on branches, or on the ground—practically never by hawking. The family includes also the subfamilies Monarchinae (paradise flycatchers and allies of Africa, Asia and Australia) and Pachycephalinae (the whistlers of Australia and the Pacific).

FANTAIL   *Rhipidura fuliginosa*
Maori name: Piwakawaka.
Description: $6\frac{1}{2}''$ (tail $3''$–$3\frac{1}{2}''$ beyond coverts). Readily identified by characteristic proportions—rounded head and long tail—and tail spread for display; tail closed in flight except when manœuvring. Birds of normal colour pattern (" Pied Fantail ") make up most of the population in North Island, but the " Black Fantail " (i.e. dark phase) accounts for perhaps a quarter of the population of the South Island subspecies; dark phase absent in Chatham Island subspecies. Pied Fantail dark olive brown above, darker on the head, with rich yellowish buff under-parts; white throat, and band of sooty black across the upper breast; white eyebrow stripe and faint buffy-white wing-bar; the two central tail feathers are dark, and the remaining feathers have white inner webs, producing vertical stripes on the spread tail; bill black and feet dark brown. In the Black Fantail plumage is sooty black above, chocolate brown below: a small white patch may be present behind the eye.

Lively movements include sidling and posturing with tail fully spread, but tail sometimes folded when it frequently hangs down.

Voice: Common note a penetrating *cheet*; also repetitive chattering derived from the same note. Call notes sometimes merge into a not unmusical song, which may be well sustained.

Habitat and range: Common in forest of all types, but just as familiar in town and country gardens, parks, hedgerows, shelter belts and exotic plantations; it evidently adopted man-made environments and modified native vegetation at an early stage of settlement, and has extended its range into all settled districts providing trees and shrubs. Present on most of the nearer islands, including Three Kings, Poor Knights, Hen and Chickens, Great and Little Barrier, Mayor, Kapiti, Stewart Island and outliers, but not on distant outlying islands except the Chatham Islands.

The North Island (*placabilis*), South Island (*fuliginosa*) and Chatham Island (*penitus*) subspecies are distinguished by the amount of white on the tail feathers (except for two dark central feathers): approximately half of each feather white in North Island subspecies, two-thirds of feather in South Island subspecies and three-quarters in Chatham Island subspecies. In the North Island form undersurface of spread tail greyish-white, in South Island and Chatham forms almost pure white; breast is somewhat darker in South Island and Chatham Island than in North Island form.

Breeding: Nest a compact, often tailed, cup on a slender branch or fork 6–20 feet from the ground, constructed of fibres, moss, bark, horsehair, etc., and finished off with an outer coating of spider's web. Three, four or even five broods August–January; eggs 3–4, cream, spotted grey and brown, most abundantly at the larger end where a ring of denser spots may be present. Both parents incubate and feed the chicks. Incubation period 15 days, fledging 15 days in North Island Fantails.

TOMTIT *Petroica macrocephala*
Other names: Miromiro (North Island), Ngirungiru (South Island), Wheedler, Butcher-bird (Taranaki).
Description: 5″. Large-headed and short-tailed. Sexes differ: *Male.*—Prominent pattern of black and white: head and upperparts jet black, the black throat forming a clear-cut line above the breast; a small white forehead spot and *prominent white L-shaped wing-bar*; three outer tail feathers on each side white with black tips forming *conspicuous white patch on each side of tail* when spread, or partly spread; bill black; feet brown, orange-yellow soles. *Female.*—*Above greyish-brown*; brownish-white forehead spot is somewhat indistinct; wing-bar small and faint as compared with that of the male, and washed with buff; *tail-patches white*. *Immature male* resembles adult female, except that the head and throat are dark grey.

Comes readily—especially the male—to examine an intruder, and aggressive behaviour including raising of frontal feathers, wing drooping or fluttering, and darting flights accompanied by bill snapping, is characteristic.
Voice: Call note of male a penetrating *swee*; faint *seet* in female. Male song a high-pitched trill that has been vocalised as *Willoughby willoughby* (Buller); *ti oly oly ho* and *yodi yodi yodi* (Fleming). According to Fleming the female occasionally, when excited, utters a whispered warble similar to the male's song.
Habitat and range: Forest, forest remnants, mature exotic plantations, even mainly exotic cover near native forest, are inhabited by this species: original range—reduced greatly by forest clearing—is thus to some extent being recovered, and this is one of several forest species at present showing a tendency to expand under settled conditions. According to Fleming is " sedentary, undertaking few small-scale and no large-scale seasonal movements " and in most areas pairs evidently remain together, in the general area of their nesting territory, all through the year. Insectivorous, much of its food being obtained from trunks and branches, and some from the forest floor; Fleming describes the typical " darting from a watching perch to pick up insects on the bark."

The North Island Tomtit (*P. m. toitoi*) (slightly smaller than South Island and Chatham Island subspecies, male with pure white underparts, female greyish white underparts) is distributed throughout the North Island (rare in Northland where it is restricted to larger forest areas); also Hen and Chickens, Little and Great Barrier and Kapiti Islands. The South Island Tomtit (*P. m. macrocephala*) (size larger; breast and abdomen yellow, colour being of varying intensity ranging in the male from lemon-yellow, with deep orange on the upper breast, to individuals that "appear white-breasted in the field"; underparts of female faintly washed with yellow) is found throughout the South Island, on Stewart Island and outliers, and on Solander Island. The Chatham Island Tomtit (*P. m. chathamensis*) (like the South Island Tomtit, differing mainly in the browner upperparts of the female, and the greater length of tarsus) is now restricted to the larger forest remnants on the main island of the group; also Pitt Island, Mangare, Little Mangare and South East Island.

Tomtit (*Petroica macrocephala toitoi*)

The two remaining Tomtits of the New Zealand region exhibit notable departures from the description given above for the species, although they may be regarded as strong subspecies of *P. macrocephala*. The Auckland Island Tomtit (*P. m. marrineri*) is, like the South Island and Chatham Island forms, yellow-breasted; however, the female is superficially similar in plumage pattern to the male, and thus strikingly different from females of other subspecies; the upperparts of the female are dull black instead of glossy black; the fledgling plumages also differ in more nearly resembling the adult condition. Fleming, who pointed out these characters in *marrineri*, states that a tendency towards "maleness" can be observed in the plumage of many females of the Chatham Island Tomtit, *P. m. chathamensis*.

The Snares Island Tomtit (*P. m. dannefaerdi*) is entirely glossy black except for wing and tail which are brownish black; female plumage with slightly less gloss. According to Fleming, field observations in 1944 (R. A. Falla) and in 1947 (R. A. Falla, C. A. Fleming, E. F. Stead) showed that the song and habits agree with those of the New Zealand Tomtits; "the song is a typical Tomtit warble, which could be matched within the range of variation in other races of *macrocephala*." The total population is of the order of some hundreds of breeding pairs; mainly in the *Olearia lyallii* scrub that clothes much of the main island; nests well hidden in hollow logs or holes in trees, generally close to the ground, also among rocks in tussock areas.

Breeding: Nests from ground level to 30 feet; average 6–15 feet (except Snares Island Tomtit which nests near ground level). Site is generally sheltered from above in a hollow in a trunk, a rock crevice or under vegetation, but occasionally in an unsheltered position in a fork. Material moss, scraps of bark, cobwebs, with lining of feathers; built by female rarely assisted by male. Female fed by male throughout nesting period. Highly territorial; male selects nest site. Breeding August–February; double-brooded; eggs 3–5, cream, with delicate yellowish- and purplish-brown spots, usually forming a denser zone at large end. Incubation by female. Incubation period of North Island Tomtit *c.* 17 days, fledging 17–18 days (Wilkinson); incubation of South Island Tomtit, 15 days (Jensen), 16 days (Potts). Both parents feed young.

ROBIN *Petroica australis*
Maori name: Toutouwai.

Description: 7″–7½″. Dark slaty grey upper surface, together with long legs and upright stance are characteristic. Differs from Tomtit in absence of tail pattern, faint wing-bar and much reduced sexual dimorphism. *Male*—head, upperparts, sides and throat dark grey, meeting the pale underparts in a definite line; wings and tail brownish black; white forehead spot; on inner webs of the mid-wing feathers is a white spot which is not generally visible, but faint buff spots on the outer webs of the same feathers form a weak wing-bar; bill black; feet brown, yellow soles. *Female*—slightly browner and paler, with a reduced pale breast and abdomen, and with throat and sides not sharply marked off from the pale underparts.

Tameness and tendency silently to inspect the intruder are characteristic, and it has a pattern of aggressive behaviour essentially similar to that described above for the Tomtit; a habit often noted is spreading of white frontal spot especially to warn off a straying Robin in the territory, but also in display to a human intruder.

Voice: Call note is a short chirp. The song is varied and sustained, according to Wilkinson's observations on Kapiti, delivered frequently for half an hour at a stretch, and broken only by very short pauses. " Beginning with slow, almost plaintive notes, the song soon gains in volume, until it is ringing through the bush with almost startling vehemence. The variety of notes is astonishing. . . . Usually when singing, the Robin chooses a perch fairly close to the ground . . . never does it perch on an exposed branch, like the Thrush does, but always keeps well under cover.[1] When near the end of its song, the pauses become more frequent and of longer duration, until it ceases altogether. The bird then hops on to the ground, where it obtains food."

Habitat and range: The present discontinuous distribution of the Robin is difficult to explain: although " chiefly confined to native forest in districts at least moderately remote from areas with high human populations " (Fleming), it readily enters second-growth scrub (e.g. on Kapiti Island and Stewart Island); is one of the forest species

[1] Wilkinson's Robins must have been unduly secretive! Both N.I. and S.I. Robins may sing from conspicuous perches.

now increasing in the exotic plantations of the Volcanic Plateau. It was probably originally universally distributed in forest or scrub. Like the Tomtit is insectivorous, but a much higher proportion of the food is taken on the ground; it does not make darting flights like those of the Tomtit to pick up food, but unlike the Tomtit spends much time hopping over the forest floor. Food includes worms (not regularly taken by the Tomtit) and a variety of invertebrates. The habit of " caching " surplus food has been several times observed. Fleming describes the Robin as " a bird of the lower stratum of the forest."

Like the Tomtit is sedentary and probably territorial throughout the year.

The North Island Robin (*P. a. longipes*) (throat mottled white; feathers of crown and back with white shaft streaks; breast, abdomen and under tail-coverts ivory white) is distributed discontinuously in forested areas of the central North Island from Mamaku (near Rotorua) to the East Cape district, and south to East Taranaki; west of Otaki (Tararua Range); also Little Barrier and Kapiti Islands. The South Island Robin (*P. a. australis*) (largest subspecies in average dimensions, and with proportionately shorter wing and longer tail; breast washed with lemon-yellow in male, this colour being of varying intensity; female whitish below; brownish dorsal plumage) is found on D'Urville, Chetwode and Pickersgill Islands (Marlborough Sounds region); scattered throughout Marlborough and Nelson in habitats ranging from manuka scrub to deep forest tracts; west of the Alps in Westland; and in scattered localities in Otago and Southland (comparatively abundant in the Manapouri–Te Anau area). The Stewart Island Robin (*P. a. rakiura*) (similar to *australis*, but slightly darker above; breast ivory white like that of North Island Robin) is found in the Stewart Island area on the main island and on Green, Jacques Lees, Tamaite-mioka and Pokowaitai, on which two last the population is unusually dense (A.B.).

Breeding: Nest in similar situations to those chosen by Tomtit, but usually favours lower level. Nest rather bulky, of twigs, fibres, moss, etc., bound together with spider web, and lined with treefern scales or soft grasses, etc.; built by female. Breeding September–February, double-brooded; eggs 2–3, cream with purplish-brown spots, denser at the larger end. Incubation by female; male's feeding of female persists throughout the period of mating, nest-building, incubation and fledging of the young. Incubation period of North Island Robin *c.* 17 days, fledging 19 days (Parkin); incubation of South Island Robin, 20 days, fledging 21 days (Richdale).

CHATHAM ISLAND ROBIN *Petroica traversi*
Description: 5½″–6″. Entirely brownish black; bill black; legs brownish black with yellow soles.

Habits as in Robin of mainland, including the characteristic erect posture (probably a character " related to the long tarsus shared by both species " (Fleming)).

Voice: Fleming described the song as somewhat similar to that of the North Island Robin " but not nearly so full in tone, nor so varied in composition."

Habitat and range: Fleming states—" It is inferred that the species at one time ranged throughout the Chatham Islands, but it had become extinct on the main Chatham Island before 1871." The remaining population of the Chatham Island Robin (estimated at 20–35 pairs in 1937) lives in the small area of coastal forest and the ledges of scrubby vegetation on the surrounding cliffs on Little Mangare Island.

Breeding: The only description of the nest is given by Fleming: " An empty nest, which I believe was a Robin's, was situated low down at the base of a branch and almost sheltered above by a higher branch. It was fairly bulky, with a small cup neatly lined with a few feathers " (Little Mangare). It is evidently strongly territorial, the intruders being inspected on Fleming's visit by the Robins " sometimes alone, sometimes both birds of a pair."

SATIN FLYCATCHER *Myiagra cyanoleuca*
Description: 6½″. Slightly longer than a Fantail and noticeably larger in the body. Males and females are very different. *Male*—back wings and tail glossy, blackish green; throat black; lower breast and abdomen white. *Female*—crown and nape dull blue black; rest of upperparts brown with faint bluish wash; *throat and breast rust red or tinted orange-red*, brightest on lower part of the throat; underparts dull white, sharply defined from the red of the lower breast. The tail of both sexes has narrow very pale brown, almost whitish, outer edges. Bill broad and short with typical flycatcher hairs round the base. Feathers at rear of crown slightly raised, but not forming a crest. Maintains a constant tremulous movement of the tail.

The female of the duller and slightly smaller Leaden Flycatcher (*M. rubecula*), a summer visitor to eastern Australia which might straggle to New Zealand, is very similar; but the red on throat and breast is less vivid and the lines of demarcation between the red and adjacent areas are less clearly defined.

Voice: A cheerful, loud piping whistle, *chee-ee*, *chee-ee*; and also a short rasping note.

Habitat and range: A fairly common summer migrant to the eastern states of Australia, reaching Tasmania in some numbers. Has been noted on board ships during its crossing of Bass Strait. Moves north in autumn to North Queensland and apparently to New Guinea and adjacent islands.

Only once recorded in New Zealand, a very active female near Gisborne, June 1963.

WARBLERS: Sylviidae

A large family of four rather diverse subfamilies, typical members small and with thin bill; bristles at base of bill well developed or absent. With few exceptions have a musical—often powerful—song; movements active as they search for food in foliage and crannies of twigs and branches. Insectivorous.

Subfamily Sylviinae (Europe, Africa, Asia, Indonesia, Australia and the Pacific) contains approximately three-quarters of the total species including *Bowdleria* of New Zealand. The Regulinae (goldcrests, known as kinglets in North America) are Eurasian and North American; Polioptilinae (gnatcatchers) restricted to the New World (United States to Brazil); Malurinae (East Indies to the S. W. Pacific, Australia and New Zealand) contains the blue wrens (*Malurus*) and their near allies of Australia and New Guinea, and some 20 aberrant genera, among which are *Gerygone* (East Indies, South-west Pacific, Australia and New Zealand), *Finschia* (New Zealand) and *Mohoua* (New Zealand).

FERNBIRD   *Bowdleria punctata*
Other names: Matata, Tataki Thrush (Foveaux St).
Description: 7″. Warm brown above, streaked dark brown; white below, with dark brown spots on throat and breast; flanks brown with dark brown streaks. Forehead and anterior portion of crown chestnut. *Tail feathers have a spine-like appearance* owing to the disconnected barbs of the webs and dark brown shafts; webs often much frayed.

Characteristically reluctant to take flight and will remain hidden

Plate 18

SOME BIRDS INTRODUCED BY MAN
(Swallow excepted)

even though movement of foliage is visible when moving through swamp vegetation, etc. Flight is for short distances (exceptionally, 50 yards). In flight the tail trails behind hanging down.

Voice: Mechanical double call consisting of a low and a sharp metallic note, also a single soft *click*. Rarely a warbled song of about six rather metallic notes (B. D. Bell). Pairs travelling through scrub may keep in touch, one calling *plik* and the other *choot*.

Habitat and range: Reduction of swamp- and fern-lands through agricultural development has greatly reduced the range of the Fernbird, which on the mainland inhabited drier swamps and adjacent scrub, bracken and the low rushes and stunted scrub clothing saltmarsh, gumland, *pakihi* and other poorer lands, up to 3000 feet. It is nevertheless widespread, although local. The early stages of settlement may have locally increased its range as bracken or low scrub regenerated on cleared forest lands, but most of these areas were subsequently developed, and became grassland. Now mainly in swamps, and the remaining undeveloped poorer lands (including the considerable *pakihi* areas of north-western and western South Island).

Pending a full study, both North and South Island Fernbirds are referred to *punctata* (size of spots on under surface used as a character to distinguish *vealeae* of North Island from *punctata* of South Island is variable); this form occurs on Great Barrier and on two of the Alderman Islands (on the latter lives in *Poa anceps* on steep slopes and low scrub); also formerly on Great Island, Three Kings group. The Stewart Island (*stewartiana*) subspecies (Stewart Island and outliers except Codfish Island) is unsatisfactorily defined, but is apparently dimorphic (either spotted on both throat and breast as in *punctata*, or with throat devoid of spots, or very faintly spotted: the latter type was described by E. F. Stead as a new subspecies, *insularis*). The Codfish Island (*wilsoni*) subspecies is distinguished from *punctata* by the heavy pattern of large spots on throat and breast, and darker upper surface (feathers black with only narrow brown edges). (*Note.*—Stewart and Codfish Island forms occur both on the coast in low vegetation—swamp, grass and low scrub—and in the scrub and adjacent grasslands above the bushline; also swamps and bogs on the main island.) The Snares Island (*caudata*) subspecies is a more uniform brown above, with obscure dark streaking, and with a strong wash of brown below; tail quills broader than in other subspecies, the barbs weakly connected; feet comparatively robust (this form obtains cover from tussock, but unlike other subspecies is also seen constantly in the open: it feeds in penguin colonies, and on the open forest floor of *Olearia lyallii* forest). The Chatham Island (*rufescens*) subspecies is believed to have become extinct in *c.* 1900: dark chestnut brown above, back streaked with dark brown; under surface lacking spots, or a few obscure spots on throat and upper breast (occurred on Chatham, Pitt and Mangare Islands: practically nothing recorded of its habits, but apparently like the mainland form kept to denser vegetation).

Breeding: Nest deep in sedges, rushes, shrubs or other low vegetation, from a few inches to *c*. 4 feet above the ground (according to Guthrie-Smith when in swamps usually above water or damper portions); a deep cup of neatly woven dry rushes, grasses, etc., with lining of feathers which frequently conceal or partly conceal the eggs. Nest built by both adults. Breeding September–February. Eggs 2–3, white or pinkish heavily flecked brown and purplish-brown, usually a denser zone (or broad band) at large end. Incubation period 12½ days; fledging 12-13 days (Soper). Both adults feed young; food given to the young: tipulids, moths, grubs and caterpillars (Guthrie-Smith, Buddle).

B. p. caudata of the Snares nests in dense ground vegetation (fern, grasses)—occasionally in a hollow log—nest resembling that of the mainland subspecies; according to Stead's observations both adults incubate; during Stead's visit in late November–early December a pair accompanied by newly-fledged young were seen building a second nest, viz. double-brooded.

BROWN CREEPER *Finschia novaeseelandiae*   *Pl. 17*
Maori name: Pipipi.
Description: 5¼″. Reddish-brown forehead, crown, lower back. rump and tail, this colour strongest on rump and tail but merging gradually with ashy grey on upper back; a zone of ashy grey, shaded with brown on nape and upper back and this passes forward without interruption to face which is pure ashy grey; wings dark brown, quills with buff edges; underparts including throat pale cinnamon brown; *narrow pale throat meets ashy grey of cheeks in a sharp line situated well below the eye*; a faint pale buff stripe behind the eye; dark brown spots at one-third from tip of each tail quill, except centre pair, form a band when tail is spread; bill and feet pale brown.

In flocks, pairs or family parties (see below); seldom silent, maintains contact with constant flocking call.

Voice: Call has some resemblance to call note of Yellowhead (*q.v.*) but with experience readily distinguished: it consists of a rapid succession of somewhat harsh notes *chi-chi-dee-dee-dee-dee-dee-dee.* Notes are rapidly repeated; may be partial or a *chi* or *dee* given singly (the single *chi* can be a prolonged note). Flocking calls may be broken with fragments of song. The song consists of from five to six highly musical notes, of which the third is emphasised viz. *chi-roh-rée-roh-ree* (or final *ree-ree*).

Habitat and range: South Island, and Stewart Island and its outliers; in forest throughout, but much more widely distributed than commonly believed and present in a surprising range of smaller native forest remnants; where remnants are adjacent to gardens, etc., containing old-established exotic vegetation it will enter this freely (e.g. on Banks Peninsula occurs in vegetation consisting mainly of oaks and other well-grown exotic trees); in second-growth forest and scrub; also reported established in pine plantations at Golden Downs, Nelson. Reaches the timber line in the mountains, but not normally found in subalpine scrub.

Flocks or pairs move characteristically through the trees when feeding; feeds among branches and in canopy, a vigorous inspection being made of bark crevices, leaf bases, etc.; frequently clings upside down to a twig or allows itself to swing down as the foliage gives under its weight. Food apparently consists of insects only.

Large flocks are sometimes formed: a flock of c. 50 was noted on 24th February in the Craigieburn Range, Canterbury (E. G. T.).

Breeding: Nest an open cup 5–30 feet from the ground, generally in canopy or in bush lawyer and other vines; sometimes in a fork. Material dry grasses, fibres, small twigs, moss, bound together with spiders' web, and lined feathers. Strongly territorial; pairs feed together in territories (observed 23/10/1961; probably shortly before nesting (E. G. T.). Breeding October–January; probably double-brooded. Eggs 3–4, of extremely variable colour and pattern (pink or pinkish-white with scattered reddish-brown blotches, white with dense brown blotching, white with scattered brown and purplish spots, etc.). Incubation c. 17 days. Only female incubates and is fed on nest by male (M.F.S.).

WHITEHEAD *Mohoua albicilla* Pl. 17

Maori name: Popokatea.

Description: 6″. Upper surface, wings and tail pale brown; this colour also extends on to the sides and flanks; rump and base of tail quills tinged to a varying degree with reddish-brown; *head and underparts white*, slightly tinged with brown; head almost pure white in adult male, shaded brown on nape and crown in female and immature; bill black, feet bluish-black.

Generally in flocks or family parties, located in the forest by flocking call.

Voice: Calls varied, the commonest consisting of a rapid series of chirping notes which may be compared with opening portion of song of Chaffinch; frequently heard is a hard single *zit* (R. B. S. found that on Little Barrier Island this could be mistaken for the typical note of the Stitchbird). Song composed of clear canary-like notes, which are commonly interspersed with harsher notes (Reischek described a song of this type consisting " first, of three notes, like ' *viu, viu, viu,*' then four, like ' *zir, zir, zir, zir* ' "). In spring it adds a five-note chime like a Bellbird's (R.A.F.).

Habitat and range: North Island; Great and Little Barrier, Arid and Kapiti Islands: now found on the mainland only south of a line approximately through Te Aroha and Pirongia. Found in the larger remaining forest areas up to c. 4000 feet (and adjacent second-growth forest), but may be close to settlement, e.g. east of Wellington; abundant on Little Barrier and Kapiti Islands. On the Volcanic Plateau one of the species established in exotic pine forests.

Main food is insects, searched for vigorously in canopy, on tree trunks, logs and " even, on occasion, the forest floor " (Wilkinson), whose observations on Kapiti show that it also eats fruits (mahoe, matipo, toro, horoeka, hangehange, kaikomako and kotukutuku); like the Brown Creeper and Yellowhead often hangs downwards on a branch or twig.

Breeding: Cup-shaped nest of twigs, rootlets, grass, bark, bound together with spiders' web; lined with fragments of bark and sometimes a few feathers; common site is canopy of shrub or low tree 4–8 feet above the ground, but may be at 30 feet or more; commonly in a fork; sometimes " hung from light twigs or branches like that of the Silvereye " (Buddle); in mainland forest (Urewera) a common site according to R. St. Paul is leaf of treefern 1–2 feet from trunk. Breeding October–February; probably double-brooded. Eggs 2–4, variable (white or pinkish-white with reddish-brown blotches; white with reddish-brown and purplish spots; densely blotched red, almost obscuring the ground colour; white with only faint indication of spots, etc.). Wilkinson, on Kapiti Island, found that the nest took about four days to build, after which there might be a delay of several days before the first egg was laid; incubation c. 17 days, by both parents; fledging 16–17 days (Wilkinson). Young fed by both adults: at a nest on Little Barrier Island (November 1947) the female returned with food approximately every 7 minutes, the male every 30 minutes; food comprised caterpillars, grubs, moths, beetles, a blow-fly, spiders (Buddle, E. G. T.).

" Quartets " combining to incubate and feed young were noted by Guthrie-Smith in his investigation of the breeding habits of this species on Little Barrier Island and in Hawke's Bay; he was doubtful whether these comprised two pairs, or a male and three females, but as according to Soper's recent observations the male Yellowhead (see below) is commonly polygamous it seems likely that the latter explanation is the correct one. Guthrie-Smith found four adults present at a majority of the nests examined, but at some there was only a single pair.

YELLOWHEAD *Mohoua ochrocephala* Pl. 17
Other names: Mohua, Bush Canary.
Description: 6″ Back olive-brown, tinged with yellow: rump and tail brownish-yellow; wing quills brown, yellowish-brown on outer edge; *head and underparts bright canary-yellow*; lower abdomen greyish white; under tail-coverts yellow; nape shaded olive-brown in female and immature; bill and feet black. Tip of tail quills nearly always much abraded, shaft projecting (see below).

Identification of the call note is even more important than for Brown Creeper and Whitehead as the Yellowhead feeds mainly in the tops of the trees; in pairs, family parties or small flocks.

Voice: A louder and more mechanical call than the Brown Creeper's, consisting of 6–8 notes rapidly repeated; a high-pitched ratchety buzzing (notes have a vibrating quality that has been compared with a pneumatic drill); the call is much varied, e.g. Soper found that during incubation the male's call increases in volume as soon as the female leaves the nest; according to Soper a characteristic call note, *lukaart, lukaart,* is given by the female for the few days prior to hatching and after hatching. Song a variable number of musical, canary-like notes; sometimes ends in a guttural *curr*. When the notes are much drawn out they have a strong resemblance to certain notes of the Bellbird.

Habitat and range: South Island, Stewart Island (doubtful). In the large areas of native forest, i.e. Marlborough, Nelson, Westland, and western Otago and Southland (also some smaller areas of forest near Dunedin); formerly Banks Peninsula but last recorded in *c*. 1900.

Soper states that although it feeds mostly in the tops of the trees, it has " a fondness for rooting through the accumulations of rubbish that fall down and collect in the forks . . . they grip the bark with one foot . . . dig their tail, which is supplied with spines, into the trunk, and scratch vigorously with the other foot sending down a shower of debris." In the search for insects, it thoroughly investigates leaves, twigs, branches and higher portions of the trunk. The tail feathers rapidly become abraded, presumably through use in feeding on branches and trunks, and it is quite normal for the spines formed by the projecting shafts to be ¼″ in length (similar abrasion appears in the Whitehead but is much less marked). Actions are vigorous, hanging head downwards from a twig, or swinging on tips of smaller branches to examine foliage. So far as known entirely insectivorous.

Breeding: Differs from the Brown Creeper and Whitehead in that it is apparently always hole-nesting: according to field studies by Soper, the site may be 8–60 feet above the ground, but usually over 30 feet. All the nests he examined were in cavities in dead or dying trees; nest cup-shaped, composed of moss, rootlets and spiders' webs, lined with fine grass (Soper suggests that hole-nesting has been comparatively recently acquired, as the construction of the nest conforms to that used in the open by the related Brown Creeper and Whitehead). Breeding November–December; eggs 3–4, pinkish-white evenly blotched with reddish-brown. Incubation by female, at least 21 days (Soper). Soper found that for the first five or six days after hatching the chicks were fed by regurgitation; later they received " insects, grubs and caterpillars of all kinds " (fed by both adults); the chicks left the nest on their eighteenth day. He records courtship feeding early in the season, and, according to his observations at one nest, the nest site is chosen by the male.

Soper has shown that polygamy is of regular occurrence in this species. He was able to observe the breeding cycle closely at five nests and found that three birds (a male and two females) were associated at two of the nests, the females being of different ages and thus distinguishable by the degree of shading on the nape. The number of eggs in these nests was three or four, the same number as in nests with one female; both females shared the work of incubation.

GREY WARBLER *Gerygone igata*   Pl. 17
Maori name: Riroriro.
Description: 4¼″. Greenish-grey above; pale grey throat and breast; white abdomen and under tail-coverts; a yellow tinge varying in

intensity on sides and flanks, but this may be absent (not present in juvenal); on anterior margin, at bend of wing, a narrow white streak may be visible; *short, rounded tail*; conspicuous *white patch on either side of dark brown tail seen in flight* (the tail quills have a subterminal or terminal white spot except the centre pair); bill black; feet blackish brown.

Song, heard throughout the year, is its most familiar feature; commonly seen fluttering on perimeter of foliage or emerging for a short flight to the next feeding point; usually in pairs.

Voice: Song a sweet trill, may be varied by reduction of the number of notes, or suppression of the latter part; also delivered in a somewhat rambling fashion (this, however, may be a local variation). A shorter song consisting of three comparatively weak, unmusical notes is commonly repeated at intervals when feeding; these notes sometimes given as a preliminary to the trill. (*Note.*—Local variations are commonly distinguished, but further study is required.) In calm weather the warble has remarkable carrying power.

Observations in Dunedin by Marples showed that while the Grey Warbler sings at all times of the year, a marked diminution occurs in the winter months during which there are usually a few weeks when it is not recorded. He found that the main peak of singing activity came in September or October, but it fell to a low level in December, reaching another peak in February or March.

Habitat and range: A familiar bird of all settled districts, having like the Fantail adopted modified native forest and exotic trees and shrubs. It entered the man-made habitats resulting from settlement rapidly, and Buller could refer to it in 1873 as " the familiar frequenter of our gardens and hedgerows." Now occurs in exotic vegetation, e.g. willows, pine shelter belts, gorse hedges, gardens, remote from forest or forest remnants; also in pine and other exotic plantations, in remnant or second-growth native forest and scrub up to *c.* 4500 ft. a.s.l., and in larger native forests. In forest it is evenly distributed, but appears to be more abundant in modified and second-growth forest than in unmodified forest.

Insects and spiders provide main food; searches leaves, twigs, bark and characteristically flutters at foliage to feed; has been seen hovering to catch a spider in front of web (H. C. Abraham); " hawks " small moths on the wing (Moon).

North, South, Stewart Island and nearer outlying islands, including the Solander Islands. Study of possible subspecies is required: several have been described but present information does not justify their recognition.

Breeding: Suspended nest is pear-shaped and has a side entrance near the top, frequently hooded; composed of grasses, moss, sometimes small twigs, spiders' webs, thistledown and even wool, lined with feathers. Nest situated 5–25 feet from the ground. (Of 23 nests examined by Moon most were hanging from the canopy of the outermost branches; the point of suspension was " firmly woven around a branch, with the lower part secured at one or more sides to prevent it from swinging.") Built by female, male assisting with gathering of material; a nest observed by P. C. Bull was built in 7 days. Breeding August–January; double-brooded. (*Note.*—August–September broods escape parasitism by the Shining Cuckoo, *q.v.*: the latter is then arriving in New Zealand from winter quarters, lays in November–December.) Eggs 3–6, pinkish white evenly covered with small reddish-brown or purplish spots, a dense zone or band at larger end (sometimes almost unspotted except at large end). Incubation period 17–19 days, fledging 17–19 days (J. M. Cunningham). Both adults feed young (fed in nest at intervals of 3–6 minutes: Moon); according to Moon's observations most of the foraging is done within a short distance of the nest. Chicks fed for three weeks after departure. Chicks have a most distinctive, high-pitched call *cheef* in addition to the begging call at this stage.

CHATHAM ISLAND WARBLER *Gerygone albofrontata*

Local name: Woodpecker.

Description: 4¾″. Olive-brown above; upper tail-coverts and base of tail pale reddish-brown; forehead, line above eye and whole of under-parts white; only obscure whitish spots on outer tail quills; sides and flanks tinged yellow; bill and feet dark brown. The Chatham Island Warbler has a much larger bill than the Grey Warbler.

Voice: " Three rather weak notes repeated several times with a break in between " (B. D. Bell).

Habitat and range: Originally in forest throughout, but now of very local distribution. Fleming in 1937 gained the impression that it was " not nearly so abundant in the changed conditions in settled country as is its New Zealand representative [the Grey Warbler]." Since 1937 it has become more restricted in distribution on the main island, being found only in bush remnants of the southern half (B. D. Bell). Also in bush remnants on Pitt Island; present on South East Island (abundant) and Little Mangare Island.

According to Fleming its general habits and movements resemble those of the Grey Warbler, as do its feeding habits, differences apparent to the observer being " merely correlated with the Chatham bird's larger size."

Breeding: Nest very like Grey Warbler's: materials recorded are roots, fibres, moss, leaves, cobwebs, with lining of feathers. Two nests recorded by Fleming on the main island were 20–30 feet from the ground, one in a tangle of vine and the other hanging from a lofty limb in the open; a nest on South East Island was about seven feet up in a tangle of *Muehlenbeckia*. Breeding recorded November–January, but this is probably the second brood (parasitised by the Shining Cuckoo). Eggs 4, pinkish white with reddish-brown spots, a dense zone at the large end. The behaviour of the adults when feeding young in the nest closely resembles the behaviour of the Grey Warbler; family parties of three or four young with their parents are normal (November–January).

THRUSHES: Turdidae

The true thrushes are a very big almost cosmopolitan family, missing only from much of Polynesia and New Zealand; though one variable species, the Island Thrush (*Turdus poliocephalus*) is widely distributed in the south-west Pacific and came as close to New Zealand as Norfolk Island. Song Thrushes and Blackbirds were first introduced from England in 1862; since when they have proved such successful colonisers that they are now among the most numerous birds in the country.

SONG THRUSH *Turdus philomelos*

Description: 9″. Above warm olive-brown, with paler underparts, boldly spotted breast and reddish buff under wing. Bill brownish; legs pinkish brown. Young have mantle speckled buff. By midsummer upperparts of many adults are grey-brown with bleaching.

Voice: Song, April–January, a " fine careless rapture ", bold, varied, musical, the clear-cut phrases often repeated with brief pauses, usually delivered from a conspicuous perch. Alarm note a loud *chuk* or *tchik* rapidly repeated; flight note a thin *seep* or soft *sip*. Occasionally a mimic; has been heard to incorporate notes of Pied Stilt and Red-billed Gull in its song.

Habitat and range: Throughout New Zealand in all types of country including dense bush up to *c.* 4000 feet. Now present on most off-shore and outlying islands north to Kermadecs and south to Campbell. Feeds mostly on the ground using regular " anvils " for smashing snails; but also takes some berries and small fruit.

Breeding: Nest, seldom high, often conspicuous, smoothly lined with mud or wood-pulp, a mixture of rotten wood and saliva, where no mud is available, e.g. Rangitoto. Eggs, June–January, 3–6, clear greenish blue with black spots. Incubation period 13–14 days; fledging 13–14 days.

BLACKBIRD *Turdus merula*

Description: 10″. Male a robust all black bird with clear orange-yellow bill; female dark brown with grey chin and brown bill; juvenile more rufous-brown with some speckling (hence popular fallacy of hybrids between Blackbird and Song Thrush). Partial albinos are not uncommon, but seem to be much more numerous in some years than others.

Voice: Song clear, fluent, tuneful, mellower and more fluty than that of the Song Thrush. Song period, July–January, considerably shorter than that of Song Thrush. In late summer and early autumn Blackbirds may sing quietly a soft inward warble while remaining hidden in the heart of a thick leafy shrub. Alarm notes an anxious *tchook*, an angry screech and a persistent *tchink*, *tchink* which becomes particularly resonant when vermin, cat or owl, is being mobbed.

Habitat and range: Throughout New Zealand up to *c.* 4500 feet. Rather a more thrustful coloniser than the Song Thrush of off-shore and outlying islands from Kermadecs to Campbell. Wild and shy in insular habitats. Feeds mainly on ground, but much more partial to fruit than the Song Thrush.

Breeding: Nest generally low and ill-concealed, strengthened but not lined with mud; frequently now in out-buildings. Eggs, 2–5, July–December, bluish-green freckled with red-brown, but showing considerable variation. Incubation period 13–14 days; fledging 12–15 days.

ACCENTORS: Prunellidae

A small palaearctic genus of rather colourless sparrow-like birds but with fine pointed bills, probably related to the thrushes and warblers. None native to New Zealand. One species, first introduced in 1868, has shown itself a most successful coloniser.

HEDGE SPARROW *Prunella modularis* *Pl. 18*
   Local names: Dunnock, Hedgie.
   Description: 5¾″. Upperparts brown streaked black; throat and chest slate-grey, underparts paler with heavily streaked flanks. Inconspicuous rather than skulking. Perhaps most evident in autumn when song restarts, males are challenging and pairs are formed. Seldom seen to fly far. Feeds on ground, moving with a slow shuffling gait, often with a flicking of the wings.
   Voice: Call-note a sharp insistent *tseep*. Song, a hurried warble faster and stronger than that of a Grey Warbler (*weeso, sissy-weeso, sissy-weeso, sissy-wee* (W. Garstang).
   Habitat and range: At home in all kinds of cover from sea-level to 5000 feet; saltmarsh, mangroves, gumlands, gardens, shrubberies, sand-dune lupins, wind-flattened taupata, gorse hedges, pine plantations, mountain scrub. Has spread to most off-shore islands and into the sub-antarctic as far as Campbell Island.
   Breeding: Nest usually low down in thick cover. Eggs, August–January, 3–5, clear deep blue. Incubation period *c.* 12 days. Fledging 11–15 days.

PIPITS AND WAGTAILS:
Motacillidae

The pipits and wagtails are largely insectivorous birds, characterised by slender form and comparatively long tail. The wagtails are with one exception restricted to the Old World, being absent from New Zealand and occurring only accidentally in Australia; pipits nearly cosmopolitan, although absent from the Pacific islands.

NEW ZEALAND PIPIT   *Anthus novaeseelandiae*

Other names: Pihoihoi, Sandlark (Chathams).

Description: 7½″. Brown above (feathers with darker centres) and white below with dark-brown streaked upper breast; *fairly prominent white eyebrow-stripe* and *white outer tail feathers*. The Skylark, with which it is commonly confused, lives in pasture land where the Pipit is generally absent, but ranges of the two species overlap in rough open country, etc. The main field differences between Skylark and Pipit are the more slender form (including comparatively long tail) of the latter, and the raised head feathers forming a short crest in the Skylark; colour of Skylark generally more strongly buff; both have white outer tail feathers. Skylark's aerial song is unmistakable (Pipit sings briefly from a prominent perch, only occasionally on the wing: see under " Voice " below). Both Pipit and Skylark walk and run,

rarely hop. Note also the distinctive habit in the Pipit of spasmodically moving tail up and down either when walking or standing.

The juvenal plumage characterised by crescentic warm buff dorsal feathers, and zone of dark streaks on upper breast more distinct than in adults.

Voice: Common call a high-pitched *scree* or a rasping drawn out *zwee*; in spring male repeatedly calls from a prominent perch *pi-pit* and sometimes gives the musical trilling song; *tsew-tsēr weet-tsrrr*; or more briefly *tzu-weet*; song may be delivered from a prominent perch or in flight as the bird descends in short glides, wings and tail elevated; the song flight commonly ends in a quick run on alighting.

Habitat and range: The most obvious habitat restriction under modern conditions is the avoidance by the Pipit of pure pasture land as mentioned above, but elsewhere on rougher farmland, roadsides and in open country generally it is found throughout and fairly common. Under conditions of early settlement it probably greatly increased in range as forest was cleared, although it was perhaps limited in abundance by introduced predators; before European settlement probably restricted to lowland and alpine tussock grasslands, river-beds and the coastal zone. In mountain districts widely distributed on the open rocky tops. Almost entirely insectivorous, insects occasionally captured on the wing; some seeds also taken.

A member of the wide-ranging species (from East Europe to Australia and New Zealand) including *A. n. richardi*, Richard's Pipit. On most coastal islands surrounding New Zealand, and Chatham, Antipodes, Auckland and Campbell Islands (straggling to Kermadec and Snares Islands). The populations of New Zealand sub-antarctic islands may prove to differ subspecifically on examination (several subspecies have been described but these are doubtful).

Breeding: Nest a deep cup—the lining of dry grass generally substantial—well concealed at the base of a tussock, or amongst grasses, low bracken and similar vegetation, which may enclose nest in a tunnel. Two- to three-brooded. Breeding August–March; eggs 3–4 (heavily blotched brown or purplish-brown, and grey). Incubation period *c.* 14 days; fledging 14–16 days; young fed by both parents. When visiting the nest, adults alight at some distance off, but usually fly directly off the nest after feeding chicks.

HONEYEATERS: Meliphagidae

A family restricted—but for the doubtfully assigned South Africa genus *Promerops*—to Indonesia, Australia and New Zealand and the South-west Pacific (also Hawaii); in Australia, the main centre of distribution, there are a number of common and conspicuous species. Tongue brush-tipped.

STITCHBIRD *Notiomystis cincta*   *Pl. 16*
Maori name: Hihi.
Description: *Male—7½″. Velvety black head, throat, upper breast and mantle,* with a *tuft of white feathers on each side of head behind eye* (white tufts can be erected when disturbed); *a band of golden-yellow* passes from the shoulders and lesser wing-coverts across the breast; *white wing-bar;* back olive-brown; wings and tail brown with olive-brown outer webs; underparts pale greyish brown, with irregular streaks of dark brown mainly towards sides. *Female—7″. Olive-brown above;* a faint white spot on each side of head corresponds to ear tuft of male; *pale brown below,* darkest on throat and upper breast, obscurely marked with dark brown streaks; a faint yellow wash on lesser wing-coverts; *white wing-bar.* Bill brownish-black; feet pale brown (both sexes). Plumage of immature male similar to that of female; female and immature might be mistaken for female Bellbird but can be distinguished by less slender build, comparatively short tail and white wing-bar.

Tail is commonly tilted.
Voice: The common call *tzit* (from this the bird's name is derived as, in Buller's words, " it has a fanciful resemblance to the word 'stitch' ") is

given by both sexes. Female also has a repeated *pek, pek, pek, pek* (like alarm note of Bellbird); feeding call of young is a continuous, high-pitched *sit, sit, sit*. Sibson also recorded a softer call *tseet*, in addition to the common *tzit*; and also on one occasion heard " a two-note call like part of the exuberant bubble-song of the Bellbird." The male has a vigorous song: Sibson's description states that " it began with the typical *tzit*, and went to *tsiu, tsiu, tsiu*; it ended quite abruptly and was not repeated." Also a soft warbling by the male (recorded both in spring and in mid-December, i.e. towards the end of the nesting season).
Habitat and range: Originally the North Island, and Great and Little Barrier and Kapiti Islands, but has been extinct on the mainland since about 1885. It is doubtful whether it was originally evenly distributed on the North Island mainland; however, Buller described it as " comparatively common in the southern parts of the North Island " in 1872. It was apparently rare north of a line approximately through northern Taranaki and the Bay of Plenty; according to Maori tradition, was plentiful in the Upper Wanganui, Rotorua and Urewera districts. A last remnant of the species exists on Little Barrier Island, but here it is well established.

It inhabits forest of varying types at all altitudes on Little Barrier, although not frequently seen in the second-growth manuka of former clearings; like the Bellbird and Tui it is strongly attracted to nectar-bearing trees and shrubs, and a marked attraction to the coast when flax (*Phormium*) was in flower was noted by Parkin. Food includes insects and fruits (Buller states that A. Reischek found "some minute seeds as well as insect-remains" in stomachs of specimens); however, observations on Little Barrier Island, especially (see below) feeding of the young in the nest (Guthrie-Smith, Sibson), suggest that it is more dependent than the other New Zealand honeyeaters on nectar. On Little Barrier it has been recorded feeding on the nectar of pohutukawa, kohekohe, *Alseuosmia* and flax.
Breeding: In holes in trunks and branches, 8–60 feet from the ground; nest substantially built of sticks and rootlets, lined with treefern scales and a few feathers (Guthrie-Smith). Breeding November–December; eggs 3–5, white. Guthrie-Smith's observations on Little Barrier showed that both parents feed the young; he believed that nectar alone was given to the chicks (he notes that the parents often wiped the bill on a branch as if sticky, and that insect or other food was not at any time seen in the parent's bill). At two nests found more recently (Sibson, Parkin) the same observations were made: however, at the nest discovered in early January, 1948, Sibson found that only the female came in with food. The nest observed by Parkin contained small young on 21st December, 1955, and the young left the nest on 3rd January, 1956: fledging thus occupies not less than two weeks.

BELLBIRD *Anthornis melanura*   *Pl. 16*
Other names: Korimako, Makomako, Mockie.
Description: *Male 8″. Soft olive-green,* yellowish green on sides and

abdomen; gloss of iridescent purple on forehead, crown, face and chin (this is of variable extent); *tuft of yellow feathers on each side* situated near angle of closed wings; *under tail-coverts pale yellow*; wing and tail quills brownish black. *Female—7½". Plumage is much more drab than the male*: olive-brown above, yellowish-brown with tinge of olive below; purple on head much reduced; the tuft on the sides and the under tail-coverts yellowish-white; *a narrow white stripe from gape passes below eye.* In both sexes: bill black; feet blue-grey, claws brown. Iris cherry-red (male); brown (female).

Located by song throughout the year; movements vigorous and lively, and silhouette distinctive, with slender proportions, distinctly arched bill and slender tail with shallow fork.

Voice: Song a sequence of liquid notes, of which the more powerful at a distance sound remarkably bell-like. Songs consist of phrases which, as recorded by numerous observers, vary from district to district (see Marples's observations below). Female sings in comparatively short phrases, and song weaker.

Marples recorded the songs heard in the Town Belt of Dunedin over 3½ years (1941–4): he noted a different periodicity for three different and easily recognisable songs. The song he designated as No. 1, a distinct phrase of seven notes, was heard constantly at all times of the year, but there was a peak of this type of song in May and a period of minimum song in October (in 1941 there was a late peak in August). Song No. 2 consisted of two notes followed by a *zizz*, followed by the two notes again, and finally a phrase of six notes, the third being a high one heavily accented—at times groups of male Bellbirds were seen sitting a few feet apart, all singing this song with great energy: periodicity of No. 2 song was similar to No. 1, the peak falling in June or July; however, it was not heard at all during four or five spring and summer months. No. 3 consisted of a series of descending notes, usually four but sometimes three or five, in which the last note was slurred or accented; periodicity of this song was identical with that of No. 2 but nothing comparable with the group singing of No. 2 was noted. Marples's observations included records of four other songs, well marked and easy to recognise, but only heard for short periods; is was suggested that these records were of strange birds passing through the area.

Alarm call a series of rapidly repeated harsh notes *pek, pek, pek, pek* or *yeng, yeng, yeng, yeng.*

Habitat and range: Found in forest, forest remnants and second-growth forest throughout New Zealand (except around and north of Auckland: see below); also in exotic vegetation, orchards, gardens, etc., in some districts, but mainly in the neighbourhood of forest remnants. It may, however, be in the process of expanding into settled districts. Established in the large exotic plantations. In winter, like the Tui, reaches nectar-bearing trees and shrubs at some distance from its breeding areas.

Up to *c.* 1860 it was abundant but a marked decline, which it is

suggested may have been due to disease, subsequently affected populations throughout New Zealand. It decreased in numbers until *c.* 1910
but after this recovered in nearly all districts (Stead states that in Canterbury numbers were maintained until *c.* 1900, recovering after about
10 years of low ebb in *c.* 1910). In North Auckland and about
Auckland became locally extinct: recolonisation in this area has only
recently occurred at two isolated points (Whangarei Heads,
Warkworth). There was no decrease of the populations of the Three
Kings, Poor Knights, Hen and Chickens, Little Barrier, Kapiti and
other off-lying islands.

Food the same as that of the Tui—insects, fruits and nectar. More
information on the proportions of the three types of food in the diet
of these two species is required, but the Bellbird's feeding habits suggest
that it takes a higher proportion of insects: it appears to spend much
time at all seasons searching for insects in crevices in bark, and on
twigs and branches; and sometimes on the ground.

Common sources of nectar in forest are: rata, pohutukawa, kowhai,
rewarewa, native fuchsia, kohekohe; also flax (*Phormium*), and
numerous exotics including tree lucerne, gums, wattles, *Banksia* and
various garden shrubs. Honeydew (produced by mealy bugs) is a major
food in much southern beech (*Nothofagus*) forest (the sooty mould
which grows on the trees in association with the mealybug gives a
characteristic appearance to forests where honeydew is available).
Artificial foods (sweetened water, honey, etc.) freely taken.

Fruits include those of a number of native trees and shrubs (including
Coprosma spp., native fuchsia, cabbage tree and mistletoe), and of berry-
bearing exotic trees and shrubs of all kinds; may also take grapes, and
figs, apples and peaches if close to orchards.

Mainland (*melanura*) subspecies (mainland and most nearer islands)
is also found on the Auckland Islands; the Three Kings (*obscura*)
subspecies is a little larger and plumage less yellow, with patches on
sides and under tail-coverts creamy-white instead of yellow; Chatham
Island (*melanocephala*) subspecies larger, head deep purple and reduced
patch on the sides (extinct since 1906).

Breeding: Usually in fork at 4–40 feet from the ground; generally in
dense cover but sometimes conspicuous from the ground; sometimes
in an open cavity in a trunk; rarely almost at ground level. Nest has
a somewhat loosely-constructed base of dry twigs and fibres, and a deep
well-lined cup (lining fine grass, sometimes wholly feathers). Breeding
September–January; double-brooded; eggs 3–4, pinkish (pale pinkish-
white to rich pink) with reddish brown spots and blotches, densest at
large end. Incubation by female; may be fed on nest by her mate.
Incubation period 14 days; fledging 14 days. Young are fed by both
adults, feeding continues for about 10 days after departure from the
nest. Stead found that the young were fed entirely on insects; Buddle,
at a nest observed on the Poor Knights, noted that for three days after
hatching the chicks were given nectar alone; insects were then added
to their diet in increasing numbers.

TUI *Prosthemadera novaeseelandiae*   *Pl. 16*

Other name: Parson Bird.

Description: Male 12½″, female 11½″. Iridescent metallic green with bluish-purple reflections (varies according to light and appears black at a distance); the back and scapulars dark brown with bronze reflections, and the abdomen and sides reddish brown; under tail-coverts metallic green; *double white throat-tuft* composed of curled feathers; a lacy white collar on back and sides of neck (formed by white-shafted filamentous feathers which curl forwards on the side of the neck); *white wing-bar*. Bill and feet blackish brown.

Female has smaller throat-tufts, and paler reddish brown abdomen.

Immature plumage slaty black, except wing and tail quills which have metallic green outer webs; a crescentic mark or extensive patch of greyish white on the throat; dusky white wing-bar. Buller states that a well-grown fledgling taken from the nest and kept in captivity began to sprout throat-tufts within a month; at the end of another six weeks it was changing into the full adult plumage, and metallic coloration appeared first in irregular tracts on the breast and sides of the body.

Movements are vigorous like those of the Bellbird, and flight is often noisy especially when darting through the trees at a high speed; performs aerial acrobatics, often plunging down with closed wings from some height.

Voice: Closely resembles that of the Bellbird, and like the Bellbird varies song from district to district. However, it has a much greater tendency than the Bellbird to intersperse harsher sounds among the notes (variously described as croaks, coughs, clicks, grunts, rattles, wheezes and chuckles). Richer notes are more fluid and resonant than any notes of the Bellbird.

Also has notes evidently of high frequency and beyond the range of human hearing, for the bird is seen singing energetically although only faint squeaky sounds are to be heard.

A high-pitched plaintive cry *ke-e-e-e* is apparently an alarm note. Also sometimes uttered is a high-pitched jackdaw-like *tchack*.

Habitat and range: Although like the Bellbird often seen obtaining nectar in settled districts, the Tui has remained primarily a forest bird. Nests occasionally in exotic vegetation, e.g. hawthorn, adjacent to forest or forest remnants, but unlike the Bellbird has not expanded into exotic vegetation and apparently appears only as an occasional visitor in the larger exotic plantations. Found in most of the larger forest tracts, up to *c.* 3500 feet and even in comparatively small remnants; also second-growth forest, and manuka scrub if this contains some forest remnants. Does not favour southern beech (*Nothofagus*) forests e.g. almost absent on the eastern side of the divide at Arthur's Pass but abundant on the western side.

Food insects, fruits and nectar: fruits probably bulk larger in the diet than for the Bellbird. The following have been recorded (probably many others): for fruits, mahoe, *Coprosma*, supplejack, maire, makomako, karaka, totara, kiekie; for nectar, rata, pohutukawa, kowhai, rewarewa, native fuchsia, flax (*Phormium*). In settled districts tree lucerne, wattles, gums and a number of others provide nectar, while fruits are obtained from various ornamental trees and shrubs; Tuis commonly feed on nectar from garden flowers at the homestead of Little Barrier Island sanctuary, such flowers as freesias and lachenaleas being visited eagerly. May be fed artificially.

The typical subspecies (*novaeseelandiae*) is distributed over the mainland of New Zealand, Stewart Island, many of the off-lying islands (including formerly the Three Kings), and the Kermadecs and Aucklands; Chatham Island (*chathamensis*) subspecies larger, with longer throat-plumes and bluer breast (main island, and Pitt and South East Islands).

Breeding: Generally in a fork in the outer branches or canopy, 10–50 feet above the ground; base a bulky structure of sticks and twigs up to ten inches in diameter, and the cup is lined with treefern scales, grasses or other finer material, or with moss; sometimes a few feathers. Breeding November–January (occasionally September and October); probably often double-brooded. Eggs 2–4, white or pale pink, with reddish-brown specks or blotches mainly at the larger end. Incubation by female; throughout incubation male sings from a nearby tree. Incubation period 14 days; fledging *c* 21 days. Moon noted that the female alone fed the chicks for the first four days, the male subsequently assisting. He found that the movements of the adults were so rapid that it was only with the aid of a slow-motion movie camera and electronic flash exposures that the food could be identified—insect food and possibly nectar during the first 4–5 days and later a number of berries and larger insects (insects identified included moths and stick insects).

RED WATTLE-BIRD *Anthochaera carunculata*

Description: 13½″. Brownish-grey strongly streaked with white above; pale grey with brown and white streaks below; tail and wing quills with white tips; *a yellow patch in middle of abdomen*; *small red fleshy wattle* hangs behind the eye; bill black, feet brownish-grey.

Voice: " Raucous notes " (Serventy and Whittell); in addition to these loud, harsh notes, has double whistling alarm call.

Habitat and range: Twice recorded as a straggler: Matakana, North Auckland (*c*. 1865) and Rahotu, Taranaki (1882). In Australia distributed from southern Queensland to Victoria (not Tasmania), and westward to the south-west of Western Australia; a partial migrant. Feeds on insects, nectar, and fruits (sometimes including orchard fruits); common at nectar-bearing trees and shrubs, including those of towns and cities.

SILVEREYES: Zosteropidae

A family of about 85 species found in Africa, southern Asia from Arabia eastwards, China and Japan, Indonesia, Australia (a recent colonist to New Zealand) and many Pacific Islands.

SILVEREYE *Zosterops lateralis*   *Pl. 17*
   Other names: Tauhou; Waxeye, White-eye, Blightbird, Blightie.
   Description: 4¾″. Head, upper surface of wings, rump and upper tail-coverts bright yellowish-green; wing and tail quills brown with yellowish-green on outer webs; upper back and scapulars grey tinged with yellowish-green; underparts pale greyish-white (throat and undertail coverts — or undertail coverts alone — may be tinged yellow, and the whole of the undersurface may be darkened to a distinct grey); sides and flanks chestnut brown; under wing-coverts white; *eye-ring white*, with a line of black in front and below. Bill brown, paler at base; feet pale brown.
   Female can be distinguished by less intense (pale cinnamon brown) colour of sides and flanks. Eye-ring absent in immature.
   Active and noisy in flocks, which are conspicuous in autumn and winter. It is the species most commonly fed artificially (fat, fruit, sugar, honey, syrup, jam, bread), and as it is readily trapped and banded has been the subject of a number of studies of life history, social behaviour, etc. Dispersal or migration is as yet largely unknown.
   Voice: Flocking call especially in flight a chirping *cli-cli-cli . . .* and a further common flocking note is a rather plaintive *cree*.
   Fleming describes the nest-alarm call as a grating or nasal *swang* (rare except in the breeding season but liable to occur if a Kingfisher, Morepork or cat is near); when birds are actually flushed from the nest this is modified as *swang di-di-di-di-di*. Special calls (modification of the *cree*) when incubating, feeding young, etc., and as a threat call. There are also according to Kikkawa a number of imitative call notes.
   Song of male in breeding season was divided by Fleming into: (*a*) *warbling song*—apparently during earliest stages of establishment of territory—of slender volume but varied, including trills, warbles and slurs; (*b*) *challenge song*—normally begins after mating and before building—made up of a rapid succession of high-pitched call notes with rare trills interposed, has less range in tone and pitch than the warbling song but louder; (*c*) *whisper song* (by both sexes), consisting of whispered trills punctuated by a normal call note: inaudible outside a range of a few yards. Challenge song somewhat similar to the song of the Hedge Sparrow, but less powerful.
   The chick after leaving nest has a characteristic begging call *ee-chéeta*.

Habitat and range: Common generally up to *c.* 3500 feet, has reached Kermadec, Chatham, Snares, Auckland, Campbell and Macquarie Islands, though curiously scarce as a breeding bird on many northern off-shore islands. In all types of settled habitat with tree-cover; also in native forest (although here numbers are relatively few) and subalpine scrub.

Distribution eastern and south-eastern Australia and Tasmania (a partial migrant). In June 1856 (i.e. the early settlement phase) large flocks appeared on the Wellington coast at Waikanae; arrived in Canterbury in July of the same year (Potts). Some other dates of appearance are Nelson, 1856; Otago, 1860; Wanganui, 1863; Auckland, 1865; Bay of Islands, 1867. It thus seems probable that spread throughout New Zealand began with the invasion of 1856, and that any further invasions have been subsequent to the dispersal of the 1856 stock throughout New Zealand. Earlier than 1856 there had evidently been scattered records in Otago and Southland (earliest was 1832, Milford Sound).

Food mainly insects and fruits, but eagerly takes nectar (Kikkawa records that when Bellbirds were drinking syrup at a feeding station they rarely allowed Silvereyes to feed: nectar-feeding from flowers in many localities may thus be limited by the two honeyeaters). In forest fruits of a number of trees and shrubs are taken, and in subalpine scrub fruits of *Coprosma*, *Hymenanthera*, etc. Many introduced plants provide fruits and nectar.

Kikkawa in a study of behaviour noted various displays associated with aggressive behaviour, including the commonly observed " wing fluttering " and, in addition, " head-up " posture, " beak clattering " and pecking. Chasing occurred among breeding birds as a means of defending territory.

Breeding: Nest, a cup woven strongly of fine grasses, fibres, fragments of moss, etc., and spiders' webs and attached to twigs or foliage hammock-wise at the rim; generally in outermost foliage at a height of 3–30 feet; other sites recorded include bracken fern and a clump of bamboo (nest between two slender stems 6 feet above ground). Kikkawa found that mated birds remain together in the winter flocks; flock disintegration is brought about as pairs leave the flock to establish individual territory, and the first-year birds form pairs while in the winter flock. Strongly territorial; eggs, August–February, two, and sometimes three, broods in a season. Eggs 3–4, pale blue. Incubation by both parents; incubation period 10–11 days, beginning with the second egg; fledging 9–12 days. Both adults feed the chicks. Moon found that the food as recorded on a series of flashlight photographs comprised grubs, caterpillars, fruits and occasionally adult insects and spiders. The first flocks—probably resulting from fusion of family parties and young of early broods—were noted by Fleming in mid-February (at Auckland).

FINCHES AND BUNTINGS:
Fringillidae

A huge family of seed-eating birds with short strong bills. Males are usually more brightly plumaged than females; and juveniles resemble adult females. None is native to New Zealand but six species were successfully introduced from 1862 onwards and five of these are now among the commonest passerines in the North and South Islands. In winter these birds form flocks, which sometimes contain thousands of individuals of several species, frequenting untidy arable wastelands, paddocks where hay is fed out, and especially saltings and rough land along the coast. Because finches have plump bodies and comparatively short wings their flight is undulating.

GREENFINCH *Chloris chloris*   *Pl. 18*
Local name: Green Linnet.
Description: 6″. A plump stockily built finch with a short distinctly forked tail and a pale heavy bill. Male, olive-green with yellower rump and with bright yellow patches on the fore-edge of the wings and at the sides of the black-tipped tail. Female and juvenile much duller, the green having a brownish wash.
Voice: The distinctive spring and summer call is a harsh drawn out *dzwee*. A pleasant twittering song with slower variants *chichi-chichichit-teu-teu-teu-teu* may be delivered from a conspicuous perch or during an ecstatic, darting, bat-like flight. Young in family parties call persistently.
Habitat and range: Widely but unevenly distributed and locally abundant up to *c*. 2000 feet. Self-introduced to Chatham Islands, and a straggler to many sub-antarctic islands: but not a persistent coloniser of off-shore islands. Apparently partial to exotic pines. Forms large flocks in autumn. Winter roosts often with House Sparrows in thick hedges and shrubberies.
Breeding: Nest in a bush or tree usually below 20 feet. Eggs, September-January, 4–6, dirty white with reddish spots or streaks, rather variable. Incubation period 13–14 days; fledging 13–16 days. Usually double-brooded.

GOLDFINCH *Carduelis carduelis*   *Pl. 18*
Local name: Goldie.
Description: 5″. The gayest of the finches. Sexes alike. Head a striking pattern of red (crimson mask), white and black; back brown; rump whitish; wings black with broad band of bright yellow and white terminal spots on the quills; tail black with white tips, forked; under-parts white, washed with brown on the flanks. Juvenile streaked and comparatively sober-hued.

Sociable. Larger flocks or family parties (charms) fly with a light lilting motion. Commonly seen feeding on thistleheads.

Voice: Call, a shrill clear *pee-yu*. Song a distinctive, fast, liquid, tinkling *tswitt-witt-witt*, which in spring can be elaborated into a vibrant canary-like song.

Habitat and range: Abundant over large areas of the North and South Islands, becoming scarce above *c.* 3000 feet and apparently uncommon in Westland. Self-introduced to Kermadecs and strays to sub-antarctic islands south to Campbell; but breeds only sparingly away from main islands. Big winter flocks often frequent coastal saltings especially in the north, e.g. *c.* 2000 feeding on *Salicornia australis* in the Firth of Thames. Many birds remain together in flocks feeding on close-mown turf well into the spring, when local breeding birds already have nests and eggs.

Breeding: The nest, one of the most beautiful, is usually among green leaves, between 5 and 12 feet from the ground. Eggs 4–7, bluish white with spots and streaks of reddish brown. Incubation period 12–13 days; fledging 13–14 days. Normally double-brooded. Some young are on the wing by the end of October.

REDPOLL *Carduelis flammea*   *Pl. 18*

Description: 4¾″. The smallest of the introduced finches; streaked grey-brown; but close observation reveals *crimson forehead, black chin,* and buff or whitish double wing-bar. Male in summer has pink flush on breast. A sprightly acrobat as it feeds on the swaying heads of rushes or catkins of birch and alder. The distinctive flight-call (q.v.) is often the first indication that these superficially drab finches are present. Flight commonly rather high, 50–200 feet; airy and confident.

Voice: Flight call a metallic twitter *chich-ich-ich-ich.* Alarm a plaintive *tsooeet.* Song a short rippling trill, often preceded by flight-call, and delivered either in flight or from a perch.

Habitat and range: Now at home in New Zealand in a remarkable variety of habitats. Rather rare in the north, but a few breed near the sea on the sun-baked gumlands of Parengarenga and there is a long thin zone where breeding occurs among the sand-dunes and broken scrub country of the Auckland west coast. Redpolls become more plentiful on the Volcanic Plateau and breed commonly above the bush-line in the ranges especially, e.g. Egmont, and in the south of the North Island. In the South Island they are abundant from sea-level to 5000 feet. Self-introduced to most sub-antarctic islands, they are now perhaps the commonest passerine on Campbell Island and are established on Macquarie. After the breeding season mixed flocks of finches in the lowlands may contain large numbers of Redpolls. In winter coastal wasteland is a favourite feeding ground.

Breeding: Nest, small and compact, in scrub, seldom above 10 feet. Eggs, September–January, 4–6, bluish-green, glossless, spotted and streaked light-brown, sometimes unmarked. Incubation period 10–12 days; fledging 11–14 days. Sometimes double-brooded. Redpolls are sometimes almost colonial nesters, forming local pockets, e.g. where a patch of rough country remains among tamed green farmland.

Note: From a critical examination of many Redpolls trapped at Lincoln College, D. Stenhouse has concluded that Redpolls in New Zealand are descended from two subspecies, Lesser (*cabaret*) and Mealy (*flammea*). Some individuals with white rather than buff wing-bars are too large and too pale to be considered typical *cabaret*, but more closely resemble *flammea*. It may be significant that in the winter before the first introduction of Redpolls to New Zealand, great numbers of Mealies appeared in Britain and many are likely to have been caught in the bird-catchers' nets.

According to Stenhouse (*a*) the bulk of the population is composed of *cabaret* type individuals; (*b*) perhaps 10–15 per cent of the population are of *flammea* type; (*c*) the two types are inter-breeding.

In the North Island, Redpolls showing strong " mealy " characters have been noted in the Firth of Thames and on Great Mercury Island.

CHAFFINCH *Fringilla coelebs*   *Pl. 18*
Description: 6″. Males are strikingly handsome; *crown and nape slate-blue*; forehead black; mantle chestnut; rump greenish; sides of heads and *underparts pinkish-brown*; wings blackish with conspicuous *white patch on the shoulder* and lower a white wing-bar; tail blackish with *white outer tail feathers*. Females and juveniles lack the bright colours and look greyish-green or yellowish-brown. In flight the white in wings and tail shows clearly.
Voice: Ordinary call-note a metallic *pink* or *chwink*; also in summer from males, a loud but rather plaintive *cheet*; flight-note a soft *tsip*. Song, a loud bustling rattle leading up to a terminal flourish—*chip chip chip tell tell tell cherry-erry-erry tissi cheweeo* (W. Garstang). At the start and end of the singing season, July to January, the terminal flourish is missing or incomplete. Broken snatches of song can be heard in autumn.
Habitat and range: The commonest finch in New Zealand, though sometimes obvious only to the ear, evenly distributed wherever there are trees or shrubs from sea-level to 4500 feet and penetrating the bush as no other finch has done. It can, e.g. be the dominant singer in the beech forest of the North Island above 3000 feet. A vigorous coloniser of off-shore and sub-antarctic islands, breeding as far south as Campbell Island. Winter behaviour in New Zealand needs studying. Small flocks of brightly plumaged males have been noted near the coast; also larger loose flocks of females and juveniles.
Breeding: Nest, " a beautiful piece of workmanship," firmly placed in a crutch or fork, usually below 20 feet. Eggs, 4–6 September–January, generally greenish-blue with spots and streaks of dark purplish-brown. Incubation period 11–13 days; fledging 13–14 days.

YELLOWHAMMER *Emberiza citrinella*   *Pl. 18*
Description: 6½″. Adult males with bright *yellow head and underparts*

are unmistakable; but extent and depth of yellow varies; upperparts chestnut streaked black; across chest a streaky cinnamon band not always easily seen; rump chestnut; *white on outer tail feathers* conspicuous in flight. Female duller with much less yellow and head decidedly dusky; closely resembling female Cirl Bunting except in *chestnut* rump. Juveniles and young females still duskier, only faintly yellow below.

Voice: Call notes a ringing *tink* or *chip*; a single *twick* used in flight and a more liquid *twitup* or *twitic*, characteristic of winter flocks. Song popularly worded as " Little bit of bread and no cheese " (*tintintintink-sweee* or *chitty-chitty-chitty . . . swee*) the " cheese " (*swee*) omitted at start and end of singing season, August–February, and emphasised in full song; usually delivered from conspicuous perch. In early spring some males still in flocks start singing. Song continues well into February after other introduced songsters have fallen silent. A soft tuneful warbling has been heard in May from birds in flocks at Kaipara, Rotorua and Lake Forsyth.

Habitat and range: Widely distributed in all types of open country, sometimes ranging to alpine tussock at 5000 feet, often feeding on exposed sea beaches and occasionally breeding on saltings, and along the ditchbanks of marshes. In autumn and winter flocks visit gardens, parks and playing fields and stragglers cross considerable distances of open sea to off-shore islands, e.g. Little Barrier, Mokohinau. Southward, has established itself as a breeder at Chatham Island, and stragglers have been reported from the remoter sub-antarctic islands. Northward it is known from Lord Howe Island and has been found breeding at Raoul in the Kermadecs.

Breeding: Nest usually close to the ground in scrub, fern, gorse, bramble; commonly on rough roadside banks and in hedge-bottoms. Eggs, October–February, 3–5, whitish or pinkish cream, pencilled with fine hair-lines of dark brown and few spots (hence local English names of Scribbling Lark and Snakebird). Incubation period 12–14 days; fledging 12–13 days. Usually double-brooded.

CIRL BUNTING *Emberiza cirlus*   *Pl. 18*

Description: 6½″. Resembles Yellowhammer, but adult males at once distinguishable by *black throat*, bold black eye-stripe, with yellow stripes above and below, *dark crown* and *greyish-green*—not cinnamon —band across chest; sides of breast and back rich chestnut, underparts below chest-band yellow; flanks streaked; *rump olive-brown*, not chestnut. Female and young only reliably separable from Yellowhammer by *olive-brown rump*. Cirl Buntings look compact; Yellowhammers longer.

Voice: Call note a thin *zit*, *sip* or *zib-zib*, sometimes run together in flight to form a sibilant *sissi-sissi-sip*. Song a monotonous metallic rattle or sharp high-pitched trill *tirrrr*, recalling a Yellowhammer's song without the " cheese," but readily distinguishable with practice. Singing season in New Zealand not recorded, probably

August to February, possibly longer. Males near Oamaru often sing from telegraph-poles and wires.

Habitat and range: Rather rare, except perhaps in a few favoured localities, e.g. limestone country near Oamaru. The population may fluctuate. Recently reported from the southern portion of the North Island, and widely in the South Island east of the Alps from Marlborough to Otago. Nomadic in winter, frequenting farmlands and coastal wasteland.

Breeding: Nest usually within a few feet of the ground in thick cover (more precise details for New Zealand lacking). Eggs 3–5, greenish or bluish with almost black streaks and hairlines, generally more boldly marked than eggs of Yellowhammer. Incubation period 11–13 days; fledging 11–13 days. Usually double-brooded.

SPARROWS AND WEAVERS: Ploceidae

HOUSE SPARROW *Passer domesticus*

Description: 5¾″. Females and juveniles are dull brown above, with dark streaks on mantles and shoulders, and dingy white below. Adult males easily separable by dark grey crown, chestnut nape, black throat, whitish cheeks and short white wing-bar.

Partial albinos, particularly with the white in wings or tail, are not uncommon.

Gregarious, garrulous and quarrelsome.

Voice: Has a variety of penetrating calls, but not a note of real music; though chirping by several males together may develop into a " fairly regular song of 8–10 notes with some approach to rhythm."

Habitat and range: The survivors of several shipments were liberated in the 1860s. Their descendants are now widely distributed and not always in association with man. Sparrows are said to have introduced themselves to the Chatham Islands about 1880 and have straggled to other sub-antarctic islands. In the north they have followed settlement of the off-shore islands. In northern districts where no grain is grown large flocks visit saltings and even mangroves in winter.

Breeding: Commonly nests in buildings; but colonies of untidy nests may be seen near the top of tall trees, e.g. 80-foot gums; and a few birds nest in remote sea-caves. Eggs 5–7, variable on a whitish ground. Incubation period, *c.* 13 days; fledging 15 days. During the lengthy breeding season, five or even more broods may be reared (Kirk).

STARLINGS: Sturnidae

Though there are no native members of this family; the European Starling, first liberated in 1862, is now one of the most familiar birds in New Zealand; and the Indian Myna, which was widely introduced in the 1870s, is firmly established over much of the North Island.

Starlings are stocky birds with short tails, long pointed bills, an upright stance and a jaunty walk. They are noisy, perky and self-confident. They feed mostly on open ground, sometimes in trees. The sexes are alike.

STARLING *Sturnus vulgaris*

Description: 8½″. Blackish with a green and purple gloss; wings short and pointed; tail short; bill robust, pointed, yellow in nesting season, otherwise dusky. Winter plumage speckled with white, especially on the underparts; females appearing more richly spangled than males. Juveniles drably brown with whitish throat.

Voice: A drawn out descending whistle, *cheeoo* is characteristic. Song a " lively rambling medley of throaty warbling, chirruping, clicking and gurgling notes interspersed with musical whistles and pervaded by a peculiar creaky quality." Some Starlings are clever mimics, choosing especially to imitate the calls of the Californian Quail. A Starling has been seen attempting to imitate both voice and actions of a Fantail on a wire.

Habitat and range: Abundant everywhere except in dense bush and above *c.* 4000 feet. In large numbers on Kermadec and Norfolk Islands. Has colonised even the remote sub-antarctic islands, e.g. Campbell and Macquarie. In winter large flocks converge at dusk on favoured roosts, several of which are on islands, even as far off-shore as Motuharakeke (Cavallis) and Kapiti. Near the coast, Starlings often feed on the foreshore and have been dubbed in jest " pseudo-waders."

Feeding flocks will rise in a cloud to mob a passing Harrier, Bush Hawk or even a Black Shag.

Breeding: Nests in a hole commonly about buildings but also in trees, clay banks—often in disused Kingfisher tunnel—and sea cliffs. Eggs 4–7, very pale blue with a faint gloss. Incubation period *c.* 13 days; fledging period *c.* 21 days. Usually single-brooded. Family parties of Starlings descend upon the paddocks when the first hay is cut.

MYNA *Acridotheres tristis*   *Pl. 18*

Description: 9½″. Rather bigger than a Starling; but a showy bird in flight when *white patches* in broad rounded wings and *white tip to black fanned tail* are very conspicuous. Head and neck black, glossed green; body *mainly vinous brown*, paler underneath; abdomen and under tail-coverts white. Bill, bare skin on face and legs *yellow*.

Voice: A rowdy medley of notes, raucous, gurgling, chattering, even bell-like, in rapid sequence. Adults with young utter a harsh *skwark*, and the call of flying young is a noisy, persistent *chi-chi-chi*.

Habitat and range: Released widely in the South Island from which it is said to have disappeared before 1890; but two seen near Nelson, 1956. Common in the North Island, north of Wanganui and southern Hawke Bay; increasing on Volcanic Plateau where it first became established in middle 1940s, ascending above 2000 ft. a.s.l. at Mamaku and Kaingaroa and above 3000 ft. on Desert Road, 1966; still spreading northwards and reached Bay of Islands, 1960, and Doubtless Bay, 1965. Now in many parts a characteristic bird of the roadside. Large flocks occur about dumps and rubbish-tips; smaller parties often feed on the seashore. Often perches on sheep and cattle. Local night roosts in winter may be found by following flight lines. Biggest roost so far described (Ardmore) contained nearly 1000 birds. In districts where they are grown, Phoenix Palms are favourite dormitories.

Breeding: Rather a late nester. Nest usually in a building; sometimes in a hole in a tree or bank. Eggs 3–6, pale blue, rounder than those of a Starling. First broods fly in late December; some young are still in the nest in mid-March.

CROWS: Corvidae

This almost cosmopolitan family is now represented in New Zealand only by the introduced English Rook. An extinct crow (*Palaeocorax moriorum*) once widespread, is known from sub-fossil bones. Between October 1945 and January 1949 there were several sightings on the outer islands of the Hauraki Gulf of a large corvine bird which may have been an Australian Raven (*Corvus coronoides*).

ROOK *Corvus frugilegus*

Description: 18″. Almost entirely black with purplish gloss; but *face bare and whitish*. Bill greyish-black. Thighs of rooks on the ground look shaggy. Walks sedately with occasional hops. Flight strong and direct. Very sociable. Juveniles have the face feathered—an important point to note in the identification of stray " crows."

Voice: Usual note is *caw* or *kaah*; but a variety of other notes is used especially at rookeries and roosts. A rookery in spring is pleasantly noisy.

Habitat and range: Rooks were liberated in Nelson, Auckland and Christchurch, between 1862 and 1873 but only the Christchurch liberation was successful. Rooks are now well established in two North Island districts (Hawke Bay and Southern Wairarapa) and in three South Island ones (Christchurch, Banks Peninsula and Peel Forest); a rookery near Feilding was destroyed about 1925. Most of the rookeries are located in districts of yellow-grey earth where the growing of crops is an important aspect of farm management. In 1956 the main centres of population were near Hastings and near Christchurch, but subsequently the latter population was much reduced by systematic poisoning. Communal winter roosts may contain some thousands of Rooks. Only rarely do stragglers appear far away from the main breeding centres, one at Maungaturoto in Northland in 1953 being quite exceptional. In the mid-1960s odd birds appeared on Awhitu Peninsula and an isolated nest was found in 1967. An occasional visitor to the Hutt Valley.

Breeding: Carrying of nesting material has been observed in August. Nests mainly in tall eucalypts and exotic pines, especially *P. radiata*, occasionally in Lombardy Poplars and Norfolk Island Pines. Eggs September–October, 2–5, pale bluish-green fairly evenly marked with blotches of dark and light brown. Incubation period 16–18 days: fledging *c*. 30 days.

AUSTRALIAN BELL-MAGPIES:
Cracticidae

White-backed Magpies (" white crows that sing ") were imported from Australia and liberated widely in New Zealand in the third quarter of the nineteenth century. They have proved successful and aggressive colonists. Evidently at the same time some Black-backed Magpies were introduced. Though their increase has been slower, there are pockets of country in which they are now strongly entrenched. The two species may sometimes interbreed. Grassland farming, with its attendant shelter-belts of pines and gums, suits these magpies. In some districts both species occur side by side.

BLACK-BACKED MAGPIE *Gymnorhina tibicen*
Description: 16″. Head, *back* and underparts black; hindneck and lower back white; shoulders of wings and base of tail white. Female similar to male, but with hindneck mottled grey.
Voice: " To describe the note of this bird is beyond the power of my pen " (Gould). " Wonderfully modulated whistle unequalled among European birds " (Alfred Russel Wallace).
Habitat and range: Formerly known in New Zealand only from North Canterbury, whence it has spread into Marlborough. First recognised in the North Island near Hastings in 1946, and now known to be widely distributed in Hawke's Bay and some districts to the south. Stragglers have appeared as far north as Manukau and Kaipara.
Breeding: Badly in need of study in New Zealand.

WHITE-BACKED MAGPIE *Gymnorhina hypoleuca*
Description: 17″. Common and conspicuous over large areas. About the size and shape of a Rook. Male similar to Black-backed Magpie but with *hind neck and back white*. The back of the female is grey.

Adult males, females and young of the two species appear to be readily distinguishable, if the colour of the nape and back can be seen.

Voice: A " glorious carol " of flute-like notes, similar to that of *tibicen*; at its best soon after daybreak or in the evenings when the birds are going to roost. *Quardle oodle ardle wardle doodle* (Denis Glover).

Habitat and range: Widely but unevenly distributed in the North and South Islands, ranging up to 4000 feet in the Tongariro National Park and up to 3000 feet on the eastern side of the Southern Alps; still spreading, e.g. on Volcanic Plateau as more sheep-country is broken in; missing from the extreme north and south of both islands and from the western side of the Southern Alps. Occasionally reported as a wanderer to off-shore islands, e.g. Kapiti, Little Barrier. Readily becomes a suburban dweller, frequenting parks, playing fields and airports.

Breeding: Nesting may start as early as June. The nest is usually in a tall tree; but hedges of gorse and hawthorn are mentioned as sites in Canterbury. Eggs 2–5, very variable on a bluish-green ground.

NEW ZEALAND WATTLE-BIRDS:
Callaeidae

Various relationships have been suggested for this endemic family; it is included by Mayr and Amadon (*Am. Museum Novitates No. 1496*: 1951) in the group of Australian and Papuan families comprising the Cracticidae (Bell Magpies), Grallinidae (Magpie-larks, White-winged Chough, Apostlebird), Ptilonorhynchidae (Bower-birds) and Paradisaeidae (Birds of Paradise): probably closest to Grallinidae. Mayr and Amadon regard these families as the descendants of a very early crow-like stock.

SADDLEBACK *Philesturnus carunculatus*   *Pl. 16*
  Maori name: Tieke.
  Description: 10″. Glossy black (bluish iridescence on head and breast); wing quills dark brown with glossy black outer webs; *bright chestnut saddle*, composed of back, scapulars, wing-coverts, rump and upper tail-coverts; under tail-coverts chestnut; *wattles orange*; bill and feet black.
    Immature: see under subspecies.

Voice: The two common calls, the first of which especially has a strongly penetrating quality, are difficult to represent on paper—one is a rapid *cheep—te-te-te-te,* and the other has been described by Guthrie-Smith as *che-che-u-che* (sometimes *che-che-u-che-che*). The birds repeat the calls constantly (Buller's description of the Saddleback as a " clamorous " bird is apt). Softer notes are commonly interchanged between the two birds of a pair: a reedy *wheea,* a musical *kluoo,* and a double, clicking note (E. G. T.).

The male's song is soft and musical.

Habitat and range: Originally in forests of North Island, South Island, Stewart Island and outliers, and Little Barrier Island, Great Barrier Island, Cuvier Island, Kapiti Island and Stephen Island. It had greatly decreased in most areas by 1880 (Buller in 1873 described it as more abundant in the South than in the North Island, but it was still well established to the south of the lower Waikato; by 1888 it was " extremely scarce in the North Island "). Richard Henry's observations in Fiordland show that the Saddleback, Kokako and New Zealand Thrush remained in thriving populations until the 1890s, but a decline was observed at about this time quite suddenly; Henry attributed the decline to stoats which arrived in the area in the 1890s. However, the decrease of the three species mentioned as pointed out by Williams had begun throughout much of New Zealand before stoats and other mustelids could have had any effect. (Present range under subspecies.)

Its progress through the trees typically consists of short flights, and rapid hops from branch to branch; flight although strong is rather erratic. Pairs remain together all through the year, and are seen moving through the forest examining crevices for insects, often tearing away loose bark with the powerful beak. Feeds in twigs and foliage of second-story trees or shrubs but does not commonly enter the high canopy. Commonly feeds on the forest floor (on Hen Island observed almost hidden in the litter). Roosts in holes in trees, or dense vegetation (E. G. T.).

Food, insects and other invertebrates and fruits; occasionally nectar. A wide variety of fruits is probably taken: on Hen Island pate (*Schefflera digitata*) and whauwhaupaku (*Neopanax arboreum*) are an important berry source.

The North Island (*rufusater*) subspecies has a narrow yellowish-buff line along the front of the " saddle." The two subspecies differ in the pattern of the immature plumage: in the North Island subspecies the immature is like the adult (plumage brownish-black, with dull chestnut " saddle "); in South Island subspecies the immature plumage is markedly dissimilar (described as a separate species and known in early literature as the " Jack-bird ") (uniform olive-brown, a little paler below, with reddish-brown upper and under tail-coverts). Wattles of immature comparatively small in both subspecies; adult plumage is not assumed until two years old; however, Stead considered that some " Jack-birds " may take three years to attain full adult plumage. Stead noted a " Jack-bird " in transitional plumage apparently mated to a fully adult male and considered that the birds may breed before passing into adult plumage (i.e. at one year old).

The North Island subspecies is now known to survive for certain only on Hen Island, North Auckland; and South Island subspecies only on three of the South Cape islands (to south-west of Stewart Island). On these islands the birds are well established.

There are unconfirmed reports from both North Island (East Cape district) and South Island (north-west Nelson); no recent reports from Stewart Island.

Breeding: Nest in a hollow tree or in dense cover of epiphytes, etc., mainly close to the ground on South Cape Islands (Guthrie-Smith) but 6 feet or more above ground on Hen Island. Guthrie-Smith found a nest in a flax kit which was hanging inside a mutton-birder's hut. Nest strongly built of twigs, with lining of finer material (fibres, grasses, bark, treefern scales). Breeding October–January; eggs 2 (occasionally 3), pale grey or white, with reddish-brown and pale purple spots or blotches. Observations by Guthrie-Smith on the South Cape group showed that the female incubates, and afterwards broods the chicks; incubation period *c.* 21 days, begins with the second egg; food is gathered mainly by the male but on his return to the nest female takes part of the food to distribute among the chicks. The male also feeds the female off the nest when incubation and brooding are in progress. The young probably accompany their parents for some months—a number of family groups were still together on Hen Island in May, although some families had broken up as immatures not attached to adults were observed (E. G. T.).

HUIA   *Heteralocha acutirostris*

Description: Male 18″ (bill stout, arched); female 19″ (bill slender, scimitar-shaped). Wholly glossy black, with bluish iridescence; rounded orange wattle; tail tipped for 1″–1¼″ with white. Bill ivory-white, greyish at base; feet bluish-grey, pale brown claws.

Immature duller black plumage, and white tips of tail feathers tinged with reddish-buff; wattles small and pale-coloured; bill of immature female only slightly curved (Buller).

Voice: " A soft and clear whistle "; also a loud whistling note of higher pitch, and various chuckling and whining notes (Buller).

Habitat and range: Presumed extinct. Restricted to the North Island, and apparently confined to parts of the Rimutaka, Tararua, Ruahine and Kaimanawa Ranges and immediately adjacent forests. It survived longest in the rough mountainous portions of its range, but has probably been extinct since *c.* 1907. Collectors obtained skins in such numbers that its fate would probably have been sealed whether affected by other factors or not.

Buller's fairly lengthy account indicates that it was almost invariably met with in pairs (once a solitary male bird was recorded, and sometimes parties of " four or more "). It flew only when necessary to traverse an opening in the forest, or cross from one tree to another.

It normally moved rapidly along the ground or from tree to tree " by a series of bounds or jumps."

Food both insects and fruits. Buller records wetas and other orthopterous insects, grubs, caterpillars and spiders. Wood-boring larvæ, especially the huhu—the large, succulent grub of the longicorn beetle *Prionoplus recticularis*—were obtained from rotting wood. Buller states that a pair in captivity immediately attacked a log of decayed wood, the male breaking off softer material and the female probing holes in harder portions, to obtain the grubs; when a grub was extracted, the bird would place one foot firmly upon it in order to tear off the hard parts, and then, throwing the grub upwards to secure it lengthwise in the bill, would swallow it whole.

Breeding: In a hollow tree or in a mass of dense vegetation; nest a substantial structure of sticks and twigs, with finer material lining the cup. Potts recorded the finding of a nest containing one chick on 18th November; it was taken from the nest and reared on huhu. A further nest reported to Potts containing three young was also found in November. Supposed egg in Dominion Museum pale brownish-grey, with brown and dull purple spots and blotches.

KOKAKO　*Callaeas cinerea*　　　　　　　　　　*Pl. 16*
Other names: Wattled Crow, Organ-bird, Gill-bird, Bluegill (N. I.).
Description: 15″. *Dark bluish-grey*, shaded olive-brown on wing-coverts, lower back, rump, upper tail-coverts, lower abdomen and under tail-coverts; wing and tail quills blackish-brown with a slaty wash; a broad band of velvety black passes back from base of bill to the eye and encircles eye as a narrow ring. Wattles blue or orange according to subspecies (q.v.). Bill and feet black.

In immature plumage the brown shading extends on to the upper back; wattles smaller and paler than in adult.

In silhouette the long legs are distinctive, and this and the large size (distinctly larger than Tui) are aids to identification; almost invariably located by voice.

Voice: A variety of notes, in addition to the rich musical song, have been identified in the course of recent observations by H. R. McKenzie and others in the Hunua area, south of Auckland. Maning has summarised the calls as : (*a*) an alarm or curiosity note *took-took-took-took* (audible only at very close quarters); (*b*) a low mewing note, also of small range, apparently used by the pairs in keeping touch; (*c*) a double call (short bell-like note followed by a sharp *kik*); (*d*) abbreviated versions of these calls.

The full song according to Maning is a sequence of " two long rich organ notes followed closely by three short-clipped whistled ' pips ' or 'pipes,' audible up to about one mile " (the two organ notes are quite often given alone and the " pips " more rarely so).

Song and calls are given most often in the morning and evening.

Habitat and range: Although originally throughout forests of North, South and Stewart Islands, it seems probable from Buller's account that the Kokako was of somewhat uneven distribution before it could have been affected by European settlement. However, it was locally common in many districts. By 1880 it had greatly decreased (like the the Saddleback and New Zealand Thrush). (Present range under subspecies.)

Its characteristic mode of progression is to hop vigorously up trunk and limbs; it then glides to the next tree, perhaps losing a good deal of height, the process being repeated. It rarely makes a sustained flight, but is likely to be seen gliding between trees, or making longer glides of up to 60 yards across a gully. Pairs keep together all through the year.

Buller mentions that the foot is used, parrot-fashion, when feeding.

Food mainly vegetable, insects may be included but not conclusively recorded in recent observations. Much of its time is spent on the outer branches where leaves, flowers and fruits are obtained (fruits of bush lawyer, pigeonwood, supplejack, native fuchsia and *Coprosma* recorded); has also been seen examining moss on larger branches (for insects?) (J. W. St. Paul).

North Island Kokako (subspecies *wilsoni*) has *ultramarine-blue wattles*; well-developed olive-brown shading on wing-coverts, etc.; there is a narrow zone of pale grey round margin of the black facial area shading off into the blue-grey plumage. In the South Island Kokako (subspecies *cinerea*) the *wattles* are *rich orange*, blue at the base; olive-brown shading on wing-coverts, etc., reduced; no pale edge to the black facial area; tail quills dark bluish-grey like the body plumage, with only tips ($1\frac{1}{2}$″–2″) blackish-brown.

The North Island Kokako is apparently still quite widely distributed: it has been recorded recently from North Auckland (Mangamuka, Pakotai, Tutamoe and possibly other localities); Great Barrier Island; Waitakere and Hunua Ranges, near Auckland; near Ngaruawahia; near Raglan; Mt. Pirongia; south of Kawhia; some parts of the King Country; North and South Taranaki; the Coromandel Range south to about Te Aroha; parts of the Volcanic Plateau; and the Bay of Plenty side of the Urewera forest area.

The South Island Kokako is likely to survive only in a few isolated areas: the only recent records are from the head of Lake Monowai, 7 with Bush Canaries, February 1946 (W. Axbey); the Wilkin Valley, North-west Otago in 1958 (A. Chapman) and from near Havelock in 1962 (unconfirmed). Last reported on Stewart Island in the 1940s (Martin).

Breeding: A somewhat massively-constructed nest in a fork or tangle of branches 9–30 feet above the ground; composed of a platform of small branches and twigs up to 2 feet long, and above this finer material and fragments of rotting wood; cup consists of moss and finally treefern scales or other fine lining. Breeding November–March; probably single brooded. Eggs 3 (occasionally 2); pale brownish-grey, with brown and purplish-brown spots and blotches. Little was recorded of breeding habits until the discovery of a nest in the Hunua Ranges

in December 1950, subsequently observations have been made at two
further nests by H. R. McKenzie (December 1952) and R. and J. W.
St. Paul (January 1962). Observations by McKenzie and a number of
others showed that incubation was performed by the female, but the
male helped to feed the chicks; food consisted mainly of fruits and
supplejack, pigeonwood and *Coprosma australis*, together with macer-
ated foliage (the quantity of the latter was increased as the chicks grew
older). Fledging 27–28 days. R. St. Paul in January 1962 found that
the male helped to build the nest, and his observations showed that the
incubation period was *c.* 25 days. The nestling has a little dark brown
down on the crown, back and legs; mouth inside purplish red, bluish
towards gape.

NEW ZEALAND THRUSHES:
Turnagridae

An endemic family of doubtful position: its relationships are probably
with the southern crow-like birds including the Callaeidae.

NEW ZEALAND THRUSH *Turnagra capensis*   *Pl. 16*
Maori name: Piopio.
Description: 10½″. Olive-brown above; wing quills dark brown on
inner webs; below olive-grey (with white throat) or broadly streaked
brown and white, according to subspecies (q.v.); *upper tail-coverts and
tail quills except centre pair rust red*; centre tail quills olive-brown.
Bill and feet dark brown.
Voice: Buller states that the common call (whence the Maori name
Piopio is derived) is a "short, sharp, whistling cry, quickly repeated."
The song according to Buller is remarkably varied and sustained: it
consists of "five distinct bars, each of which is repeated six or seven
times in succession"; the bird often stops abruptly to introduce a
variety of other notes, including a rattle and a loud rasping cry; there
is also a short flute-note. When singing, spreads the tail and slightly
droops wings (Potts).
  Potts states that both the male and female use a low purring *chur-r-r*
as a threat to intruders at the nest.
  Sighting of the North Island Thrush were made in the Waikaremoana area in April 1953 and April 1955 by G. E. Sopp and others;
on the first occasion the song ("a beautiful loud clear song") was heard,
and in 1955 several birds were heard giving the alarm call; this was
a harsh *pek*, *pek*, *pek*, *pek* like the alarm notes of the Bellbird but louder
and slower (the call often heard over the year by G. E. Sopp is usually
given three times with very short pauses between).
Habitat and range: The early settlers found the native Thrush a common bird of the forest, yet, like the Wattle-birds, it was reported to be

fast disappearing by 1880: Buller attributed the decrease to the ravages of cats and dogs, " to which this species, from its ground-feeding habits, falls an easy prey." In Fiordland, and possibly other more remote areas, it remained well established, like the Saddleback (q.v.) and Kokako, until the 1890s.

All early accounts give prominence to its tameness—thus Buller quotes James Hector to the effect that it was very abundant during Hector's exploration of the West Coast in 1862-3; Hector ". . . on one occasion counted no less than forty in the immediate vicinity of his camp. They were very tame, sometimes hopping up to the very door of his tent to pick up crumbs."

Its flight is evidently direct and powerful: Buller describes the flight as " short and rapid," and adds: " It haunts the undergrowth of the forest, darting from tree to tree, and occasionally descending to the ground, but rarely performing any long passage on the wing."

Food apparently extremely varied: insects and other invertebrates, and vegetable matter, including fruits, seeds and foliage. Henry saw it eating fruits of native fuchsia. Leaf-roller caterpillars were obtained by the bird observed by G. E. Sopp in 1955. It evidently obtains much of its food from the forest floor, and Buller's account includes mention of one seen " grubbing with its bill among the dry leaves and other forest debris." Buller found that in captivity it was markedly omnivorous (grain, raw meat, earthworms, insects, fruits, green vegetable matter).

North Island Thrush (subspecies *tanagra*) has *white throat*; olive-grey breast and abdomen, darkest on breast (the abdomen and under tail-coverts with a wash of yellow); olive-brown sides. The South Island Thrush (subspecies *capensis*) is *broadly streaked with brown and white below* (the striped plumage on the throat and sides of the neck tinged reddish-brown); yellow wash on abdomen and under tail-coverts; feathers of forehead, crown and face tipped rust red; feathers of wing-coverts tipped irregularly with rust red. (In immatures of the North Island Thrush the feathers of forehead, crown, face, upper breast and wing-coverts are tipped with rust red, and breast is brown; in the South Island Thrush the amount of the red coloration on the head, throat, sides of neck and wing-coverts much increased.)

The only fully authenticated recent records of the North Island Thrush are those by G. E. Sopp in forest north-east of Lake Waikaremoana mentioned above (April 1953 and April 1955); in November 1955 G. E. Sopp, with H. R. McKenzie, heard the calls of the Thrush in the same area. Other recent reports which seem acceptable are from the Okataina-Tarawera bush; the upper reaches of the Ruakituri River (W. Axbey) and the Wanganui River between Pipiriki and Retaruke (W. P. Mead). Unconfirmed reports of the South Island Thrush from near Lake Hauroko, Southland, in 1947 (J. V. Dunckley and C. M. Todd), and from north-west Nelson in 1948 (E. M. Moore). **Breeding:** Nest compactly built of twigs and moss, lined with grasses, treefern scales or other fine material; from 4 to 12 feet from the ground, usually 7 or 8 feet (Potts). All eggs recorded found in December; Potts considered that it probably bred twice in the season. Eggs 2, white or pinkish-white, with scattered black or brown spots, and sometimes with additional purplish blotches at the larger end.

ADDITIONS TO THE NEW ZEALAND LIST

Since the text of the first edition of the Field Guide was completed in 1964, the following species have been acceptably recorded as stragglers and added to the official New Zealand list.

Emperor Penguin	*Aptenodytes forsteri*	Oreti Beach, 1967
Northern Shoveler	*Anas clypeata*	Lower Waikato, 1968
Brolga	*Grus rubicunda*	Punakaiki, 1968
Bristle-thighed Curlew	*Numenius tahitiensis*	Macauley Island, 1966
		Norfolk Island, 1966
Common Sandpiper	*Tringa hypoleucos*	Taranaki, 1964
Great Knot	*Calidris tenuirostris*	Manawatu, 1967
Long-tailed Skua	*Stercorarius longicaudus*	Muriwai, 1964

ACKNOWLEDGEMENTS

BIBLIOGRAPHY

INDEX

ACKNOWLEDGEMENTS

Special thanks for encouragement, helpful criticism and precise information on some doubtful points are due to Messrs. A. Blackburn, president of the Ornithological Society of New Zealand, B. D. Bell, D. H. Brathwaite, A. T. Edgar, D. G. Fenwick, F. C. Kinsky, M. E. FitzGerald, Dr. C. A. Fleming, B. D. Heather, J. R. Jackson, J. Kikkawa, H. R. McKenzie, K. H. Miers, G. J. H. Moon, H. L. Secker, M. F. Soper, P. A. S. Stein, G. R. Williams, Mrs. A. E. Woodhouse, Miss M. M. Davis. The editor is grateful to Mrs. B. F. Shimmin, Mrs. L. E. Walker and Miss S. S. Millar for long hours of typing; and to the New Zealand staff of the publishers for their guidance, patience and forbearance.

R. B. S.

BIBLIOGRAPHY

The literature listed in two bibliographies has been frequently and profitably consulted to check, from the one list, the discovery, history and changing fortunes of New Zealand birds; from the other, their migrations, range, distribution and affinities in other lands.

(a)

1882 POTTS, T. H., *Out in the Open.*
1882 BULLER, W. L., *Manual of the Birds of New Zealand.*
1888 BULLER, W. L., *History of the Birds of New Zealand*, 2nd edition.
1905 BULLER, W. L., *Supplement.*
1914 GUTHRIE-SMITH, H., *Mutton Birds and Other Birds.*
1925 GUTHRIE-SMITH, H., *Bird Life on Island and Shore.*
1927 GUTHRIE-SMITH, H., *Birds of the Water, Wood and Waste*, 2nd edition.
1936 GUTHRIE-SMITH, H., *Sorrows and Joys of a New Zealand Naturalist.*
1925 MONCRIEFF, PERRINE, *New Zealand Birds and How to Identify Them.*
1926 THOMSON, G. M., *Introduced Birds and Fishes in New Zealand.*
1930 OLIVER, W. R. B., *New Zealand Birds*, 1st edition.
1932 STEAD, E. F., *Life Histories of New Zealand Birds.*
1937 FALLA, R. A., *B.A.N.Z.A.R.E. Reports (B).*
1939 FLEMING, C. A., *Birds of the Chatham Islands, Emu, vol.* 38.
1947 TURBOTT, E. G., *New Zealand Bird Life.*
1951 BUDDLE, G. A., *Bird Secrets.*
1952 WILKINSON, A. S. and A., *Kapiti Bird Sanctuary.*
1953 FLEMING, C. A. *et al., Check List of New Zealand Birds.*
1955 OLIVER, W. R. B., *New Zealand Birds*, 2nd edition.
1957 MOON, G. J. H., *Focus on New Zealand Birds.*
1959 WILSON, R. A., *Bird Islands of New Zealand.*
1963 SOPER, M. F., *New Zealand Bird Portraits.*
1965 SOPER, M. F., *More New Zealand Bird Portraits.*
1967 MOON, G. J. H., *Refocus on New Zealand Birds.*
1967 TURBOTT, E. G., *Buller's Birds of New Zealand.*
1939–50 *New Zealand Bird Notes*, I–III.
1950– *Notornis*, IV–X.

(b)

ALEXANDER, W. B. (1955), *Birds of the Ocean.*
AUSTIN, O. L. and KURODA, N. (1953), *The Birds of Japan: their status and distribution.*
CONDON, H. T. and MCGILL, A. R. (1960), *Field Guide to the Waders.*
DELACOUR, J. and SCOTT, PETER (1954–9), *The Waterfowl of the World.*

246

Emu, The Quarterly Magazine of the R.A.O.U.

GLENISTER, A. G. (1951), *Birds of the Malay Peninsula.*

HENRY, G. M. (1955), *A Guide to the Birds of Ceylon.*

HINDWOOD, K. A. (1940), *Birds of Lord Howe Island.*

HINDWOOD, K. A. and MCGILL, A. R. (1958), *The Birds of Sydney.*

LEACH, J. A. (1958), *An Australian Bird Book.* New edition.

MATHEWS, G. M. (1928), *Birds of Norfolk and Lord Howe Islands and the Australian South Polar Quadrant.*

MAYR, E. (1941), *List of New Guinea Birds.*

MAYR, E. (1945), *Birds of the Southwest Pacific.*

MAYR, E. and DELACOUR, J. (1946), *Birds of the Philippines.*

MURPHY, R. C. (1936), *Oceanic Birds of South America.*

SERVENTY, D. L. and WHITTELL, H. M. (1948), *Birds of Western Australia.*

SHARLAND, M. (1958), *Tasmanian Birds*, 3rd edition.

SMYTHIES, B. E. (1960), *The Birds of Borneo.*

SMYTHIES, B. E. (1953), *The Birds of Burma.*

VAURIE, C., *Birds of the Palearctic Fauna.*

WHISTLER, H. (1949), *Popular Handbook of Indian Birds.*

WITHERBY, H. F. *et al.* (1938–41), *Handbook of British Birds.*

Song chart for eight introduced European birds near Auckland

Continuous line—most adult males in full song
Dashes—some adult males in full song; others tuning up or fading
Dots—incomplete song by a few males or tentative song by young birds

NOTE. Auckland, at latitude 37°s, has a milder climate than most of New Zealand. Accordingly adjustments to the song chart must be made for latitude and altitude

INDEX

Figures in bold type refer to pages opposite illustrations.